100 THINGS
GIANTS FANS
SHOULD KNOW & DO
BEFORE THEY DIE

Dave Buscema

TRIUMPH
BOOKS

Triumph Books and colophon are registered trademarks of Random House, Inc.

Library of Congress Cataloging-in-Publication Data

Buscema, Dave.
   100 things Giants fans should know & do before they die / Dave Buscema.
      p. cm.
   ISBN 978-1-60078-571-9
   1. New York Giants (Football team)—Miscellanea. I. Title. II. Title: One hundred things Giants fans should know and do before they die.
   GV956.N4B88 2011
   796.332'64097471—dc23

                           2011025169

This book is available in quantity at special discounts for your group or organization. For further information, contact:
   Triumph Books
   542 South Dearborn Street
   Suite 750
   Chicago, Illinois 60605
   (312) 939-3330
   Fax (312) 663-3557
   www.triumphbooks.com

Printed in U.S.A.
ISBN: 978-1-60078-571-9
Design by Patricia Frey
All photos courtesy of AP Images unless otherwise noted

To my mother, who is always willing to tell me 100 things I should know or do. Like any good New York fan, sometimes she boos because she wants to cheer. But when you earn those cheers, they're the best around.

To my father, who might not stack up too well with Bill Parcells as a football coach, but could certainly teach the ex-realtor a thing or two in that field.

Contents

Acknowledgments

Writing a book requires a lot of other folks' time but more importantly their patience. Whether it's interview subjects graciously sharing stories, professionals helping you reach them, or just about anyone around you who can tolerate the increasingly maddening world you enter when delving into a subject (or 100), a mere thank-you can never be enough. Given the state of the media business these days, I'm afraid it will have to do.

Thank you to:

Wallace Matthews, ESPN New York's talented writer and journalist who pushed me in the direction of this project and is one of the best friends you can have in the New York sports media scene.

Mike Vaccaro, the *New York Post* columnist who cares as much about the business and the people in it as he does the words he so carefully crafts.

Herb Gluck, the author of the original bestselling Mickey Mantle book, *The Mick*. Herb's encouragement to a young stranger on the other end of a phone many years ago helped him believe he could one day write books.

Tim Leonard, a good friend and great old-fashioned New York/New Jersey sports writer, who let me bounce things off him and pointed me in some good directions.

Paul Dottino, the Giants' exceptionally knowledgeable, long-time beat reporter for WFAN, who shared some memories and thoughts on the list.

Bob Trainor, an old-school New York City sports media guy, who's always ready to talk New York sports.

My old bosses, Paul Vigna and Jeff Gilbert, who have become old friends always ready to read an e-mail or take a phone call if you need an extra set of eyes, or an ear.

The Giants public relations staff, which has long been one of the best in the business and offered me gracious assistance, especially Pat Hanlon, Avis Roper, and Phyllis Hayes.

The Giants players, coaches, staff, and relatives of players—past and present—who donated their time and shared details that helped flush out their stories. A special thanks to former trainer John Johnson, who had 60 years worth of memories to reflect on, and former running back Joe Morris, who shared an especially large portion of his time.

All the other interview subjects of this book, who helped provide more well-rounded stories.

All of my friends and family across the country, who help spark creativity, help me start again when I stall, or just offer general support.

Michelle Buscema, my favorite adult cousin in Virginia with a broken wrist, who can offer a supportive ear, good advice, and a quick wit—all traits that have made me grateful for the conversations that helped along the way and proud of the strong woman she's become.

Jenni Maples, my favorite adult cousin in the Midwest without a broken wrist, who also is a go-to person when the creative juices are stalled and you want to speak to a person you respect.

Scott Dodd, for editing skills, football knowledge, and most of all phenomenal friendship. Just remember the next time you get hold of one of my stories that with great power comes....

Henry Dodd, for reinforcing the importance of teamwork and the ability to smile at any time.

Wayne Lockwood, one of the best editors I've had, a phenomenal writer, a rockin' musician, emerging publisher and, above all, one of the most supportive, incredible friends a person could have when needed most.

Ditto on the rockin' musician and incredibly supportive friend part to Luis Bravo, who, along with his brother Manuel—another treasured friend—offered valuable feedback from true Giants' fan perspectives. The thanks to you two never ends for me, and that goes deep into the wide-spread Bravo clan, as well.

Mike Flick, one of the most genuine, caring people I know, who you can turn to for creative advice, support or just the chance to hear an old-fashioned song sung with sincerity.

Ellen Battersby, a selfless, special friend whose pep talks or willingness to offer feedback during the writing process were greatly appreciated. Ditto Mindy Arbaugh, Zakia Gadsden, Anna Dubrovsky, Ted Palik, Scott Pruden, Lyzz Treffinger Jones, Kevin Cooper, Rebecca Colbath Carlino, Marc Lucas, Jordan Zolan, and my cousins, Heather and Heidi.

John Pennisi, one of the most talented artists around and an even better person, who reminds me to keep searching for the human side of sports because fantastic people like him will read those stories.

Matthew and Madison McVey, who spark creativity because whenever I think of them I can't help but remember the kid inside and "choose joy."

My nieces, Jelany and Jenaya, and my nephew Julius, who make me smile just by looking at a picture of them or by hearing their voices.

My brother, Requillo, and sister, Djeane, who have hearts bigger than the name of the team this book is about. My stepmother, Mimi, whose laugh is as contagious as her spirit and who cares deeply about those who inspire it.

Kevin Jungerman and Nelly Tjalim, who remind me what strength and character are built by having dealt with adversity that goes well beyond the clichés that often come out of the locker room.

Gabriella Marino, whose emerging talent as a writer inspires me to hone my craft and whose ever-present sensitivity as a human being pushes me to be a better one.

Jeske and Mikah Maples, whose bubbling passion for sports reminds me who I write for, and whose wonderful energy can lighten stressful times.

The women who have given me an extra set of mothers because they all grew up together with mine on the type of old-fashioned New York City block Sam Huff and Charlie Conerly would have appreciated: Olympia Costagliola, Vivian Costagliola, my Aunt Jeannie Murphy, and my godmother, Irma Rossi.

Tucano, Abara, Sabre, Indio, and all my classmates at Capoeira Brasil, who helped me push myself in a new challenge, which can always help you meet old ones.

Scott Rowan at Triumph Books, who brought me on board and made me feel good about working on a project with him because his professionalism and passion came through the first time we talked.

Adam Motin, my editor at Triumph, who offered enthusiastic support and encouragement for the project while helping guide me to a finish line that sometimes seemed too far out of sight.

A special thanks in memory of Bill Shannon, the legendary New York sports writer and scorekeeper, who shared so many late-night chats, stories, lessons, and infectious laughs—all of which came from a true New York City character and one of the most utterly decent men I've known. You are missed beyond words, Bill.

And most of all, thanks to Jesus—for everything.

Introduction

Welcome Giants fans to my tutorial on what you should know about your favorite team and what you should do to enjoy the experience of rooting for one of the most tradition-filled members of the NFL.

Okay, I'll let you in on a secret.

I don't consider this so much a tutorial as a shared experience, a conversation on moments you might remember fondly or with a sudden, unexplainable twitching horror because I took you back to the bad place.

Sorry. That cannot be helped. You know as well as I do that's part of being a fan.

So there will be those wonderful moments. Even as an impartial sportswriter who for years has been trained only to root for the most compelling story, I still cannot get the images of Super Bowl XLII out of my head.

I still remember the locker room after the game when it quieted down and was nearly cleared out—my favorite time because you get those precious few moments when players drop their guard and reveal at least a tiny piece of themselves instead of the rehearsed clichés. I still remember Giants spokesman Pat Hanlon calling to Amani Toomer and saying, "I see you, A–1! It took seven years to get it right, but we got it right." Toomer, who felt the sting of the Giants' Super Bowl XXXV loss to the Ravens all that time, smiled. "Boy," he said, "did we get it right."

David Tyree, the receiver who came back from so many personal issues to help make the greatest play in Super Bowl history—heck, maybe the greatest play in NFL history—screamed to no one in particular, "Home of the gritty, baby! Home of the gritty!"

These are the type of moments I've enjoyed covering the most and the type I hope to bring you in this book.

Good or bad, I hope we can go behind the scenes or at least on the scene through so many historic Giants moments whether it's looking at the emergent new world of the NFL in New York through the 9-year-old eyes of Wellington Mara as we do at the start or the faithful thoughts of a revered fan who befriended him as we do at the end. Or anywhere in between, where we learn to adjust our view of sports teams from the past when we labeled our players heroes and thought they could do no wrong. Lawrence Taylor gave Giants fans so many reasons to cheer and marvel at an uncanny ability to play the game—but he also sobered young fans as they learned to separate a man's athletic ability from the rest of his life.

We'll relive the excitement of Ottis Anderson making a dream come true by earning a Super Bowl MVP award in 1991 after his career seemingly reached its peak—and see the flip side of Buffalo kicker Scott Norwood's dream scenario turn into a nightmare.

There will be a trip back to the '50s and the glamour of a championship team filled with characters from Frank Gifford to Sam Huff, all of whom hit the famed Toots Shor's bar in New York City to celebrate with the rest of the town during a golden era that helped usher football into a new level of public interest.

We'll go all the way back to the 1930s and the Giants' first championship teams and also salute men who earned the name hero through their military service, including former Giants such as Al Blozis, who offered the ultimate sacrifice for his country.

We will remember with pride players like Emlen Tunnell, who not only became a Hall of Fame safety but was renowned for his graciousness and courage in saving the lives of two shipmates while in the Coast Guard.

There's a reminder that for all the pride of the past, there was some shame as Tunnell broke a Giants color barrier that never should have existed in 1948. We can only attempt to take some solace in the progress the club made by hiring Tunnell as the first African American assistant coach in the NFL and watching Jerry Reese, the team's first African American general manager, win the Super Bowl decades later in his rookie year.

Bill Parcells is here, of course, with tales of his flexible coaching style, patting some players on the back, kicking many more in the butt. But there's also a perspective on Parcells seen less often—from his old boss at a real estate company when the football coach tried once to live a normal life at the request of his family.

In between all the familiar names and games, we'll take a fun look at some things you should do. One I should have mentioned, but ran out of space for, is to read Pat Hanlon's Twitter feed. The man who was built to throw barbs is perfect for that media form. Also, of course, be sure to read the work of old-fashioned reporters, whether you get it from their websites, blogs, or Twitter accounts. In a new media age, fans are tempted to dismiss newspaper journalists as dinosaurs, but keep in mind most of the stuff that is blogged and tweeted about wouldn't be known without the original, responsible reporting that often originates from traditional journalists.

Here are some things you might already enjoy but can take pride in doing now that you know they began with your team—spike a football, dump some Gatorade on someone, and simply chant "DEE-Fense!" The Giants—or their fans—started each of those traditions.

Just *please* do not throw a snowball. At least at a game.

Granted, with a team featuring a legacy as large as the Giants, there might be a little more focus on things you should know. And, of course, there will be those moments or players you so desperately want to find but don't see in the contents.

Don't worry. It's likely that if you don't see your favorite moments or players, there's at least some mention of them embedded in another entry or pulled out in one of the many sidebars.

And if I missed one of your favorites? Well, that brings us back to how I don't consider this as much a tutorial as a conversation. That's part of what you should know as a sports fan, right?

Things are always up for debate. So keep an eye out for a Facebook page where we can meet and continue the conversation.

There's one more thing a Giants fan should do:

Hope you enjoy the book.

1 The Duke and his Dad: The Mara Family Legacy

The 9-year-old boy departed the Sunday Mass with his family earlier that fall day in 1925, then they checked on his father's new business. Timothy Mara later told his son, Wellington, the franchise's price would have been worth it for "an empty store with chairs in it in New York."

When the family arrived, Wellington sat not in a chair but on the end of a bench full of imposing men. He saw not an empty store but a stadium with 27,000 people. And they all cheered for his father's new franchise, the New York Football Giants.

The 9-year-old's ears perked up when he heard a coach bark at players as he shoved them into the Giants' first game in New York, a 14–0 loss to Frankford.

For the rest of his life, Wellington Mara told this story.

"'Get in there and give 'em hell!'" the coach said.

"Boy," the 9-year-old thought, "this is a really rough game."

It was a rough game. A rough sport. It remains so in the 86 years since Mara followed his father into the Polo Grounds and a family legacy.

So let's start by looking through the eyes of Wellington Mara because, through all those years when he took over the franchise his father founded, there was always a glimpse of that 9-year-old boy.

* * *

Tim Mara did not set out to own a football team or eventually take his place in the inaugural Hall of Fame class. The legal bookmaker who grew up watching his parents scrape to make ends meet in the Lower East Side attempted to purchase part of boxer Gene Tunney's contract. That did not happen, but another conversation started about how the National Football League sought to start a team in New York City.

The price was right and Mara, despite his lack of football knowledge, founded a team that endured the struggling early days of the NFL, the Great Depression, and eventually grew large enough in stature and wealth to live up to the name Mara adopted from the city's National League baseball team.

Mara lost money early but helped save the franchise by setting up an exhibition game against Chicago and its legendary star Red Grange. Fans flocked to that game, and through the years Mara made several other moves to draw in more, including a short stint for Jim Thorpe as well as the purchase of an entire team for popular quarterback Benny Friedman.

Friedman helped turn the franchise around—and helped show Mara's philanthropic side as the Giants earned $115,000 in a charity exhibition game against Notre Dame and its Four Horsemen in 1930. The money went to the unemployed as posters besieged fans to "Smash that line! The Bread Line."

There were shameful early days, too. In 1926, Mara's Giants refused to take the field until Sol Butler, an African American player for the visiting Canton Bulldogs, agreed that he would not play, according to the accounts of African American newspapers and historians.

The Giants were also part of the league's unofficial ban on players of color, failing to sign their first black player until 1948, when Mara told Emlen Tunnell he would give him a tryout since the safety "had the guts" to seek one unannounced. Tunnell and the Mara family bonded, and the team later hired Tunnell as the first African American assistant coach in the NFL.

* * *

Wellington, 14, and his brother, Jack, 22, became the team's owners in name only in 1930 when their father attempted to protect his team from creditors during desperate financial times. The sons eventually took over the day-to-day operations and did not let go—except when Wellington served in the navy—until their deaths 40 years apart.

"His father wanted him to go to law school after his graduation from Fordham in 1937," John Mara said in his eulogy of his father, Wellington, in 2005. "'Just give me one more year with the team,' he pleaded. My grandfather agreed, and that number turned into 68."

Nearly everything there is to know, or suggestions on what to do, as a Giants fan can be seen through the eyes of that 9-year-old boy who became an 89-year-old patriarch.

Mara led the football side, his brother, Jack, led the business side. Nicknamed "The Duke of Wellington" by players when he started hanging around as a boy, The Duke grew into an NFL legend, whose nickname now adorns the official game ball in tribute.

He became as respected as he was present, always quietly taking in the action, looking for ways to improve the franchise without interfering with the team as it worked on the field.

The Duke was there for the famous Sneakers Game in 1934. He scouted Hall of Famer Tuffy Leemans in the '30s while in high school, and he drafted fellow Hall of Famers Frank Gifford and Roosevelt Brown in the '50s. He traded for stars that led the Giants to six championship games in the late '50s and early '60s, including Andy Robustelli, Y.A. Tittle, Dick Lynch, Del Shofner, and so many others.

He watched the Giants move from the Polo Grounds to Yankee Stadium, ushered them into Giants Stadium, and walked out of his son John's meeting on the future New Meadowlands Stadium by saying it had all become too complicated.

He was loved for his gentle spirit, admired for his faith, and respected for his earnest, even-handed ability to keep peace in a brutal sport.

From long-time trainer John Johnson remembering his old friend "Well" throwing Polaroid pictures of plays down from the Yankee Stadium press box to the field with weighted socks, to raucous tight end Jeremy Shockey rushing to the beloved owner's bedside before his death, Mara embodied the family business credo of "Once a Giant, Always a Giant."

"The Maras treated my wife and I like we were kings and queens," Tittle said, echoing the sentiments of so many Giants over the years. "The Mara family has always cared for their players, period. Period. They treat us so nice. That's the main thing, I think. Class organization, and the family is, too."

* * *

Mara loved the game almost as much as the people, but he wisely knew which order to maintain. His son, John, the team's current co-owner, once recalled a game when he was screaming while watching a player, wondering what on earth he was doing.

He felt his dad's hand on his shoulder.

"What he's doing is the best that he can," the father told his son.

There would be the glory of the '50s, when the Giants helped football reach across the city, then through the country while playing in one of the most famous games in the sport's history—the 1958 NFL Championship Game against the Colts.

There would be the relationships, as always, like Mara had with Gifford, who in 2003 threw a surprise party for The Duke. Knowing Mara's humility would keep him from attending such a party, Gifford told him the event was for Gifford's wife, Kathie Lee. Of course, Mara attended and everyone finally got to say thank you.

"He was as close to me as my father," Gifford said. "And then later he became like a brother. When I went into the Hall of Fame, he was my sponsor; when he went into the Hall of Fame, I was his. He was one of my dearest friends; he made a difference in my life."

Mourning The Duke

When Wellington Mara died in 2005, he took a piece of the organization's soul with him—one that fans, players, and staff still miss.

The Giants won the game two days before Mara died on a last-second touchdown pass from Eli Manning to Amani Toomer. In the locker room, the players chanted "Duke! Duke! Duke!"

In the first home game after Mara's death, Kate Mara, one of The Duke's 40 grandchildren, sang the national anthem in an emotional moment.

Then Tiki Barber, days after appearing at the owner's bedside, rushed for 206 yards against Washington in a 36–0 win. After the victory, the Giants presented the game ball to Wellington's son, John, the oldest of his 11 children, and the man who would take the reins.

"I think a lot of people just felt like," O'Hara said. "'You know what? We won that game for him.'"

He made a difference in so many lives, from the parking lot attendants to the Hall of Famers. Or at least he always tried. Lawrence Taylor often said through his bouts with drug abuse that Mara treated him better than he did himself. Former running back Joe Morris remembered Mara gently telling him he needed to "take care of yourself" as he battled weight problems after his career.

The 9-year-old was surely still in Mara when he helped the Giants sacrifice personal revenue for the good of the league in the early '60s when New York's large market could have commanded a much bigger share of the emerging television world. But Mara said they should all stick together. The result of such sacrifice might be of use to note for current owners and players.

The franchise and the league became worth well more than a store with some empty chairs.

While the Giants grew, Mara's ego did not. When fans wrote to him, he took time to respond, often calming an angry correspondent by writing back "in sorrow more than anger."

There were more joyful exchanges with Donald Thum, a fan who wrote the Giants owner for three decades and eventually became one more friend of Well's.

Mara endured the awful stretch in the 1970s when Giants fans, sick of losing during a stint of 18 playoff-free appearances, questioned his motives and burned him in effigy. Even Mara's eventual rebuke came with self-recrimination. "People said we were cheap and didn't care if we won because all our games were sold out," Mara told *The New York Times* years later. "That got under my skin. We weren't cheap. We were just stupid."

He endured the pain of embarrassing public battles with his nephew, Tim—his brother Jack's son—who inherited the team after his father's death in the '60s.

The Duke celebrated in the '80s when the Maras hired general manager George Young, who later brought in coach Bill Parcells and drafted the players who helped the Giants finally win one Super Bowl title, then another.

Mara savored his final championship on "this field of painted mud," as he said, after the 2000 NFC title game victory over Minnesota. When the Giants shocked the Patriots seven years later, everyone said the underdog team would have been one of Mara's favorites.

Center Shaun O'Hara keeps the funeral card of his former boss hanging in his locker because he can still remember the times Mara stopped by just to tell him he recognized the pain he endured when he battled an injury. "Just things like that kind of hit you hard," O'Hara said. "The fact that he knew what you were going through, took the time to acknowledge it, and thank me."

There are similarities in John Mara's understated manner, demand for accountability of effort from his team, and loyalty for his coach, as he showed to Tom Coughlin in 2010 by quickly squashing rumors about his job being in jeopardy.

But Giants fans who remember Wellington Mara's loyalty couldn't help but wish there were still those 9-year-old boy's eyes peeking behind the face of an old patriarch when the team moved to its new $1.6 billion stadium—and said it could only be financed by charging thousands of dollars for Personal Seat License fees that forced decade-old fans out of the stadium.

As the Giants entered the 2011 calendar year, the NFL dealt with concerns of a lockout off the field and the effects of concussions sustained on it.

The 9-year-old boy was right all those years ago.

The game can really be rough.

But it can be a lot easier to remember the joy it causes when you think of the 89-year-old patriarch who took care of the game by caring about the people who loved it as much as he did.

"I've figured it out," former punter and broadcaster Dave Jennings once told *The New York Times*. "Wellington Mara was the greatest Giant of them all."

2 Lawrence Taylor vs. LT

The nightmares came as if in fast-forward, sometimes at a speed the mind could not comprehend. The snarling, storming presence of Lawrence Taylor appeared in a blink like no linebacker before or since. In these nightmares that turned into reality on Sundays, Taylor was an unprecedented force known simply as "LT."

"I'm coming to get you!" he might yell in warning. "I'm going to kick your a--!"

The blocker? A formality. LT was on the quarterback or running back in an instant. He flew into view, unleashing an attack that went from stalking to conquest with a shocking jolt.

It was terrifying by football standards, because the hit so often came abruptly from a blind side, LT recklessly flinging his entire 6'3", 240-pound body onto his victim's back, his right hand clubbing down in his famous tomahawk motion, an attempt to devour the ball along with the ball carrier.

The nightmares began for opponents in LT's rookie season in the NFL, and warning ripples went out around the league. The No. 2 draft pick behind running back George Rogers angered his teammates by requesting the ridiculous sum of $250,000 a year. But when he started playing, he prompted even more ludicrous statements from those so viciously introduced to him.

"Who is this guy?" Steelers Hall of Fame quarterback Terry Bradshaw later remembered thinking after facing LT in Taylor's rookie year, 1981. "He dang near killed me. He kept coming from my blind side and just ripped my ribs to pieces."

Packers offensive coordinator Bob Schnelker knew who the guy was before his team even played Taylor for the first time, comparing the 21-year-old rookie to all-time greats Dick Butkus and Ray Nitschke.

"Guys, let me tell ya, I've seen Butkus, I've seen Nitschke, I've seen 'em all," Schnelker told his team according to *LT: Over the Edge*, Taylor's 2003 autobiography. "He's better than all of 'em." Schnelker was proven right.

LT caused those nightmares his whole career, whether it was offensive linemen who prepared to play dirty just to get him the heck off their side of the field to quarterbacks who played with one eye staring downfield, the other twitching as it nervously scanned for No. 56.

"Where's LT?" they would all stammer before a play. "Where's LT?"

"He is the Michael Jordan of football," Giants teammate George Martin said the week of Taylor's Hall of Fame election in 1999. "There is just that dominance."

LT did not just dominate the NFL from his outside linebacker position. He altered it. "He changed the position of outside linebacker, plain and simple," former teammate and offensive lineman Karl Nelson said. "The typical linebacker dropped back into pass coverage.... LT totally changed that. The outside linebacker became the blitzing position.

"The offenses had to change their offense because of LT. When I came into the league, running backs were responsible for outside linebackers. If you waited to do that with LT, give him a three-, four-step head start, he'd kill you. Started doing fan protection, get a big guy on LT quicker. It changed offenses."

Giants running back Joe Morris remembered watching LT in an early practice and shaking his head. "I've got to block this guy one-on-one? What the hell? He's running over tackles," the 5'7" Morris remembered thinking. "Didn't make sense to me. Who wants to block this guy by himself? Head coach Bill Parcells said. 'What are you gonna do if Lawrence blitzes on you?'"

"I'll do what I have to do," Morris recalled responding. "Bill looks at me and says, 'Yeah.'"

It was all so riveting that Taylor fed off the intoxicating world he created as LT, able to impose his will on anyone from opposing linemen to his disciplinarian Coach Parcells, who allowed his talented linebacker to play by a different set of rules.

"Let's go out there like a bunch of crazed dogs and have some fun," was not just something LT famously exhorted his teammates to do once; it was his credo.

The whole time, Giants fans scrambled to get their own No. 56 jerseys, happily escaping after another weary work week, shaking their heads in disbelief and pride at having one of the

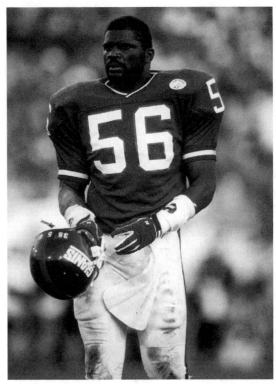

Lawrence Taylor displayed a dizzying level of speed and ferocity to become one of the NFL's greatest players, but off-the-field issues have always been part of the action-filled package.
(AP Photo/NFL Photos)

greatest football players to walk the planet on their team. "LT! LT! LT!" they deliriously chanted, and he ate up every moment.

"Sunday is a different world," Taylor once said. "It's like a fantasy world which I'd rather live in. "Then I go back to the rest of the world, and that's when the trouble starts."

The rest of the world. That's right. There was one outside this intoxicating bubble of testosterone and adrenaline.

The real world. The place where the nightmares for opponents long ago ended. Where the fans' eyes no longer see only a star his teammates dubbed Superman manically tearing toward a quarterback. In the world outside that Sunday fantasy, the pictures of Taylor can be sobering. Still.

There's no moving allowed when the police ask you to pose for another mug shot. From his past battles with cocaine and crack to his 2011 plea bargain of sexual misconduct and solicitation of sex with a 16-year-old girl—just three years older than the daughter he asked a court to decrease child support payments for two months later—Taylor has snapped all those adrenaline-filled fans back into stark reality.

The seemingly larger-than-life character that became LT—the "plain, wild dude" as he dubbed himself early in his career—could be the best and worst thing to ever happen to Lawrence Taylor.

"I just recognize the fact that there's a public persona to everyone and then there's a private life to everyone," teammate and long-time friend Harry Carson said. "Everyone sort of looks at Lawrence and they call him 'LT' and that whole 'LT' thing is what he ascribes to, but that really is what tends to get him in trouble.

"If he would just commit LT to the side…and allow Lawrence Taylor to live, he's one of the sweetest individuals; it's not about playing the game anymore."

* * *

The trouble is, Giants fans could be as addicted to LT as he was to himself. Even if they didn't like everything the package included.

When he wasn't imposing his will on blockers or speeding back to cover receivers, Taylor showed a charisma that earned him post-career fame in everything from movies like *Any Given Sunday* and gritty video games to a stint on *Dancing with the Stars*.

When he played, you could frown at his lack of desire to practice or take care of himself but nod in reluctant agreement when he boasted to teammates that they could receive special treatment when they accomplished what he did on a football field.

Parcells has often recalled the time Taylor was supposed to drop back in coverage against Cardinals quarterback Neil Lomax but instead rushed him for a sack—twice. The second time, after Parcells warned Taylor not to do it again, the linebacker sacked

Lomax and George Martin recovered a fumble and returned it for a touchdown.

Regardless, Parcells remained in authoritative coach mode, telling Taylor the play was not in the team's playbook. "Well," Taylor said, "maybe we better put that one in on Monday, because that play's a dandy."

Parcells laughs about stories like that. But the coach who let Taylor play by his own rules at practice and ignored a wealth of off-the-field transgressions has also admitted he helped make Taylor a better player but wondered if he should have done more for Taylor as a person.

The sense of entitlement and recklessness grew, and Taylor later admitted to *Sports Illustrated* that he would have done things differently. But he wondered if it would have made him less of a player.

All that time Taylor spent changing football thanks to his unrestricted abandon, he refused to restrict other aspects of his life. He did not train as hard as other players. He didn't worry about taking care of himself physically.

"A lot of people say if LT had taken care of his body, he could have played a lot longer, but the thing that made LT great was his lack of respect for his body," Nelson said. "Flying around and doing whatever he had to do. I think if LT would have respected his body…he would not have done what he did on the field. Flying around the field and crashing his body into people."

But Taylor also grew more reckless off the field. The tales have come from everywhere, including his own books. They detail his bouts with alcohol, cocaine, and crack, as well as how he sometimes drove as recklessly as he played and how he fathered several children from different mothers.

There were also the sordid stories he told in 2003 on the news program *60 Minutes*. How he hired escorts—for himself, and for opponents with the idea of tiring them out.

Lawrence Taylor Career Highlights

Years: 13

Awards/Honors:
- Inducted into Pro Football Hall of Fame, 1999
- No. 3 on NFL Network's Top 100 all-time players list, 2010
- NFL MVP, 1986
- Three-time NFL Defensive Player of the Year (1981, 1982, 1986)
- Rookie of the Year, 1981
- 10-time Pro Bowler
- No. 56 jersey retired by Giants, 1994
- Member of inaugural Giants Ring of Honor class, 2010

Key Stats:
- 132.5 career sacks (not including 9.5 his rookie year, when sacks were not an official stat)
- 20.5 sacks, single season (1986)
- 4 sacks, single game (vs. Tampa Bay, 1984; vs. Philadelphia, October 1986)
- 12.5 sacks—Number against both rival Eagles quarterbacks Ron Jaworski and Randall Cunningham, most Taylor had against individual quarterbacks.
- 97-yard interception return—Taylor commanded the national spotlight not with a hit but with his speed and dramatic flair on Thanksgiving Day 1982 when he scored the game-winning touchdown to beat Detroit 13–6.

There was one outlandish, unlawful tale after another, including the opening scene to his *LT: Over the Edge* biography, which featured the line, "The sonuvabitch had a gun to my head" as he detailed his post-football life full of drugs.

There were admissions Taylor played high, failed several drug tests, and received urine samples from teammates to help him pass.

"Lawrence is a very different man," Morris said. "A father, a good teammate. Watching him play is a pleasure—he was just a great, great player. I could think about all the games and all the people he hit; it will always be in my mind. But sometimes I think of the other part of it. I'm sad for him."

* * *

Taylor could be the best teammate or the worst, depending on the situation. For the most part, he motivated by words or play. He famously played with a torn pectoral muscle for the Giants when they were without Harry Carson and fellow linebacker Carl Banks in 1988 against New Orleans.

Taylor's arm was in a harness, the pain driving him to his knees several times. But the 7–5 Giants were fighting for a playoff berth, so each time he got up and played on.

Broadcaster Joe Theismann called LT a "gladiator" on the air. Theismann should know, of course. Taylor sent him to the booth three years earlier when his tackle snapped the former Washington quarterback's leg. (In that famous moment, the country saw beyond LT's ferocious exterior into a glimpse of the real Lawrence Taylor that Carson knows. As Theismann writhed on the ground, Taylor frantically waved his arms for help from the sideline, holding his hands to his helmet in horror.)

LT finished the Saints game with three sacks, four tackles, and two forced fumbles, helping the Giants to a 13–12 win. "I wanted to cry because I felt like somebody had torn my shoulder off," Taylor said after the game.

Parcells pulled him close in the middle of the locker room.

"You were great tonight," Parcells told him.

"I don't know how I made it, Bill," Taylor responded.

Taylor was not as lauded when he crossed the players' picket line during the 1987 strike, famously saying after the Giants' replacement players had gone 0–3 that he had to return because "the Giants are losing, and I'm losing money." He also admitted, "I'm a football player first, and I really have not adapted myself to anything but football."

* * *

For a long time, it looked like Taylor would be remembered as more than a football player. He would be recalled as a recovering addict, one who bravely turned his life around.

Taylor displayed his vulnerability as he cried on *60 Minutes* in 2003 while discussing the support of his family, including his son, Lawrence Jr., who presented him at Taylor's Hall of Fame induction a few years earlier.

"Thank you for putting up with me all those years," Taylor told his family in his speech that day.

He reportedly remained sober for a decade, using his love of golf as a refuge from the demons that turned his life into too much chaos. He humbled himself by apologizing publicly over and over and attempting to help other addicts by sharing his story. He went on annual trips with his old Crunch Bunch buddies, the linebacker crew from the Giants' early 1980s teams, including a project where they built a house for the homeless with Habitat for Humanity.

"I've had more chances than I deserve, and I've been very fortunate that I've made them work," Taylor told *The New York Times* in 2003. "LT died a long time ago, and I don't miss him at all. All that's left is Lawrence Taylor."

But in 2010, Taylor's name was in the news again and his mug shot back. A 16-year-old girl, allegedly forced into prostitution by a pimp who allegedly beat her, knocked on LT's hotel room door. Taylor later admitted he engaged in sexual acts with the girl, but told the court she had said she was 19. He did not explain why he apparently ignored the bruises on her face.

Facing statutory rape charges in January 2011, Taylor was given six years probation as part of a plea bargain deal, and he had to register as a sex offender. Prosecutors said one of the reasons they accepted the plea was because of the assistance Taylor provided to investigations of human trafficking after he was charged.

Two months later, Taylor was back in court for a hearing in a child support case, where he asked the court to reduce his $456 weekly payment.

It was all an extremely long way from all those rabid Sundays when Taylor became one of the best NFL players of all time—a player whose name still drew one of the loudest ovations at the Giants' Ring of Honor ceremony in 2010, although he did not attend.

Away from the cheering of the Sunday fantasy world he relished, reality had once again hit Taylor harder than all those nightmares the player known as LT had caused.

3 Super Bowl XLII: The Perfect Upset

The ball arced high above Plaxico Burress' head, gently falling toward his hands, a whisper amid a riot. As Eli Manning's pass descended toward his receiver, the final remnants of doubt seemingly fell with it and eyes widened across the University of Phoenix Stadium.

Throughout the stadium and across the country, the fans' frenzy grew as they watched Manning lead the Giants down the field in the final minutes of Super Bowl XLII. With each play, the fans grew increasingly riveted by the seemingly impossible scenario.

Eli Manning, Peyton's awkward little brother, was leading the Giants to the most shocking Super Bowl upset of all time, a win over Tom Brady and the 18–0 Patriots. New England was a 12-point favorite. A team on the cusp of a coronation set to cap its dynasty with its fourth Super Bowl championship and join the Miami Dolphins as the only teams to finish a season undefeated.

Brady had just shaken off a ferocious Giants defensive effort to lead one of his famous last-minute marches, hitting Randy Moss for a touchdown and a 4-point lead with 2:42 remaining. The Patriots withstood the Giants' onslaught, and New York would be remembered for providing a fitting final test for the NFL's greatest team.

But Manning stormed the Giants sideline, looking not like the 12-year-old kid with tussled hair he often did but an adrenaline-filled man acquired for just this type of drive. With a fire in his eyes that fans and media often criticized him for lacking, Manning told his teammates they would score.

He *liked* the 4-point deficit. It meant he couldn't settle for a field goal. He needed a touchdown. "No, that's the situation you want to be in," Manning said when asked three years later if the magnitude of the moment was intimidating. "You've got the ball in your hands; try to go win a championship."

In the huddle, running back Brandon Jacobs recalled Manning acting calm as ever, the same old "Easy E." Some of his teammates pinched each other and joked around.

"I was like, 'Yo, you guys are crazy,'" Jacobs said. "I was nervous." Nervous or not, Jacobs came through on a fourth-and-1 play with the Giants' season resting on the carry.

Manning kept driving, stirring the crowd with each completed pass—especially the legendary scramble-and-throw on third down to David Tyree, who inexplicably pinned the ball against his helmet for a 32-yard gain. Finally, after another third-down completion to rookie Steve Smith, the Giants reached New England's 13-yard line.

There, Manning lofted the ball to a wide-open Burress, who made Patriots cornerback Ellis Hobbs bite on a slant-and-go route, heading to the left corner of the end zone wide open. As the ball floated toward Burress, the frenzy of the Giants' final drive paused for a few fleeting seconds of tranquility.

Then…bedlam.

The ball landed in Burress' hands, his feet already down in the back of the end zone, Hobbs grasping in vain on a play already completed. As Burress fell to one knee, the stadium erupted with a roar from those fans whose mouths did not fall open in shock. Silent or screaming, they twisted their heads to meet the person next to them, each one wondering the same thing.

Did that just happen?

Manning released a primordial howl of release and disbelief rolled into one. The Giants turned to each other, embracing, celebrating, exhausted after taking the 17–14 lead. They had responded to Brady, the Patriots, and the questions of whether the wild-card Giants could possibly upend a team vying for the title of the NFL's best ever.

Oh, Brother: Back-to-Back MVPs

Eli Manning watched his brother, Peyton, win the Super Bowl in 2006 and earn MVP honors, and it provided one more glimpse of a little brother's envy.

Eli would turn that experience into an ambition that led to a mutual celebration the next year. Eli Manning's last-minute, game-winning touchdown drive earned him a coveted spot in Super Bowl history along with the Giants' 17–14 win over New England.

Eli (19-of-34, 255 yards, 2 TDs, 1 INT) was named the game's Most Valuable Player, making the Manning brothers the first siblings to win back-to-back Super Bowl MVP awards.

Peyton was seen clapping his hands raw as his little brother led the Giants down the field before hitting Plaxico Burress for the game-winning touchdown.

After the game, Peyton visited the Giants' locker room, beaming about his little bro's performance, especially the inexplicable scramble out of a pile of Patriots who seemed to sack Eli, only for him to escape and fling a 32-yard pass receiver David Tyree caught—against his helmet.

"The scramble will go down as one of the greatest plays of all time," Peyton said after the game. "It was fun to say you were here to witness it, and the fact that I'm related to the quarterback who threw it makes it pretty neat, as well."

In the middle of the jubilation, Giants head coach Tom Coughlin paused long enough to look at the scoreboard and come to a stunning realization. "Holy cow," he remembered saying later. "There's still 35 seconds left?"

Thirty-five seconds left for Brady, who had thrown 50 touchdown passes that season. Thirty-five seconds for Moss, who caught 23—and had scored the go-ahead touchdown two minutes earlier. Thirty-five seconds left for the Patriots, who averaged 36.8 points a game, to march right back and steal the Giants' joy.

"Man," Giants center Shaun O'Hara thought, "that's a lot of time with Tom Brady."

On the Giants sideline, Michael Strahan and his defensive mates reached for their helmets. All night they had stunned the football world with a dominant defensive performance that allowed Manning and the offense to make history. After giving up a touchdown on their last drive, the Giants defense had to stop one of the greatest quarterbacks in NFL history one more time.

* * *

A few days earlier, Strahan rushed into the locker room and ordered his teammates to hit the remote control. "Turn on the TV," he said.

On the television, Brady smirked when asked about Burress' prediction that the Giants would win Super Bowl XLII 23–17. "We're only going to score 17 points?" Brady said. He laughed. "Okay. Is Plax playing defense? I wish he had said 45–42 and gave us a little credit for scoring more points."

The Giants stared at the screen, then turned to each other, at first exchanging looks, not words. "The whole room was just kind of quiet," defensive end Justin Tuck remembered three years later. "Like, *really*?"

The words were relatively innocuous. The Giants felt capable of stifling the run and pressuring Brady, but they also understood the challenge of shutting down a team that averaged nearly 40 points a game.

But Brady did not just matter-of-factly offer an opinion. He did something else. "He laughed," Tuck said, his eyes displaying a hint of fire even three years later. "That's the thing I remember. I remember saying, 'He's up there laughing.' Like he expected to score every play.

"Yeah, the laugh was more than the statement. The laugh was just like, 'Yeah, right.' Like we didn't have a shot."

* * *

The Giants earned their shot after a season that started with them firing blanks. Coming off another disappointing first-round playoff exit in 2006, the Giants lost top running back Tiki Barber and general manager Ernie Accorsi to retirement. Everyone else— including Barber as a broadcaster—wondered if the Giants should lose their head coach because he couldn't control his emotions and their quarterback because he didn't appear to have any.

But Coughlin improved team chemistry by adjusting his prickly personality, even taking the team bowling in training camp. After allowing 80 points in a 0–2 start, the Giants won six straight. They finished 10–6 and scared the Patriots in the season finale that New England won 38–35.

In the playoffs, Manning suddenly looked more like the first overall draft pick in 2004 and less like the New York City whipping boy who threw four interceptions against Minnesota earlier in the 2007 season.

The Giants beat Tampa Bay, surprised NFC East champ Dallas, and stunned Green Bay on Lawrence Tynes' field goal in overtime to reach the Super Bowl, gaining confidence with each step.

They arrived in Arizona for Super Bowl week decked out in black suits accessorized by matching bravado. Dubbed the Road

Warriors, the Giants won an NFL-record 10 straight road games, and they wanted to shed their underdog status, led by linebacker Antonio Pierce, who was always ready to offer a smirking boast.

Seventeen years after Bill Belichick devised a plan to neutralize the Bills' supposedly unstoppable offense in Super Bowl XXV as the Giants' defensive coordinator, his old team refused to be intimidated by Belichick's genius label as the Patriots' head coach.

While news of the Patriots' infamous "Spygate" scandal persisted—the team was found to have illegally videotaped other teams' walk-throughs—Steve Spagnuolo, the Giants' latest rising young star of a defensive coordinator, plotted.

The Giants had to get to Brady. They had to do the unthinkable and find a way to rattle a man known to be "very, very, very cool" under pressure, as Giants defensive end Osi Umenyiora said that week.

"We will absolutely lose if the defensive line doesn't play well," said Umenyiora, the Giants' lone Pro Bowl selection. "They have the quarterback who does all this stuff when people are in his face—imagine if you're not there."

They had a chance thanks largely to their top trio of linemen, Strahan and pupils Justin Tuck and Umenyiora. The Giants led the league in sacks and, in one game, bombarded Philadelphia's Donovan McNabb 12 times—with Umenyiora registering an eye-popping six.

The Giants sacked Brady only once in the regular-season finale, but they remained confident. Years later, Spagnuolo admitted to the *New York Daily News* he pulled back a few things from the game plan, saving them for the playoffs.

"We just knew we could rush him," Tuck said of Brady. "We knew we could get after him with our four down linemen, and it really freed up a lot of things we could do on our back end; confuse him and show him different looks.

"I don't think any of us expected to shut them down like we did. [But] we expected to play well."

* * *

New York began the game with a record drive, taking 9:59 off the clock immediately and settling for a field goal by Tynes for a 3–0 lead.

The Patriots response was not encouraging. Brady, unflappable as ever, drove right back on the Giants for a touchdown on a 1-yard run by Laurence Maroney.

It looked like the Patriots were ready for one of their typical games. They were not. Brady spent most of the game on the ground. The Giants knocked him down 23 times and sacked him five times, bursting through a line featuring three Pro Bowlers to do so.

New England wouldn't score again until Brady finally hit Moss with 2:42 left in the fourth quarter, the 7–3 score entering the final quarter going down as the second-lowest in Super Bowl history.

In between, Tuck sacked Brady twice, including the second of back-to-back sacks with linebacker Kawika Mitchell in the second quarter. More importantly, Tuck forced a fumble and Umenyiora recovered when Brady drove the Patriots toward a score at the end of the first half.

Strahan rose in a big spot of the biggest game of his career, sacking Brady on third down in the third quarter after the Patriots appeared poised to break open the game following a Giants penalty that allowed New England to keep the ball after a punt.

Then, on fourth-and-13, Belichick inexplicably went for the first down instead of a 48-yard field goal within kicker Stephen Gostkowski's range. The pass went incomplete, and the score remained 7–3. It would not stay that way for long.

Rookie Kevin Boss, starting for injured tight end Jeremy Shockey, caught a 20-yard pass from Manning at the Giants' 40. Then Boss took off, sprinting from the Patriots all the way to the New England 35-yard line.

Finally, after straining the defense all game due to an inability to stay on the field, the offense showed life. Manning hit Smith on a third down, then eventually found Tyree—who had just four catches all season—in the end zone for a 5-yard touchdown, his first of the year. The Giants led 10–7 with 11:05 left.

The Patriots tried to answer, but twice Umenyiora pressured Brady, who threw incomplete.

On their next possession, the Giants looked for an instant as if they would put the game away, but Manning overthrew a wide-open Burress down the left sideline. Instead, they punted and Brady got the ball back with 7:54 left.

Then Brady did what he does best. And the exhausted Giants defense finally wore down. Having shut down Moss most of the game, the Giants watched the Patriots' other Pro Bowl–caliber receiver, Wes Welker, tie a Super Bowl record with 11 receptions, three on the drive.

Brady hit his stride, seemingly set for one last championship run, having previously led New England on three game-winning Super Bowl drives in the fourth quarter.

The Giants forced New England into a third-and-goal from the New York 6-yard line, one play from forcing a field-goal attempt to tie the game. But then Corey Webster—the defensive star of the NFC Championship Game when he made an interception in overtime—slipped.

Moss was wide open. Brady hit him, and the Patriots led 14–10. The defense's effort seemingly went for naught.

* * *

Thanks to Manning's calm leadership and key plays from Jacobs, Tyree, and the rookie Smith on third down, the Giants came back once more for the stunning touchdown to Burress. "Manning lobs it…Burress alone…Touchdown, New York!" broadcaster Joe Buck announced on FOX.

Now there were just the 35 seconds to go—29 after Maroney returned the kickoff to the Patriots 25-yard line where Zak DeOssie and a pile of Giants decked Maroney.

Only a few minutes earlier, Brady offered a familiar smile, having seemingly rescued the Patriots yet again. Now a look in Brady's eyes produced an unfamiliar vibe, one that no longer left him looking so "very cool" as Umenyiora said the week of the game. One that was a long way from the laugh he offered in response to Burress' prediction that the Patriots would score only 17 points.

He no longer seemed sure he could reach that number. "For the first time, you see doubt," Strahan later told NFL Films. "I've never seen Tom Brady look like that. I've never seen Moss. But really, for the first time you looked across that line and you saw doubt that, 'We're really not going to be 19–0.'"

The first pass went deep down the right sideline, with no one near the incompletion.

Second down.

Rookie Jay Alford came bursting through the middle, the latest and last Giant to sack Brady.

Third down.

On the Giants sideline, O'Hara exhaled deeply, his eyes wide open. "You almost felt like it was too good to be true," O'Hara said. "That, man, we could possibly win this game—'cause nobody gave us a shot. And I remember thinking, 'I'm not gonna celebrate 'til we have the ball and the clock reads zero.'"

Good thing the Giants didn't yet celebrate. Brady's next pass went deep again for Moss, who had a step. Webster, who slipped on the Moss touchdown, pursued. He tipped the ball away.

Fourth down.

Gibril Wilson broke up Brady's final pass.

The Giants had done it. They had beaten the unbeatable Patriots. Correction. "Every team is beatable, you know," Coughlin said.

"Can anyone get me a copy of that book *19–0*?" Giants offensive lineman Kareem McKenzie asked in the locker room, referring to a book that had been available for pre-order in case the Patriots won. "I hear that's a nice addition to the fiction section."

The Giants surprised all of the NFL, wrecked the Patriots' perfect season, and showed Brady he laughed too soon.

"Other than 18–1?" Tuck said when asked if he said anything to the Patriots quarterback.

The barbs were fun, but the Giants ultimately did something greater than simply making the Patriots pay for any overconfidence. They outplayed one of the NFL's greatest teams. They earned themselves a championship no one expected and claimed "the greatest victory in the history of this franchise," as co-owner John Mara said.

"We didn't do it to prove you wrong," Strahan told reporters after the game. "We did it to prove to ourselves we could do it. We were stopping the best offense in football. Of course, they were surprised. We shocked the world. We shocked ourselves."

The Greatest Play in Super Bowl History

He spent his career in New York eluding one attack after another, but now Eli Manning couldn't shake off the latest siege with a shrug. The people telling him he could not win a Super Bowl here weren't the catcalling fans of New York or the media railing against his poor play on talk radio. It was the New England Patriots, whose onslaught took a more literal form.

Here on the Super Bowl XLII field, the Patriots bombarded Manning. There was just 1:15 left and the New England defense swarmed Manning, who had the ball at his own 44-yard line, a 4-point deficit on the scoreboard, and a defiant stare on his face.

All the criticism Manning endured didn't matter; he had a chance to shock the world and the 18–0 Patriots with one last touchdown drive. But the Patriots had him now. Linebacker Adalius Thomas closed in from one side; linemen Jarvis Green and Richard Seymour advanced from another.

The Patriots swarmed. Seymour gripped Manning's jersey as forcefully as a parent yanking a street-bound child's hand back to the sidewalk, but still the quarterback stood. He ducked under the pile, disappearing for an instant. His only open route appeared to lead to the ground, setting up an inevitable fourth-down play.

"Just try to keep the guys off your quarterback," center Shaun O'Hara remembered thinking. "I think we all thought he was gonna get sacked, and we just didn't want them to fall on him. We just kept pushing.

"All of a sudden," O'Hara said, "Eli just kind of popped free."

Mouths fell open across the country, stunned that Manning managed to escape. No amount of replays diminished the shock. Not even for the man who tore himself away.

"People were asking me how I got out of that jam I was in," Manning said the next day, "and I really don't know."

When he popped out of the pile, Manning suddenly found plenty of space. Enough to plant his back foot and fire down the middle of the field.

"Oh, no," O'Hara thought as he watched the pass, "that's a pick. That's probably an interception."

* * *

The play called was Y Sail Union, but it no longer existed by that point. In theory, top receivers Plaxico Burress and Amani Toomer would be the first options on in-routes, then David Tyree on a post pattern and Steve Smith on a corner, with running back Brandon Jacobs as a swing option if nothing else was available.

In reality, the receivers saw Manning about to go down and tried to offer a desperate man help. That Tyree became Manning's

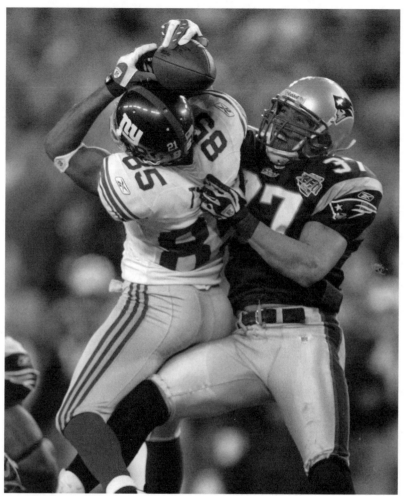

As the ball floated toward him in the waning minutes of Super Bowl XLII, Giants receiver David Tyree said he thought, "'Mine, mine, mine,' like a little kid." Tyree—the unlikeliest of Super Bowl stars who had dropped passes in practice—out-willed New England's Rodney Harrison to complete the most dramatic play in Super Bowl history. (AP Photo/Gene Puskar)

target on the greatest play in Super Bowl history made as much sense as it did not considering how improbable a play it was.

Nearly four years earlier, a month or so before the Giants traded for No. 1 overall pick Manning on Draft Day, Tyree pondered his life in a prison cell. He had decided to deal with a $10,000 fine for missing a team meeting by taking some of the pot he smoked and selling it, he later said.

That he was a wide receiver in the NFL, playing in his native state of New Jersey, did not alter Tyree's thought process at that point because little affected him. Not Leilah—the girlfriend he had back in Syracuse, where he starred for the Orange, and had one child with, as well as the one who would later tell him she was pregnant with their second.

No, Tyree had long ago succumbed to alcoholism and drug use and now had the money and status of an NFL player to add to his addictions.

But after his arrest, he sat in his cell and prayed for a second chance. As he recalled in his autobiography, *More Than Just the Catch*, Tyree began attending church, at one point crying when he discovered some members' joy, which he said left him feeling empty in comparison. He decided to become a born again Christian and credited the faith for strengthening him and helping him beat his addictions. It also helped him settle down and marry Leilah and focus on improving his game.

He was a special teams standout, earning a spot on the 2005 Pro Bowl as a "gunner"—the player charged with racing down field to tackle return men.

But as a receiver, he caught just four passes in the 2007 season, none for touchdowns. Then nearly two months before the Super Bowl, Leilah showed up at practice. Tyree's mother, Thelma, had died.

Hurting, Tyree again turned to his faith, his pain eased by the fact his mother also had been consoled by a relationship with God. Her last words, "I'm liberated," freed Tyree, as well. He was determined to make her proud in the playoffs.

But the Friday before the game, Tyree dropped so many passes that teammates rode him hard.

Manning did not. "I probably approached him just to let him know, 'Hey man, you know I'll be ready,'" Tyree told ESPN.com years later. "And even before I could finish my sentence, he said, 'Don't worry about none of that. You know I'm coming at you.'"

The quarterback did just that early in the fourth quarter when he hit Tyree for a touchdown to give the Giants a 10–7 lead. Tyree looked up, thinking of his mother. But now in the closing minutes, as Manning finally found open space, planted his back foot, and prepared to let it fly, he was again coming to Tyree.

This time because he didn't know where else to go.

* * *

When Tyree saw Manning scrambling, he doubled back, in the middle of the field. Patriots hard-hitting safety Rodney Harrison secured his 6'1", 220-pound frame as close to Tyree as possible without the two men blending into an abstract blob.

Tyree, who claimed he had the worst vertical leap on the team, jumped. So did Harrison. The Giants receiver placed his hands on the ball. Harrison put one of his there. Harrison punched at the ball, freeing it from one of Tyree's hands. But Tyree believed he would have a big game and now, along with the memory of his mother, the faith in his God, and the confidence of his first touchdown catch, he returned to the simplest of places.

"Once that ball was in the air," Tyree said after the game, "it was, 'Mine, mine, mine,' like a little kid."

Harrison mauled Tyree. His hand smacked at the ball, but Tyree pinned it against his helmet, inexplicably keeping it in place there as if attached by Velcro. Harrison bent the receiver back with his knee, looking as though he could possibly snap Tyree in half. Nothing mattered.

Mine, mine, mine.

Tyree held the ball tight against his helmet until he could bring his left hand to the ball to secure it. As the pair fell to the ground at the Patriots 24-yard line in a violent heap, Tyree held the ball above his head with both hands.

In the heat of the Giants' final drive, few people realized what they had just witnessed. From his spot, O'Hara was eager to just get off the next play before any replays could overrule whatever the heck had just happened.

"I remember looking down the field and I actually saw Tyree and, for a second, it looked like he was open, and I kind of saw him catch the ball, and I saw him come down," O'Hara said. "I didn't realize he had pinned the ball against his head and the catch was what it was until like 4:00 in the morning when I watched it."

Jacobs was one of the few players to process the play immediately, having seen it unfold.

"When David made that catch, I was in Richard Seymour's face saying, 'We're gonna win this game,'" Jacobs recalled. "'If he could make a catch like that, we're gonna win the game. If he could put the ball, stick it to his head like that, come up, we're gonna win this game. There's nothing y'all could do.'"

Seymour silently skulked back to the huddle, Jacobs said. "He knew," Jacobs said. "He knew."

A few moments later, everyone knew as Manning hit Burress for a 13-yard touchdown and the Giants held on for a 17–14 win.

The play had gone down as the greatest play in the most dramatic game featuring the biggest upset in Super Bowl history, Tyree was told after the game. "Sounds good," he said with a smile.

* * *

When the Giants returned to New York for a victory parade through the Canyon of Heroes, Tyree re-enacted the catch by playfully holding a ball against his head. It became his trademark, with everyone from players to fans shaking their head whenever they watched it.

"That play took years off my life," defensive end Michael Strahan once said.

It would also become the last catch of Tyree's career. An injury wiped out his 2008 season. The next year, he acknowledged having a bad camp and the Giants released him, Coach Tom Coughlin all but apologizing as he did so. Tyree spent a year with the Ravens as a special-teamer, then he signed a one-day contract to retire as a Giant.

He offered no regrets, opting instead to pursue business ventures as well as more work with Next in Line, a Christian ministry he runs with Leilah.

"David Tyree is such a class act," Coughlin said after announcing the receiver's release. "What a great guy he is. When he came in to see me, I had a lot of emotions running through my head. He put everything at ease; he had a big smile on his face.

"I told David he is forever etched in the annals of New York Giants history. That will never change. That moment in history will stand forever in time."

Birth of a Glory Era: 1956 Champs

Throughout the Conerly home that night, the smiles wouldn't stop forming. There were as many of the Giants as they could fit in their Concourse Plaza apartment—just a long Charlie Conerly pass from Yankee Stadium—and no one wanted the night to end.

The Giants had defeated the Chicago Bears 47–7 for their first NFL championship in 18 years just a few hours earlier. They had earned their place on the grandest stage in sports in their first year in Yankee Stadium, rolling to the title two months after the Yankees' Don Larsen pitched a perfect game there.

The Mara family had waited 18 years for this. Others arrived to help claim the moment more recently. They all earned it together.

Conerly, booed years earlier, endured the city's worst and would now enjoy its best.

Frank Gifford, the pretty-boy L.A. movie star, became a heck of a halfback. Andy Robustelli, All-Pro defensive end and dutiful husband, led the defense after forcing a trade from L.A. so he could be closer to his pregnant wife and their Stamford, Connecticut, home.

Sam Huff, the rookie from West Virginia, was ready to quit before the season because he didn't have a position and didn't think he'd find one. Kyle Rote, the receiver so respected by his teammates more than a dozen of them would name their sons after him.

Emlen Tunnell, the Giants' first black player, who, along with offensive lineman Rosey Brown, endured the indignities of racism that barred them from team hotels on certain road trips yet they still built Hall of Fame careers and lifetime friendships with team-mates from all over the country.

All through the night, the Giants celebrated what had brought them here, how they once could never have imagined this moment. Then they soaked up each other's laughter the way they had the raucous roars at Yankee Stadium earlier that day. They earned every one of them, giving birth to a glory era for the New York Football Giants still treasured six decades later.

"We're champions of the whole world!" Charlie Conerly said over and over as his delirious teammates raised their glasses and shook their heads. "Champions of the whole world."

"They were all so happy," Conerly's wife, Perian, said years later. "They were so thrilled. They were like a bunch of little kids."

* * *

It started with head coach Jim Lee Howell dragging Conerly out of possible retirement a couple years earlier. Then future Hall of Fame offensive coach Vince Lombardi made Gifford his left half-back and not the jack-of-all trades player he had been. And future

Hall of Fame defensive coach Tom Landry made Huff his middle linebacker in his innovative 4–3 defense.

These were the men who made New York fall for football.

Two years later, in the fabled nationally televised 1958 Championship Game against the Colts, the Giants helped the entire country embrace the game.

But in New York, it began here. The Giants started taking the NFL by storm during the day, the city by night. After a win, they bustled into the famed Toots Shor's bar to mingle with Marilyn Monroe and Joe DiMaggio one night and Whitey Ford and Jackie Gleason the next.

Amid all of them would be the blue-collar fans who felt just like the players they looked up to because, well, they were not all that different. The players earned no more than some of the fans, and when they were done with a season, they headed home to find another job.

"Well, the great thing about it, Wellington [Mara] never paid you much money, and Toots never gave you a bill," Huff said. "It was a great time."

The Giants steadily built a winner during the previous few years. Lombardi's stoic mannerisms on the sidelines silently ensured players like Huff, Robustelli, and fellow linemen Rosey Grier and Jim Katcavage carried out his plans. Lombardi emoted until his face was flushed as he directed Gifford, Conerly, Rote, and running backs Alex Webster and Mel Triplett.

It all worked as the Giants went from a pair of third-place finishes the previous two seasons to an Eastern division title with an 8–3–1 record in 1956.

* * *

The Giants let the Bears sneak out with a tie earlier in the season after leading 17–0. Chicago came in as favorites, but as had been the case 22 years earlier in another Chicago–New York title game, the field was icy due to frigid weather.

In 1934's famous Sneakers Game, the Giants opted to wear basketball shoes for better traction than their cleats provided. That year, the Bears were unprepared in the Giants' upset, but this time they had sneakers, as well. But they were old and tattered.

Robustelli called on his side business—Robustelli Sporting Goods—and ordered four dozen pairs of fresh white shoes. The Giants raced around the field in them.

"Look at those pretty white shoes!" the announcer called as another Giant scored.

Triplett, the fullback, opened the scoring with a 17-yard run. Webster scored on a 3-yard run after a pair of field goals for a 13–0 lead. The 56,836 fans at Yankee Stadium roared in approval.

Bears All-Pro running back Rick Casares ran for 1,126 yards that season—an eye-popping number for the time—along with 12 touchdowns. With Huff tailing him, Casares managed just 43 yards and a touchdown.

Gifford amassed 161 total yards. Conerly threw for 195 yards and a pair of scores. When it ended, the fans tore down the goal posts, a delirious sign that the city had lost its collective head over football.

The glory era started here.

"When it came time to play the game," Howell said, "we just opened the door and got out of the way. No one and nothing could have stopped the Giants that day."

6 "The Greatest Game Ever Played"

Down the hallway, the Baltimore Colts celebrated like the giddy children the Giants had been just two years earlier. Outside, in the chill of this late December day in 1958, the 15,000 Colts fans who swooped in from Baltimore to claim tickets cackled as the 50,000 Giants fans remained as silent as they had been transfixed.

In the Giants head coach's office—past a group of spent, stunned players who fought for every inch the last several weeks of the season to reach the championship game—Jim Lee Howell managed to smile and shrug his shoulders. "We have nothing to be ashamed of," he said. "After all, we were only a few seconds and possibly just a few feet away from winning."

The Giants fell 23–17 to the Colts in the first sudden-death overtime NFL Championship Game. They rallied from a 14–3 deficit only to forfeit a late 17–14 lead as Colts quarterback Johnny Unitas drove Baltimore down the field twice.

Finally, the Giants lost when Baltimore's battering ram of a fullback, Alan Ameche, did what he could not earlier in the game. He ran it in from the 1-yard line.

With all these images and so many more embedded in his brain, Howell's calm resignation did not last. That night, the coach's head hit his pillow but his eyes did not remain shut. "I just couldn't rest," he told reporters the next day. "I kept replaying the game."

Fortunately for the NFL, so did everyone else who watched.

For once, the most important scene might not have occurred on the field. Rather it came in living rooms, hotel rooms, and anywhere else around the country where fans had gathered around the emerging medium of television.

The game stunned them, stirring a new level of interest in the NFL. "I think it grew up with that game," former Giants running back Frank Gifford said six decades later. "In '58, that game captured the imagination."

Sports Illustrated called it "The Best Football Game Ever Played." The magazine devoted five pages to it in one issue and another nine two weeks later. Over the years, it became known as "The Greatest Game Ever Played."

Even that year, cynical reporters sneered at the moniker. The teams lost six fumbles—two by Gifford that helped the Colts to their 14–3 lead. They contributed many other misplays. The players on both sides later said they had played better games just that season.

But one thing has not been debated. This game kept fans all across the country riveted like none before—even if it meant straining their eyes on grainy, scrambled signals in New York, where NFL rules blacked out the game.

Picture a Super Bowl where...no, you can't do that. There was no Super Bowl yet with a world full of fans watching. Nor would there be if this game had not generated the interest it did.

"The game really began steamrolling to the top of the sports world because it's perfectly suited for television," Gifford said. "You have the natural timeouts, you have the time between different plays, you have the halftime when people can go to the [bathroom], eat.... It was almost designed for television, and it's made a huge impact."

The greatest impact came at the end when Unitas drove the Colts down the field, over the Giants, and into the fascination of fans around the country.

* * *

The game featured 17 future Hall of Famers and plenty of traded leads and comebacks. The Giants had already caught New York's attention with their title run in 1956. They reclaimed it down the stretch of the '58 season after losing the division to Jim Brown and the Cleveland Browns in '57.

With a series of exciting games, including back-to-back wins over the Browns, the Giants earned their shot at the Colts. Baltimore featured speedy receivers Lenny Moore and Raymond Berry, and a defense that could rival the Giants' talented crew. Art

Donovan, Gene "Big Daddy" Lipscomb, and Gino Marchetti tore through most lines in football.

The match-up promised to be a contest of wills, a rematch of the Giants' 24–21 win earlier that year that left the Colts feeling the Giants did not respect them.

In the end, the game surpassed the anticipation. It offered the first look at the exhilarating concept of sudden death and a showdown between a daring quarterback and the Giants' talented defense.

The Giants were set to seal the game when Gifford seemed to get just enough for a first down in the closing minutes on a

Mara Tech and the Mad Men

The Giants may have lost the 1958 championship—and were blown out by Baltimore in the '59 title game rematch 31–16—but their popularity and profitability soared. Along with unprecedented championship-game shares of more than $3,000 for the losing players, the Giants drew commercial and broadcasting opportunities of all kinds.

The Giants featured not one but two players who modeled for cigarette ads as the Marlboro Man in the '50s and '60s—rugged quarterback Charlie Conerly and wide receiver Del Shofner. Frank Gifford and Sam Huff hawked products in all kind of ads, and several players went on to broadcasting careers, even starting while they were playing, setting a precedent future Giants followed.

They called the Giants Mara Tech—the nickname for the Mara family's stable of football players and coaches who went on to fame or success in impressive post-football careers. They were the original Mad Men, making their way to Madison Avenue at a time when television and the NFL began to take their first crawling steps together toward mass appeal.

"Having 27 years on *Monday Night Football* and to see the use of television, I have been honored to be part of that," said Gifford, who also starred in movies and other TV specials.

third-down run. But when he was tackled by Marchetti, Lipscomb fell onto his teammate—breaking Marchetti's leg but possibly giving the Colts a break.

Distracted by Marchetti's injury, the official did not immediately spot the ball. When he finally placed it, the Giants were ruled short of the first down by inches. To this day, Gifford swears he made it and that the official later apologized.

"The official, he took the ball from me and it was obvious to me [that I made the first down]," Gifford said. "Everybody's getting bloody.... I don't blame the official. He said that he made a mistake."

It's been debated for decades whether Howell then made a mistake. He sent in punter Don Chandler instead of going for the first down from the Giants' 44-yard line on fourth-and-inches. Howell later said that was not one of the plays that kept him awake; he felt it was too dangerous going for it in his own territory despite pleas from his sideline.

Giving the ball back to Unitas—and Berry—turned out to be too dangerous, as well. The pair led the Colts on a 13-play drive, with Unitas repeatedly hitting Berry, who made a record 12 catches in the title game.

Even Bob Sheppard's royal tones emanating from the public address system could not soothe the Giants' aggravation. "'Unitas to Berry, Unitas to Berry, Unitas to Berry,'" Huff said with a grumble in an NFL Films spot years later. "I mean, I got tired of hearing the announcer say it, you know? You couldn't stop them."

Finally, Colts kicker Steve Myhra attempted a 20-yard field goal with the championship on the line. He had hit just 4-of-10 for the season. Huff blocked a kick earlier in the game. Weeks earlier, the Giants won a game on a block by Harland Svare to keep their season alive.

The crowd tensed. Myhra did not. The kick was good. The teams were going to overtime.

New York won the coin toss but went three-and-out. Unitas led the Colts down the field once more. They reached the Giants' 8-yard line when the fans, inching off their seats at home, suddenly were shocked.

The picture cut out. The game that sent football soaring in popularity was about to end, and the people watching were going to miss the best part. Until a fan ran on the field, causing just enough of a delay for NBC to restore its picture, after fixing a broken cable.

While the story has skeptics, legend has it that the man who caused the delay was a network executive sent to disrupt the game. "They didn't know what to do. The game went black all across the country," Gifford said, remembering what teammate and future broadcaster Pat Summerall once told him. "So they sent some guy down, he ran on the field...so we had to delay."

There was no more delaying the inevitable for the Giants, though. A few plays later, on third down, Ameche took it in from the 1-yard line. The Giants lost.

The memories of the Giants' comeback from their 14–3 deficit that almost became 21–3 fell into the background. Their earlier stop of Ameche from the 1 on fourth down—when he misunderstood the play and tried to run instead of throwing to an open receiver—was no longer such a big play. Nor was Giants running back Alex Webster recovering Kyle Rote's fumble after a long pass to set up the Giants' first touchdown.

Giants quarterback Charlie Conerly, who hit Gifford with the go-ahead touchdown and was voted the game's MVP by the writers a few moments earlier, lost the most. With the award came a new Corvette. Instead, Unitas received the honor and the car. For years, Conerly's wife, Perian, lamented that "Mrs. Unitas was driving around in my Corvette."

Regardless, all of it would be remembered, even if Unitas and Ameche stole the final scenes. From Howell's restless bed to the recovered film that surfaced years later as well as the fans' memories, that game has always been replayed.

It is known as the game that helped push the NFL to the front of the national sports conversation. "In sports, you always hope you'll do things they'll remember," Charlie Conerly once told the *New York Daily News*. "We just didn't know we were playing on one of those teams people'd never forget."

7 Young Saves Feuding Maras, Giants

The family squabble between a cocksure younger relative and a staid older one had spilled out of the Giants Stadium offices and into the type of circus the club was known for avoiding. Giants co-owners Wellington Mara and his nephew, Tim, held dueling press conferences that February day in 1979, finally confirming publicly what had only been whispered before.

There was a family feud between the men, who each owned a 50 percent share since 1965, when Jack Mara left his half to his son, Tim. The stress of too many losing seasons boiled over with the infamous play known as "The Fumble" in 1978. The Giants blew a game when they just needed to take a knee, and the fans attacked the club's management—especially Wellington. Tim, who had mostly been a silent partner, agreed with the fans.

When the pair couldn't decide on a director of operations to replace Andy Robustelli, who resigned following the '78 season, Wellington called a press conference saying he wanted to hire a coach first. When Wellington's press conference ended, Tim's began. He wanted to hire an operations man first to hire the coach—and to ensure his uncle would not meddle.

"I'm tired of the losing," Tim Mara said. "I want to have a winner. Well wants to have a winner, his way. Well's way has had us in the cellar the past 15 years."

Many of the barbs the younger Mara unleashed in critiquing his uncle's management were considered as true as they were shocking. Tim had barely spoken publicly; now he was cruelly cutting down a man respected throughout the league. One who, despite his recent poor decisions, previously made many that led the Giants to success.

For his part, Wellington acknowledged his mistakes and said he did not want as much power as his nephew indicated. He just wanted to hire a coach to get things going.

At a bitter impasse that divided the men and their families for years, they reached out to NFL commissioner Pete Rozelle to mediate and help select an operations man. The commissioner, the story went, suggested the Giants hire their first general manager— George Young, legendary Miami Dolphins coach Don Shula's right-hand man.

Years later, current co-owner John Mara, Wellington's son, told *The New York Times* the candidate had actually been recommended to Wellington by former Giants Frank Gifford and Tom Scott. Rozelle, though, was asked to act as if the idea was his. At that point, John Mara said, neither his uncle nor his cousin would have listened to the other's suggestion.

However the move came about, it ended up as one of the greatest in Giants history. Young not only saved the Maras from continuing to embarrass a once-proud franchise, he also laid the foundation for unprecedented glory. The former high school teacher, scout, and personnel man slowly built a team that won two Super Bowls through the NFL draft and wise coaching decisions.

His first overall draft pick was quarterback Phil Simms, who was greeted with boos and left with his jersey retired. Young's No. 2 overall pick two years later, in 1981, was Lawrence Taylor.

George Young: Giant Highlights

Years: 19
Record: 155–139–2
Playoff Appearances: 8
Super Bowl Appearances/Victories: 2
NFL Executive of the Year: 1984, 1986, 1990, 1993, 1997

Best Draft Picks

Name	Year	Round	Pick	Career
Phil Simms	1979	1	7	Giants all-time passer
Mark Haynes	1980	1	8	3-time Pro Bowler
Lawrence Taylor	1981	1	2	Hall of Famer
Joe Morris	1982	2	45	No. 3 Giants all-time rusher
Leonard Marshall	1983	2	37	All-time Giants great DE
Carl Banks	1984	1	3	All-time Giants great LB
Jeff Hostetler	1984	3	59	SB XXV-winning QB
Mark Bavaro	1985	4	100	All-time Giants great TE
Dave Meggett	1989	5	132	All-time Giants great PR/KR
Rodney Hampton	1990	12	4	No. 2 Giants all-time rusher
Michael Strahan	1993	1	24	Likely future Hall of Famer
Jessie Armstead	1993	8	207	All-time Giants great LB
Amani Toomer	1996	2	34	No. 1 Giants all-time receiver
Tiki Barber	1997	2	36	No. 1 Giants all-time rusher

Young brought in head coach Ray Perkins, who helped the Giants end a string of 17 seasons without a playoff appearance in 1981. Just as importantly, Perkins brought in an assistant coach named Bill Parcells, who eventually led the Giants to their two Super Bowl victories.

Young was smart enough to hire Parcells to succeed Perkins. And—despite flirtations with then-University of Miami coach

Howard Schnellenberger—Young retained Parcells after his disastrous debut at 3–12–1.

Not only did Young craft the foundation of the 1986 and '90 Super Bowl champions, but he offered future Giants fans a parting gift near the end of his 19-year tenure with the team. He drafted Tiki Barber, Amani Toomer, and Michael Strahan, each of whom helped the Giants reach one Super Bowl, the latter two helping them win another in the victory John Mara called the franchise's greatest.

Young also hired head coach Jim Fassel, who gave the Giants a playoff appearance in 1997, Young's final year with the Giants, and just four years before his death.

The Giants' most successful general manager even hired the Giants' next two eventual GMs, Ernie Accorsi and Jerry Reese. Both men contributed heavily to that Super Bowl XLII championship team through various moves.

"Without his support and help," Parcells once said, "it would have been impossible for anyone to succeed, and I will always be grateful to George for that."

For all his contributions to the Giants' success, he was not, of course, perfect. Many former players recalled Young's irascible nature with a mix of amusement and dread.

"He was cranky, but he was cerebral," said former Giants quarterback Scott Brunner, an early Young draft pick who was traded when Simms claimed the job after losing it. "He was almost caring in a condescending way. He was not loveable, by any means.

"But you knew you were one of his guys—you were a draft pick of George Young. He saw something in you and cared about you and cared about you being successful, but he would certainly never give you the satisfaction of saying that."

Young and Parcells feuded over personnel decisions at times, as the GM also did with agents as the modern game threatened his old-fashioned, conservative sensibilities. He made several poor draft choices later in his career, though they were dwarfed by the moves that made him an unprecedented five-time NFL executive of the year.

He hired the woeful Ray Handley to succeed Parcells after the coach left due to health issues in 1991. He acquired the dreadful quarterback Dave Brown in the 1990s. He struggled with many selections in that decade and did not take kindly to the new free agency rules.

But Young's shortcomings are far outweighed by his historic accomplishments. "I'm happy here," Young once said. "The Maras gave me my break."

He returned the favor many times over.

8 Bill Parcells

He tried once to break the game's hold on him, to ignore the passion for football that drove him to fame and success with the Giants, but not always contentment. It would not be easy for Bill Parcells to walk away because the idea to do so was not completely his own.

As a boy, Parcells stubbornly changed his given name of Duane to Bill because he didn't like it. As a veteran coach, his intense demands left some former Giants searching for words to politely describe him while others quickly found them—"He was a pain in the a--," one bluntly said.

But as a young man two months into his first pro job, Parcells tried to get the coaching addiction out of his blood just when he realized a dream. This was long before he proved that was impossible, before all those times Parcells came out of retirement to the knowing eye rolls of folks accustomed to the routine of a football lifer.

This was at the beginning, two months after then-Giants head coach Ray Perkins hired Parcells as a linebackers coach in 1979. Parcells had grown up in Hasbrouck Heights, New Jersey, adoring the Giants. As a boy, he regularly watched *The Giants Quarterback Huddle* with legendary broadcaster Marty Glickman interviewing Parcells' favorites like Charlie Conerly or Alex Webster.

This was everything he wanted. But he still quit.

His wife, Judy, and his children had grown tired of the football life that dragged them from one place to another, eight stops at that point. They enjoyed Colorado, where Parcells had spent the previous year as the Air Force head coach.

Parcells initially headed east while the family remained in Colorado as he started on mini-camp. But two months later, Parcells found himself telling Perkins he had to resign. His family didn't want to move again, and Parcells recognized their sacrifice by making one of his own.

He returned to Colorado, where he no longer was the Giants linebackers coach or the Air Force head coach. Parcells was simply unemployed. So he sat in the office of David Sunderland, president of Gates Land real estate, interviewing for a job in sales.

There the infamously restless football nomad, who later traveled from team to team and un-retired several times, convinced Sunderland of something he never quite got around to believing himself. "He was tired of moving around," Sunderland recalled Parcells telling him three decades ago. "When we first started to talk to him about 'Why? What are you doing?' that was his story. It was a family matter, basically. He loved football, but he got tired of moving."

So he became Bill the realtor, attempting to sell custom home lots on which owners could build upper mid-scale houses. Instead of burying his head in playbooks, he stuck his nose into the research of his new career. He was a 9-to-5er, no longer able to bellow orders at players, offer mocking putdowns to one or an amiable pat on the back to another. His job was to make the sale, learning as he went.

The customer, not the coach, was always right.

Parcells brought some similar traits to sales calls that he did to the field, giving his customers a glimpse of the personality his Giants players later saw. "Intense," Sunderland said, when asked to describe Parcells' sales style. "I sat down in a couple meetings with customers in tow. And he was intense. That was his style. It's more like staring into your soul. That's the kind of intensity he had."

The coach known to throw cutting daggers at struggling players might have appreciated a speech from Alec Baldwin's character as a brash real estate boss in *Glengarry Glen Ross*. Baldwin most likely would have told Bill the realtor to put the coffee down because it was for closers.

"We weren't getting a lot of results," Sunderland said. "He didn't like it. He was frustrated by that. He would just…he would be more determined. 'We're gonna get this done.'"

But overall, did Parcells have the makings of a good salesman? "He wasn't here long enough to get good," Sunderland said. "He wasn't here long enough to build up a customer base that a good realtor has to."

No, he was not. He wasn't there long at all. Parcells tried. He lasted about six months before his wife told him to forget it and just go look for a football job again. For better or worse, the guy was a football coach.

* * *

Credit Perkins and the Giants for recognizing Parcells' talent and not questioning his dedication even after his detour. Perkins recommended Parcells for a job as a linebackers coach with New England, then hired him again in 1981 as the Giants defensive coordinator.

Bill Parcells: Coaching Highlights
Years as Giants Head Coach: 8
Years as NFL Head Coach: 19
Giants Record: 77–49–1 (.611 winning pct.)
NFL Record: 172–130–1 (.570)
Giants Playoff Appearances: 5
NFL Playoff Appearances: 10
Giants NFC Championship Appearances: 2 (2–0)
NFL Championship Game Appearances: 4 (3–1)
Giants Super Bowls: 2 (2–0)
NFL Super Bowls: 3 (2–1)

Running back Joe Morris remembered playing pick-up basketball with Parcells when he was an assistant. Quarterback Scott Brunner recalled morning breakfasts at the team hotel on the road. But after Perkins took his dream job at Alabama in 1982, general manager George Young named Parcells as Perkins' replacement.

Breakfast and basketball were out now that Parcells was the head coach, but so was the progress the team started to make under Perkins. Parcells infamously went 3–12–1 in his first season in 1983 and reportedly was in jeopardy of losing his job to University of Miami coach Howard Schnellenberger, although Young denied the rumors.

Parcells' greatest struggles came off the field as both his parents died that year. As he mourned his parents and heard the rumors of his job status, Parcells vowed to do things his way if he returned. That meant remaking the roster, acknowledging he made a mistake in choosing Brunner over Phil Simms, and forming the core of what would be two Super Bowl teams.

Parcells' new determination also helped produce countless headaches for the players he prodded to greatness. His relationship with players could take the form of love, hate, or both depending on the player, the situation, or the day.

Bill Parcells returned the Giants to prominence and won the team's first two Super Bowls. The needling taskmaster also was labeled a "pain in the a--."
(AP Photo/Paul Spinelli)

"How can I put this?" Morris said when asked to describe Parcells. "A complex man with a lot of things on his mind. He wanted more than you could give. Very difficult man to get along with. [If] you didn't compete, you didn't play for him."

Offensive lineman Karl Nelson was less tactful. "Ahh, he was a pain in the a--," Nelson said. "Bill's biggest asset is whatever you had in you, he'd get out of you, if you let him. Some guys, he put his arm around you, some guys, a kick in the a--.

"Bill screwed with your head more than any coach out there. He played mental games. There were days I'd come home I didn't know if I could put one foot in front of the other. He'd break you down, then build you back up."

In the end did Parcells' results, including the Super Bowl ring he helped Nelson earn in 1986, make it all worth it? "Don't know.

Because we had the success that we did, I think it was worth it," Nelson said. "I have that little trinket on my finger, so I respect him. If I didn't have it, I wouldn't respect him."

Center Bart Oates, a law school student at the time, remembered Parcells' piercing Jersey accent bombarding him with cries of "Counselor! Counselor! are you writing a brief today?"

"It irritated the guy he was getting on," Oates said of Parcells' penchant for finding specific barbs, "but it delighted everyone else. Do I like him? I do like him. I didn't necessarily like him at the time."

Morris recalled Parcells purposely putting a rock in his shoe to prompt irritation so he wouldn't let up in his quest to drive players. "He manufactured it," Morris said. "You can't be yelling all the time."

He didn't yell all the time because after sizing up a player, Parcells decided whether he should put an arm around him instead. He challenged top players like Lawrence Taylor or Simms, getting in their faces and telling them which players around the league were better than them as they worked themselves into a frenzy, often going back at the coach.

Other times he'd flash a wide grin, a quick wisecrack, and show off the charm he used when harmlessly flirting with Sunderland's wife, Brooke, back in Colorado. "Some guys he took more of a fatherly approach; some guys he would take a Vince Lombardi approach," Oates said. "But bottom line is I loved watching him work."

And it was always about the work, Parcells admitted. As irritating or maddening as he could be, as much as you could question his methods if you were a player, you were less apt to question his intent.

"I calculate everything I do," Parcells once said. "I respond for a reason."

* * *

Even the players Parcells battled most bitterly ultimately recognized a fact he later revealed: "You can only really yell at the players you trust."

After so many battles, Simms started to recognize Parcells' idea of leadership. "He used to say to me things like, 'You know, Simms, if you want them to listen, you've got to show them,'" Simms said. "He came up and told me a story about work and he said, 'Even if you don't want to do it during the offseason, come down here anyway. I want you to walk around the locker room and everywhere, let everybody see that you've got all the tapes and that pad, and you go in that room and you shut it and you lock it. I don't care if you want to watch those films or you lay down and sleep for four hours.

"'But when you come out, I want everybody to see that you've been in there for hours so that all of those people will believe that at least you're doing the work to get ready to play. And if you do that, then they'll go, "Well, hell, if he's doing it, I better do it too."'"

The work obviously paid off. The Giants, a moribund franchise for most of the previous two decades, reached the playoffs five of the eight years Parcells coached. They won the Super Bowl twice. The linebackers he was fond of collecting formed some of the best units in NFL history as he implemented a 3–4 defense to utilize them.

His sense of competition was so great he snapped at reporters interfering with his goal, once calling them "commies—subversive from within." When former NFL head coach John Madden contemplated visiting practice before announcing a game for CBS, players cringed.

"If John Madden was at our practice, Fridays were the worst day because he wanted to show he could coach," Morris said. "And you're thinking, 'Oh man, please don't come to practice Mr. Madden.'"

After all the Gatorade baths his players doused him with following victories, the rides on the shoulders after two Super Bowls, and the respect he earned from a boyhood idol when Conerly told him he was proud of him, Parcells' time with the Giants ended abruptly.

They had barely finished celebrating their surprising Super Bowl win over Buffalo—Parcells' finest moment as a Giant—when he announced his resignation. There had been rumors of job offers, but this time Parcells did not give in to wanderlust. He protected his health. Years later, he admitted a heart condition prompted him to move on from his dream job.

* * *

When his health improved, so did his drive for football that falls somewhere between love and obsession. He took on the challenge of rebuilding New England, taking the Patriots to a Super Bowl before bolting for the Jets.

There had been rumors of Parcells returning to the Giants, and he came closer than people initially realized. As then-assistant general manager Ernie Accorsi later detailed in the book *The GM*, Wellington Mara wanted to rehire Parcells in 1997, but co-owner Bob Tisch did not. Only after GM Young had been dispatched to offer the job to Jim Fassel did Tisch change his mind. By the time Mara contacted Young, the GM offered Fassel the job and Mara decided not to renege on the offer.

So Parcells kept moving after taking the Jets to the AFC Championship Game. He was done again and then he came back to coach the Cowboys. He retired once more but opted to return to a non-coaching front office position with Miami, which he has since relinquished.

Parcells is expected to be inducted into the Hall of Fame in 2012, but he also cannot be expected to ever get this love of football out of his system no matter how hard he tries.

So, Why is Bill Parcells Called the Big Tuna?

There's some debate. Parcells has always maintained that as a linebackers coach for New England, before he joined the Giants, a player tried to fool him with a ridiculous excuse. "Who do you think I am?" Parcells replied. "Charlie the Tuna?" At the time, the "Charlie the Tuna" animated character depicting a chunky tuna was part of a popular advertising campaign for StarKist tuna. The character was known to constantly be rejected by the company that offered the catchphrase, "Sorry, Charlie." Thus, the nickname Big Tuna or just Tuna was born.

Players over the years have said, however, that Parcells' hefty size at the time contributed to the nickname's origin.

Judy is now an ex-wife; the couple divorced in 2002. Parcells once wrote in an autobiography that she couldn't understand why he coaches if it makes him so miserable. He didn't have an answer. He's acknowledged that his interests and viewpoints outside of football are "pretty narrow" and that he's "not proud of that."

He also has questioned whether he could have been a better father if he hadn't been so devoted and addicted to the game he loves. It's a point with which his daughter, Suzy, might agree, considering what she once told the *Palm Beach Post*. "For most of my life, my dad was there, but not really *there*," she said in a story that detailed many family events Parcells missed. "He never made us part of his inner circle."

That might not be completely true, of course. He apparently tried especially hard once, so many years ago. Tried to have the normal job and the normal life. But then, as he said many times later, he realized he was a football coach. "It's what I am," Parcells once said. "There's nothing else to it."

For the Giants, he was a football coach who alternately charmed or tormented them. One who gave them and their fans plenty of memories and a lot better results than he managed as a realtor.

"I had some of the very, very best players that a coach could want, and we were able to collect enough of them and keep them together for a while in those days," Parcells said after getting named to the Giants' first Ring of Honor in 2010. "So I think it's just a tribute to all of those people, and I'm just happy to receive this."

Super Bowl XXV: Wide Right

The thought entered Ottis Anderson's head again, but this time he did not put it there. All those years after boasting to a college roommate, and all those months after telling one of his Giants teammates, and all those days after insisting to yet another Giants teammate that this outlandish dream to become a Super Bowl MVP in his home state of Florida would come true, there he was on the sideline at Super Bowl XXV in Tampa on January 27, 1991.

There was Scott Norwood on the field, the Buffalo kicker preparing for a 47-yard field goal try that would end the closest Super Bowl ever played. Eight seconds remained on the clock. The scoreboard displayed an improbable 1-point lead for the Giants.

Now, at the time Anderson's dream seemed most possible, the thought of him becoming Super Bowl MVP did not come from the Giants running back. It came instead from a Disney World rep charged with prepping for the postgame commercial with the game's Most Valuable Player.

Amid the screaming pleas of a stadium full of fans riveted by everything from Whitney Houston's stirring national anthem, and the F–16 flyover that made everyone in the stadium feel safer during this time of war, to one of the best Super Bowls ever played, the Disney rep blocked out the spectacle surrounding him.

He did not focus on the Giants kneeling on their sideline in anticipation and prayer, the way they had the previous week when their own kicker, Matt Bahr, sent them to this game with a 42-yard field goal.

He did not focus on Jeff Hostetler, the Giants former backup quarterback who most certainly could not win a Super Bowl if you listened to any predictions. Hostetler had one knee on the ground, one hand on his chin, and one more hope in his head that he was about to prove everyone wrong.

The Disney rep was not assigned to the Buffalo Bills sideline, where players held hands as they waited. Jim Kelly, Thurman Thomas, and the high-octane Bills could no longer worry about how the Giants had shut down their fast-break, no-huddle offense, which had scored 95 points in its previous two playoff games.

It was up to the kicker.

Nor was there time for the Disney rep to think about Giants coach Bill Parcells, who told his team before the game to throw out the paper on which the calculations would never have given the 7-point underdogs a shot. Or Bill Belichick, the Giants defensive coordinator who came up with the most uncanny defensive plan of all—let the opposing running back rush for 100 yards so you could win the game.

The Disney rep could certainly not get in Norwood's head, which only a few days earlier had been filled with thoughts of this very scenario.

"Do I visualize that?" Norwood said when asked if he pictured hitting a game-winning field goal. "Sure. You start to think about what would be the ultimate for a kicker, and that would be it."

No, the Disney rep had business to handle amid the chaos.

So while all those hearts thumped on the sideline, in the stadium, across the country, and all the way overseas to troops in the Persian Gulf War, the Disney rep made a matter-of-fact statement to Anderson. "'If he misses this kick,'" Anderson has recalled the Disney rep telling him, "'you're the most valuable player.'"

"What?!" Anderson responded as Norwood lined up for the kick he dreamed of making.

"If he misses this kick," the man repeated, "you're the most valuable player."

The 34-year-old Anderson absorbed the words, on the cusp of fulfilling a dream that started as a boast he made while at the University of Miami. It had hovered in his head after all those losing seasons with the Cardinals, but it had apparently died when Anderson prepared to retire after the Giants' heartbreaking playoff game loss in 1989. Then Giants fullback Maurice Carthon told him the next year's Super Bowl was in Tampa, and Anderson changed his mind so he could take one more shot.

Just that past week, as the Giants appeared to run out of time against San Francisco in the NFC Championship Game, Anderson had told receiver Mark Ingram not to worry, that they would be going to this Super Bowl so that he could fulfill his dream.

Now, after all that waiting, hoping, and believing, the Disney man was telling Anderson he was just eight seconds and a missed kick away?

"'I don't want to hear that,'" Anderson recalled saying in an NFL Films interview years later. "I just kind of shook him off. 'I don't want to hear that. I want to see if he's going to make this kick.'"

He never did.

He never does. Over and over, no matter how many times a Giants fan watches the replay, or how many times Norwood and the Bills might decline to view the same history-making image. Every time for the past 20-plus years, the result is the same, the dream of one man and one team realized with such glee contrasted with the anguish of another team.

"No good," announcer Al Michaels declares over and over, as the ball sails far enough but just a few yards off. "Wide right."

The Giants storm the field, Anderson among them, screaming; all but Hostetler, the back-up quarterback who wasn't supposed to do it. He remains where he was for the kick, on one knee, hand on his chin, burying what must have been the world's biggest smile. Then he joins them, helmet raised as the Bills collapse on the field and Norwood's head hangs, his hand going to his eyes.

This would be the ultimate. One way or the other.

"MVP!" the Giants chant after Anderson's 102 yards rushing. "MVP!"

* * *

Twenty years after the Giants' 20–19 win, the storylines still reverberate through the NFL and beyond. For the Bills, it was the first painful step toward the ignominious distinction of losing four straight Super Bowls. For Norwood, it was a game that inspired disappointment, endless questions, and a movie, *Buffalo '66,* that features a Buffalo kicker named Scott Wood, who misses the game-winning field goal. An enraged fan attempts to hunt him down and kill him.

But amazingly, when Norwood returned to Buffalo the next day, the 30,000 fans who greeted him aimed their hands not at his neck but around his shoulders in a figurative hug. "Scotty! Scotty! Scotty!" they chanted at an event for the Bills. Norwood emerged, fighting tears at the fans' forgiveness.

"He got so emotional, he just kind of crumpled over into my arms," receiver James Lofton told the *New York Daily News* on the 20-year anniversary. "I knew then it was a heavy burden for him. It's almost too much for someone to have to bear."

Norwood was said to have borne it, moving on to a normal life in his native Virginia as a realtor, eventually recognizing that these spectacles, as painful or glorious as they may be, constitute just one moment in a lifetime.

Anderson, Hostetler, and the Giants had earned one of the greatest wins in franchise history. Super Bowl XXV marked Belichick's farewell present to the Giants in 1990, before he left for Cleveland and his first head coaching job, so many years before he became known as Coach Hoodie, the surly genius for New England.

Super Assistants

The Giants' 1990 coaching staff was stocked with talent, featuring six former and future head coaches, including Bill Belichick and then-wide receivers coach Tom Coughlin. From the days of assistant coaches Vince Lombardi and Tom Landry, the Giants have produced some impressive resumes, with several former assistants going on to head coaching jobs and their own shots at the big game. Bill Parcells' tenure was especially productive in that regard, as he and his former assistants also utilized former players as assistants. "I do take a lot of pride in that," Parcells said. "And I think you could make a case that the coaching staff that I had with the Giants had to be among the very best."

Here's a quick look at some Super assistants through the years.

Coach	Key Giants Role	Head Coach for ...Super Bowl (Win or Loss)
Vince Lombardi	Offensive coach	Green Bay I, II (W)
Tom Landry	Defensive coach	Dallas VI, XII (W); V, X, XIII (L)
Bill Parcells	Def. Coordinator	NYG/NE XXI, XXV (W)/XXXI (L)
Bill Belichick	Def. Coordinator	NE XXXVI, XXXVIII, XXXIX (W); XLII (L)
Tom Coughlin	Wide receivers	NYG XLII (W)
Sean Payton	Off. Coordinator	New Orleans XLIV (W)

The Bills had routed the Raiders in the AFC Championship Game 51–3 while the Giants had not scored a touchdown in their 15–13 win for the NFC title.

So Belichick needed a plan so creative, so unique, so utterly unpredictable that the Giants rebelled. He wanted them to allow Bills all-pro running back Thomas to rush for more than 100 yards. The prideful Giants defense featuring Hall of Famer Lawrence Taylor, captain Carl Banks, and defensive lineman Leonard Marshall resisted but eventually relented.

They had to slow down the Bills, who had been innovative in using a two-minute offense throughout the game, tiring out defenses behind Kelly's arm, Thomas' legs, and the speed and hands of Pro Bowl receiver Andre Reed.

The Giants would give Reed catches—then punish him with hits. They hit him so often that he would say after the game—and several foot-step induced drops—that it was the most beat up he had been.

The Giants would allow the Bills yardage as long as it came at the precious cost of time. As they had in their NFC title game win, the Giants wanted to control the clock. There they had held the ball for a whopping 39 minutes to the 49ers' 21. They would top that number in the Super Bowl, setting a record with a time of possession of 40:33.

They started strong, scoring on their first drive for a 3–0 lead, Houston's inspiring anthem providing a soulful reminder of the troops watching in their war zones.

On the Giants sideline stood Phil Simms, four years removed from a Super Bowl MVP performance against Denver—and six weeks removed from playing, thanks to yet another injury in a career full of them.

He broke his leg, oddly enough, against the Bills in a 17–13 loss, and Hostetler took over the 11–3 Giants. The quarterback had been frustrated for most of his seven years with the team, but he maximized his chance, going undefeated as the Giants utilized his mobility with bootlegs and roll-outs.

Hostetler made the play that saved the Giants, even if it looked like it came on one that could bury them. Trailing 10–3, Hostetler was sacked in his end zone by Hall of Fame lineman Bruce Smith, who was shut down the rest of the night by Giants tackle Jumbo Elliott.

Smith got the safety for a 12–3 lead, but it could have been much worse. Smith shrewdly reached for Hostetler's right arm, which held the ball. But Hostetler, who had taken a beating from other rushing Bills throughout the first half, managed to yank the ball back to his chest.

A 17–3 lead could have helped finish the defensive, ball-controlled Giants. Instead, Hostetler, as he did against the 49ers, kept coming back. With just 25 seconds left, Hostetler hit Stephen "The Touchdown Maker" Baker for a 14-yard touchdown, the team's first in six quarters.

At halftime, Parcells reminded the players who had been with him when they trailed vs. Denver in Super Bowl XXI before their 39–20 win that they were in the "exact same situation as we are now."

"I told them the first drive of the third quarter was the most important of the game," Parcells said later. "We had to do something with it." What they did was go on the longest drive in Super Bowl history—9:29 of what Parcells so affectionately called "power football."

Anderson, who gained 63 of his yards in the second half, picked up 24 on a third-and-1.

Hostetler passed three times for first downs, but one is especially remembered. Mark Ingram caught a short pass on third-and-13 and appeared to be tackled over and over. But he dodged one tackle, then spun back under and around to his left before breaking another. Then he moved back right, hopping on one foot, dragging the last would-be tackler just enough to reach the first down. A few plays later, Anderson ran it in for a touchdown, giving the Giants a 17–12 lead.

Four years before, the running back had gotten a garbage time touchdown when Parcells rewarded the veteran backup to Joe Morris because he might not get back to the Super Bowl. In 1989, Anderson, a borderline Hall of Fame–caliber running back with losing Cardinals teams most of his career, emerged for a 1,000 yard season when no one expected it. But he would lose time in 1990 to first-round draft pick Rodney Hampton and only started in the Super Bowl because Hampton had broken his leg in the playoff win over Chicago.

Now he had given his team the lead.

"It's the player [who] determines when he's going to retire," center Bart Oates said after the game.

But as Anderson ground out his last chance at glory on 34-year-old legs, 24-year-old Bills running back Thomas sprinted through the Giants defense, maybe even more than Belichick had envisioned.

For the game, Thomas had 135 yards on 15 carries, numbers that would have made him the MVP if Norwood's kick had gone through. He answered yet again with a 31-yard run, and the Bills led 19–17.

The teams grew exhausted, the Giants pounding the Bills on offense, marching down field one more time for a 21-yard field goal by Bahr to take yet another lead 20–19. Then came the final drive for Buffalo, Thomas eating up yards, and the Bills simply running out of time—and timeouts—as they raced down to the Giants' 30.

Norwood had kicked on turf in Buffalo and was just 1-of-5 kicking on natural grass and over 40 yards. Years later, the theories still emerged, as documented in a *Buffalo News* retrospective on the 20-year anniversary. Holder Frank Reich remembered Norwood kicking wide left so often in warm-ups that day that he might have overcompensated.

Norwood's eventual successor at kicker, Steve Christie, remembered watching on TV and years later shared with Reich what he saw then: The laces were not lined up correctly. Off by an eighth of an inch, which Christie said could make all the difference.

The kick was certainly deep enough, but kept sailing to the right of the goalpost by a few yards and never coming back. A few yards. An eighth of an inch. That's all it took to give the Giants 20 years of memories and the iconic *Sports Illustrated* cover shot of cornerback Everson Walls, his head back, his arms spread wide in exultation. Gave Anderson his chance to bypass the traditional "I'm going to Disney World!" greeting and take the second option the persistent Disney rep offered.

"I dedicate this win to all the troops," Anderson said into Disney's camera, waving a small American flag.

That's all it took to end the dream of one man while fulfilling that of another.

"I lost it," Anderson told NFL Films years later. "I jumped. I went running. I went yelling on the field. 'We did it! We did it! We did it!'"

10 Super Bowl XXI: Return to Glory

A little more than 20 years later, George Martin put himself back in his hotel room the night before the game that would forever define his Giants team. The next night, the defensive end and his Giants teammates would play in the franchise's first Super Bowl. Thirty years after the last Giants' NFL title, the 1986 edition mirrored their tenacious defense and opportunistic offense.

Veteran Giants like Martin and linebacker Harry Carson endured the franchise's darkest days in the 1970s. Younger players like wrecking-ball linebacker Lawrence Taylor echoed the reckless abandon of predecessor Sam Huff while surpassing the skills of anyone who came before.

The Giants were once again built on defense, though they had a Pro Bowl running back in Joe Morris and a quarterback named Phil Simms who survived as many boos and injuries as his championship predecessor Charlie Conerly did in the '50s.

They would play the Denver Broncos under the white-hot spotlight of the Super Bowl, trying to finally silence the cries of the long-suffering Giants fans.

Two decades later, Martin still remembered the anticipation he felt in a silent hotel room before all the noise of the country's biggest spectacle of a sporting event. "You're thinking about your performance, what you're going to do; you have your moments of grandeur," Martin remembered. "All of us want to be the MVP. On Super Bowl Sunday, even the crimes go down. Even the criminals are watching. We played in Pasadena, 110,000 fans—your neighbors, your friends, your colleagues.

"If you sneeze, if you make a mistake, if you make a great play. You know what? You're out there performing for your legacy. Sleep the night before? C'mon."

* * *

Their legacy would cap off a playoff roll surpassing anything they could have dreamed of if they had managed to fall asleep the night before.

Their 39–20 victory offered them a resounding reward for all they endured.

Simms, the quarterback who was booed on draft day and so many days since, claimed the most accurate game in Super Bowl history, completing 22-of-25 passes for 268 yards and three touchdowns to win the game's MVP award. In the process, he dwarfed Denver's John Elway—the celebrated architect of The Drive, his famous 98-yard game-winning march against Cleveland in the AFC Championship Game two weeks earlier.

"'Joe, what if the Broncos decide they're going to stop you from running the ball?'" Morris remembered someone asking him the week of the game. His response was simple.

"If they do," Morris said, "Phil Simms will kill them."

The Giants all came out to slay the Broncos and their own torturous past. They grew week to week as they finished the season with 12 straight victories.

A comeback from a 17-point halftime deficit for a rally against San Francisco in the regular season preceded a 49–3 humiliation of the two-time Super Bowl champ 49ers in the playoffs. A 19–16 victory in a Super Bowl preview against Denver—sparked by

McConkey Makes His Mark

Before Super Bowl XXI, Bill Parcells told receiver and punt returner Phil McConkey to lead the Giants onto the field in Pasadena and to wave his towel and "make it feel like Giants Stadium."

McConkey not only did that, he made the most of a Super Bowl he couldn't have imagined at the beginning of the season when the Giants released him. His 44-yard catch on a flea flicker pass from Phil Simms left him achingly close to his dream of catching a Super Bowl touchdown as he was upended at the 1-yard line.

Showing the gritty emotion that made Giants fans love him—and Parcells re-acquire him from Green Bay after releasing him earlier in the year—McConkey raised his hands over his head, fell to the ground, and pounded the turf.

"I'm thinking, 'My God, I'm gonna score a touchdown in the Super Bowl'—what I'd dreamt about my whole life," McConkey later said in an NFL Films segment. "I'm *that* close to a Super Bowl touchdown. Ohhh, I was just elated and frustrated at the same time."

He would only have to wait a little longer, catching a touchdown after a pass deflected off tight end Mark Bavaro. McConkey then hustled in for the score of his life in the Giants' 39–20 win over Denver.

Bavaro almost couldn't reach the ecstatic McConkey, who started screaming and jumping before Bavaro finally picked him up in celebration.

McConkey pulled off one more big play—in real life. In the postgame celebration, he spotted a gun on the field where it had apparently fallen after a skirmish between security and a fan. The alert former Navy man picked up the weapon and handed it to security before heading back into the biggest party of his football career.

"I scored a touchdown in the Super Bowl, helped my team, and saved some lives," McConkey told NFL Films with a smile. "All in a day's work."

Martin's acrobatic batted pass and lumbering 78-yard touchdown return—gave the Giants confidence that would spill over through an entire postseason of dominance.

Simms came through on a fourth-and-17 play against Minnesota at a point when his season had been filled with incompletions and doubt. Now?

"I'm going to go to Disney World!" he shouted into a camera, the first Super Bowl MVP to make the exclamation of an endorsement.

Just like the regular season, when the Giants lost the opener to Dallas then took their championship baby steps before building steam, New York started slowly in the Super Bowl. Elway matched Simms' hot streak at the start, each quarterback completing their first six passes. Denver built a 10–7 lead when the Broncos reached the Giants 1-yard line early in the second quarter.

That's when the men known as the Big Blue Wrecking Crew reminded everyone how they earned the name. On first down, Elway scrambled and was met by Taylor, who only sacked quarterbacks 20½ times that season.

Second down. Time to step up for Carson—the Giants' captain so revered that Parcells selected him to go solo for the coin toss. He knocked down Broncos back Gerald Willhite.

Third down. Carl Banks, the linebacker who spent most of his Giants career in the shadow of Carson or Taylor but shone brightest with 14 tackles in this Super Bowl, was next. He recalled the Broncos using a pitch in this type of situation in their regular-season meeting, he said later. He remembered correctly and stuffed running back Sammy Winder for a 4-yard loss.

That kicker Rich Karlis missed the chip-shot field goal—and another one later in the quarter—only added to the Giants' adrenaline.

Martin couldn't sleep the night before but later gave Elway a nightmare, sacking him in the end zone for a safety and cutting Denver's lead to 10–9. "I told George Martin, 'George, if I get you to the Super Bowl, can you win it for me?'" remembered Morris, who rushed for 246 yards in the Giants' two NFC playoff victories. "'Yeah, I can.' Now think of this—he gets that safety; puts us in the driver's seat."

In the second half, Parcells called for backup quarterback Jeff Rutledge to join the punt team and read the situation on a fourth-and-inches play. Rutledge saw what he wanted, looked over to the sideline to Parcells, who nodded. Rutledge stepped to the line and sneaked for the first down.

"I think the turning point was…[the] fake punt," center Bart Oates recalled. "That kind of just turned things around for us."

A few plays later, Simms hit tight end Mark Bavaro for the first of his three touchdown passes, giving the Giants their first lead 16–10.

There would be no special drives for Elway as the Giants defense settled in and shut down the Broncos. After a three-and-out, Simms connected with energetic fan favorite Phil McConkey for the game's most memorable play—a 44-yard pass off a flea flicker that left McConkey at the 1-yard line. Morris took it in from there, and the rout was on. McConkey caught a pass off the hands of Bavaro in the end zone, and backup running back Ottis Anderson scored on a touchdown run to cap the Giants' scoring.

Afterward, they celebrated the end of the franchise's dark era, with Carson donning a security jacket to sneak up on Parcells and douse the coach with the Gatorade bath these Giants turned into a tradition. The coach then asked his linemen to carry him around the field so he could mark the moment he helped return the team of his boyhood dreams to its former glory—and opened a new chapter, one they couldn't have imagined even if they had slept the night before the game of their lives.

"In my wildest dreams," Simms said after the game, "I couldn't have hoped it would work out this way."

11 Emlen Tunnell: The "First Black Everything"

Emlen Tunnell nearly lost his life once and risked it twice more to save someone else by the time he hitchhiked his way from Pennsylvania to New York in 1948. So this trip from his home in Garrett Hill, Pennsylvania, to request a tryout with the Giants was far from his most daring decision.

The future Hall of Fame safety just wanted to play football, the sport he starred in at the University of Toledo before he broke his neck as a 17-year-old freshman and was prematurely given Last Rites—when he wasn't even Catholic. He defied doctors' predictions by playing again after wearing a neck brace for a year. He was named to the Coast Guard's football All-Star team when the army and navy wouldn't allow him to enlist due to his neck injury after World War II began.

Tunnell did a lot more than play football while in the Coast Guard. He saved one shipmate's life after a Japanese torpedo blew a hole in the side of Tunnell's ship, suffering burns while rescuing a man who had caught fire. He rescued another from drowning in frigid temperatures after he fell overboard, and Tunnell was honored posthumously for his heroics in 2011.

When he got out of the Coast Guard, Tunnell again played the sport he loved for the University of Iowa, becoming the second Hawkeye to catch three touchdown passes in a game.

So when Tunnell decided to hitch a ride on a banana truck and travel to New York, it was not the most risky decision he had ever made. But he knew it came with the potential for rejection that went beyond his football ability.

Tunnell approached the nearby Philadelphia Eagles first. But the Eagles did not consider Tunnell's impressive football resume or military service as great a priority as the color of his brown skin. "The Eagles wouldn't give him a tryout," Emlen's sister, Vivian Robinson, recalled. "They didn't know how the rest of the players would react; they didn't want to do it."

The NFL began to re-integrate in 1946, when Kenny Washington and Woody Strode broke the unofficial ban on African American players a year before Jackie Robinson crossed baseball's color line. But Washington and Strode were allowed to play for the Los Angeles Rams only after heavy pressure due to a city-financed stadium.

No African American player was drafted in the NFL until 1949, though many were drafted by the military. Unlike baseball, the NFL originally allowed black players in the league. Despite a wealth of talent across the country, though, not a single African American played in the league from 1933–46.

After the Eagles' rejection, Tunnell traveled to New York, hoping times had changed enough for Giants owner Tim Mara to give him the same "fair shake" black players received at Iowa. Twenty-two years earlier, however, Mara's Giants were reported to have contributed to the sport's shame even before the ban.

The Giants refused to take the field for a game against the Canton Bulldogs at the Polo Grounds in 1926, according to accounts from African American newspapers and historians. They wouldn't play until Sol Butler, a black player for Canton, agreed he would not.

A 2009 column in *Sports Illustrated* mentioned the incident, as well, depicting Mara as standing by the wishes of his players and not making the call himself.

Despite the accounts of that history, Tunnell once said a mutual acquaintance told him Mara might treat him fairly in 1948. The presence of the few African American predecessors in the league—including running back Buddy Young for the New York Yankees of the All-America Football Conference—should be helpful, the acquaintance said.

The friend apparently was correct.

"'If you've got enough guts to come in here and ask for a tryout, you can have one,'" Tunnell often recalled Mara saying to him years later. Tunnell proved Mara correct for admiring the man's tenacity, as he became the first African American to play for the Giants, the first to coach in the NFL in the modern era, and the first to enter the Pro Football Hall of Fame.

"Probably the best safety to ever play was Emlen Tunnell," teammate Sam Huff said. "He was a good hitter; he was everything you wanted in a safety. He was not the fastest guy in the world, but he had great moves and he was very agile."

Tunnell was not just a hitter but a healer. He earned his spot on the team not just with his play but with his ability to connect with many Southern teammates during especially turbulent racial times and to withstand racial abuse from the stands.

"Mara said they would try it out and see how people acted," Robinson recalled.

Her brother formed a close bond with the Mara family, including the owner.

"He was a great man," Tunnell told *The New York Times*, speaking of Tim Mara, after his Hall of Fame election in 1967. "I still use some of the things he told me, like he said to me once, 'Don't let other people tell you what a person is like, let your heart decide.' That works."

Tunnell was guided by his heart his whole life until it gave out when he died of a heart attack at 50 in 1975.

Before that, the legendary Giants safety—who earned the nickname "Mr. Offense on Defense" thanks to his interception, punt, and kick returns that sometimes gave him more yardage than the league's top running backs—was known for his ability to get along with anyone despite enduring racial abuse.

"He was a great guy, easy-going guy," said longtime Giants trainer John Johnson, who broke in the same year as Tunnell. "[His teammates] loved him. They loved him."

Said Robinson, "He was a very outgoing person, too. They took to him like he took to them. The players were never ugly to them. They realized he was as good as they were, maybe a little bit better."

* * *

The NFL Network apparently agreed with the unofficial scouting report of Tunnell's sister. When it listed its top 100 players of all time in 2010, Tunnell was the second-ranked Giant behind Lawrence Taylor—and the 79th player overall.

He was one of the first one-way players, remaining on defense at safety after head coach Steve Owen put him in and watched him intercept four passes against Green Bay. Tunnell helped implement Owen's famed "Umbrella Defense" that fanned out defensive backs like an umbrella and was a precursor to Giants defensive coach Tom Landry's invention of the 4–3 defense.

In 14 years (11 with the Giants), the nine-time Pro Bowler intercepted 79 passes, an NFL record when he retired, and scored on 10 touchdown returns—five punts, four interceptions, and one kickoff. He scored four times in 1951, including an 82-yard punt return in a win over the Chicago Cardinals on a day when Tunnell totaled 178 return yards.

While Tunnell eventually became part of the Giants' glory years teams, winning the NFL title in 1956 and playing in the 1958 title game against Baltimore, things did not start out smoothly for him in New York.

"I was at the first game, and it was one of the worst experiences you could go through for an African American," Robinson said. "Everyone hates what they don't understand.

"He really didn't [let it affect him]. 'If they want to cut the fool, let them go ahead.' But the first few months were really horrible and I don't know how he did it, but I'm his sister and I know how I felt about it."

While outsiders offered racial taunts, Tunnell and his teammates defied stereotypes. The player known as "Em" to teammates and friends formed an especially close relationship with Charlie Conerly, the quarterback from Clarksdale, Mississippi. The pair of players quickly alleviated concerns about potential tension on the team.

"Two or three times, maybe more, Em took [Conerly] up to the Red Rooster in Harlem," Conerly's widow, Perian, said of the neighborhood night club. "Em was such a sweet guy. He was crazy about Charlie; he really was. Of course, he was the first black [Giant] and management was worried about how the Mississippi quarterback would get along with the first black guy. They turned out to be the best of friends of anybody on the team. They just kind of hit it off."

Things were not as smooth when the team traveled to Southern cities. In the days of segregation, the man who twice risked his life to save another man was deemed unfit to stay in the Giants' team hotel.

"It was tough for him in the south," Johnson remembered. "When we had to go to Florida, he couldn't stay with us. He just took it in stride. But I know there was one time we were at a hotel, we were having a meeting. The police came to get him out of there. They knew he was in the hotel.

"Four of our guys stood in the doorway. 'You want him, you gotta come and get him.'"

Robinson remembered her brother telling stories of his teammates eventually choosing to skip restaurants that wouldn't serve him, opting instead to sit and eat with him on the bus.

"It was an ugly situation," she said.

* * *

Tunnell never got ugly, though. While he might have been the subject of unfounded hate, he often responded with compassion to strangers.

70

Robinson remembered her brother allowing cab drivers to sleep over at the house after late-night drives. *The New York Times* reported that when the Giants celebrated Tunnell with a day in his honor long after he won over the fans, a group of pan-handlers he befriended outside the stadium took up a collection and handed him $28 as a gift.

"It was the best gift," Tunnell told the *Times,* "because if they had a million bucks, they would have given it to me. They were guys who hung around the ballpark, guys I'd given a dime or quarter to when I first started playing at the Polo Grounds, and then they hung around Yankee Stadium when the Giants moved there.

"It ain't no big thing because you're a great athlete. There's great ditchdiggers, great street cleaners—that's part of life."

It was little wonder Tunnell became a favorite of the soft-spoken Wellington Mara as well as his brother, Jack, then later Wellington's son, John. The Maras hired Tunnell as an assistant coach and a scout after he finished his playing career, making him the first African American coach of the modern era.

"First black everything," Tunnell once told the *Des Moines Register.* "Player, scout, talent scout, assistant coach, and first full-time black assistant in the whole league."

Tunnell dreamed of adding to the list by becoming the first black head coach, but he died too young to fulfill the goal. He had potential to be a good one. He tutored future Giants stars such as Carl Lockhart, whom he nicknamed "Spider" and also followed legendary coach Vince Lombardi to Green Bay in the final years of his playing career. Lombardi credited Tunnell's leadership in helping the Packers win a title and building the foundation for their early dynasty.

When Tunnell was elected to the Hall of Fame in 1967, the humble man with the great talent thanked the Hall's curator Dick McGann, according to the *Times.*

"Don't thank me," McGann told him. "You did it yourself."

12 Frank Gifford

The movie-star face has wrinkled. The familiar soothing voice that helped popularize *Monday Night Football* has not been regularly heard on the air for more than 20 years. And the man who became a Pro Bowler at three positions is known to an entire generation of morning talk-show viewers as Kathie Lee's husband and Cody's father.

But for Giants fans, the team they watch today and the culture in which it's presented has the most basic of origins with the handsome and talented California kid named Frank Gifford. Before any of the superstar Giants got their own talk shows or started a career in broadcasting either during or after their football career, there was Gifford, a star built perfectly for football's introduction to television.

"I think playing for one team, and playing in a period of time where football was just happening," Gifford said when asked what he was proudest of in his 12-year, Hall of Fame career. "With the advent of national television, I was right around the beginning; the game really began steamrolling to the top of the sports world because it's perfectly suited for television."

So was Gifford. His handsome face led to movie roles while he played football at the University of Southern California. When the kid out of Bakersfield first heard he was selected as the Giants' No. 1 draft pick in 1952, he wasn't thrilled with the idea of heading to the East Coast.

Who could blame him? Football was not yet a full-time career as much as it was a passion that offered a more enjoyable way to pay the bills than the other half of the year. And now he would be traveling across the country to a whole new environment. But

Gifford eventually owned the city, raising glasses with New York's celebrity elite at legendary bar Toots Shor's and helping the Giants raise expectations on the field.

He worked for what he wanted in the game, filling in at safety his first year at USC before eventually starring as a tailback. But his dream to play quarterback remained so persistent he eventually asked Giants coach Jim Lee Howell for what would be a failed tryout at the position—the year after roommate and close friend Charlie Conerly led the team to the 1958 NFL title game.

The temerity Gifford showed in making that request, as well as his recent statement to Mickey Mantle biographer Jane Leavy that the baseball legend shared *Gifford's* locker—not the other way around—demonstrated a hint of, well, let's just say extreme confidence beneath an often graceful and humble manner that endeared him to Giants fans and *Monday Night Football* viewers.

The personality and the talent meshed together to form a popular man about town as the Giants rose to prominence in the 1950s and '60s, and Gifford learned to love his adopted city.

He starred on the field even as he endured the same fate he had in college.

Gifford started as a defensive back for the Giants and earned his first Pro Bowl appearance there, although he wanted to focus on offense. He only got his shot to focus on halfback after Howell hired a young Army coach, Vince Lombardi, as his offensive coach.

* * *

Somehow, the laid-back Californian—who was so relaxed his rookie year that then-head coach Steve Owen told veterans at practice to "hammer me down to size," as Gifford has said—connected with the passionate Brooklyn coach.

Gifford helped pave the way for Lombardi to relate to the cynical pro players who didn't instantly buy his emotional rants

Hall of Famer Frank Gifford helped the Giants capture New York City's attention in the 1950s and '60s. (AP Photo/Rooney)

and offered input along with other veterans on plays. Lombardi recognized the talent Gifford could bring if allowed to focus on one side of the ball. The coach helped Gifford work his way up to seven straight Pro Bowl appearances.

Gifford infused the offense with speed and versatility, throwing 14 career touchdowns out of the halfback option and earning the Most Valuable Player award in 1956 when he produced a league-leading 1,422 yards from scrimmage and rushed for 819 yards.

The Giants developed into a champion with Gifford at half-back, Conerly at quarterback, and flanker Kyle Rote—the No. 1 overall pick the season before Gifford whose leg injury damaged what still was an impressive career.

They started humbly at the old Polo Grounds, which Gifford remembered as "a mess" by that point. They played in front of sparse crowds at times, and Gifford laughed when recalling his status as an emerging star. "When I got home, they said, 'Where you been?'" Gifford said of his annual return to California. "That's why I said, it grew up."

While Gifford might have exaggerated, considering USC fans already cheered for him during his prominent time there, his star grew as television and endorsements merged to make him a poster boy for the Giants.

However, he points out that the 1958 NFL title game credited for the boost isn't exactly the Greatest Game (he) Ever Played since his turnovers helped the Colts pull off the win.

"Certainly not on my part," Gifford said. "My two fumbles created what people call the greatest game."

The other most famous game of his career was more painful for Gifford. Literally.

Philadelphia's Chuck Bednarik flattened Gifford in 1960 with a vicious but clean hit that gave the Giants star a concussion. He did not play the next season, though he has repeatedly said that decision had as much to do with him wanting to pursue a broadcasting career with CBS as it did lingering effects from the hit.

But a year later, Gifford decided his voice would remain intact to do one job long after his body could no longer perform another, and he returned to the Giants as a flanker. Once more, he reinvented himself and earned another Pro Bowl nod with the early '60s Giants, which were quarterbacked by Y.A. Tittle.

* * *

Gifford's versatility extended off the field as he paired with legendary acerbic announcer Howard Cosell and "Dandy" Don Meredith to form a revered *Monday Night Football* crew that made the broadcast an institution.

According to an "Outside the Lines" segment on ESPN, Gifford, so often critiqued by the acid-tongued Cosell, helped his broadcast partner decide how to handle the delicate news of musician John Lennon's death, which had been first learned of by a local ABC news affiliate.

Cosell, considered friends with Lennon, was unsure whether to announce the murder as three seconds remained in a game with playoff implications and New England kicker John Smith lined up for a field goal in a tie game.

Gifford told Cosell off the air that he should make the announcement, cautioning him to handle the news with care as "this is going to shake up the whole world."

On the air, Gifford set up the announcement by saying, "Three seconds remaining. John Smith is on the line. And I don't care what's on the line, Howard. You have got to say what we know in the booth."

Cosell then famously announced news of the "unspeakable tragedy" before throwing it back to Gifford, who called the play, a blocked field goal sending the game into overtime.

Gifford told ESPN that looking back from the age of instant information "It was almost primitive" to announce such shocking news interspersed with a football game.

Gifford eventually married Kathie Lee Johnson, the future talk-show host who famously paired with Regis Philbin and filled in barely rising viewers on the exploits of "Frank" and their young son "Cody."

The couple was less cheerful when a tabloid, *The Globe*, reported Frank had an affair with a flight attendant and published photos of the two together, resulting in a statement from the Giffords that it was a painful time.

They apparently worked through the issue and are still together after dealing with the flip side of star status.

All this time later, Gifford, inducted into the Giants' inaugural Ring of Honor class in 2010, still takes pride in his many roles in helping football and the only team for which he played to grow.

"It's pretty fantastic," he said before the ceremony at New Meadowlands Stadium. "I was out there the other day and I walked out onto the field and said, 'Wow, this is a long way from the Polo Grounds.' Of course, being selected as one of the members of the Ring of Honor is really a hell of an honor to be quite proud of."

13 Sam Huff

He can talk as quickly as he used to race to the ballcarrier. Sam Huff's mouth moves with the intensity his body once did, ready to lay a verbal licking on everything from the prima donna players of the modern era to the cheap wages he earned as the heart of the Giants' legendary 1950s defenses.

Huff will proudly tell you about how he was the first NFL player on the cover of *Time* magazine and how TV anchor Walter Cronkite wired him for sound on *The Violent World of Sam Huff*. He will also joyfully recall the punishing hits he couldn't wait to deliver.

"I love talking about the game that I love," Huff said on the phone from his office in Virginia, where he still works as a broadcaster for the Redskins.

But if all Huff did was talk, no one would have listened.

Now he's remembering how he started. How Giants defensive coach Tom Landry switched the lost kid from West Virginia trying to find a position to middle linebacker from offensive guard. How

Huff didn't know what to expect but soon relished his role as the "hit man."

"God, it was like I was born to play that," Huff said. But Landry didn't make Huff a middle linebacker just because of the vengeance-filled hits he unleashed. To hit them, Huff first had to see them.

Huff's tone softened. His speech slowed the way the game did for him. "Now as a linebacker, I can see everything," he said. "I'm sitting in my office—I can see four walls—I can see my whole office sitting in my chair. That's the way I could play football. I could see the whole offense."

When he first arrived as a third-round draft pick in 1956, Huff had little to say. He felt out of place at the team's training camp in Vermont, where his 6'1", 230-pound frame left him knocked around by Giants future Hall of Famer Rosey Brown and All-Pro Rosey Grier. Along with punter and roommate Don Chandler, Huff's homesickness got the best of him and the pair prepared to quit.

They would have, too, but offensive coach Vince Lombardi intercepted them at the airport. Lombardi lured Huff back. Landry made him want to stay. Recognizing Huff's impressive peripheral vision, Landry helped him find a new home on the field, where he started after an injury to top linebacker Ray Beck.

The Giants reeled off five straight wins on the way to their first NFL championship since 1938. While Huff helped create a buzz that left fans at Yankee Stadium roaring, they were not always as friendly in the city.

Huff spent his first year in Manhattan living on 72nd Street by Central Park—the perfect haven for a country boy lost in a world of skyscrapers. But when he first attempted to make his way to the stadium from the city, he became perplexed.

"How do I get to Yankee Stadium?" he remembered asking a hurried New Yorker.

"Take the subway!" came the response.

Huff's Revenge: 72–41

The Giants prospered under Allie Sherman for his first three seasons, even if they couldn't beat Vince Lombardi's Packers in a pair of NFL title games or the Chicago Bears in another one. But as Sherman put his stamp on the team, trading off several defensive stars, including Sam Huff, the strategy eventually backfired.

Adding to the Giants' problems, their remaining stars became unproductive with age, and the club fell into a tailspin for most of the next two decades. A lowlight for them became a highlight for Huff on November 27, 1966, as his Redskins beat Sherman's Giants 72–41 in the NFL's highest-scoring game.

Humiliated, Sherman vowed to reporters the next day his team would never lose a game like that again.

The final three points came on a last-second field goal for Washington, which Huff has claimed he called for on the sideline to rub it in.

"And by God, I did," Huff said. "And I'm not ashamed of it. When there's one guy on the field you don't want to take on, it's the linebacker."

"The subway?" Huff asked, puzzled at the concept of going underground.

After failing to understand his surroundings, Huff eventually owned them. The '50s Giants defense featuring Huff, famed defensive linemen Andy Robustelli, Grier, Dick Modzelewski, and Hall of Fame safety Emlen Tunnell endeared itself to Giants fans.

Especially after the famous 1958 NFL title game, the Giants commanded attention, and Huff—an eventual five-time Pro Bowler—was at the center of it. "CBS followed up [by] wiring me for sound," he said. "I'm the first guy with a microphone that you could hear the sounds. Did that make me a star player? Well the reason I was on the cover of *Time*, the reason I was wired for sound, I was the designated hitter."

Along with his hits, Huff also deterred quarterbacks from throwing his way, picking off 30 passes in his 13-year career.

Despite the success of Huff, Landry, and the Giants defense, head coach Allie Sherman replaced Jim Lee Howell in 1961 and eventually dismembered the successful formula. Landry went to Dallas as a head coach a year before, and Lombardi went to Green Bay the previous season.

Sherman slowly broke up the talented but aging defense, trading one part after another, prompting Huff to seek out owner Wellington Mara. Mara told the linebacker he would not be traded, but Huff was dealt to Washington in April 1964, where he played his final three seasons. Eventually, Huff took to his new home. After his retirement—and a quick stint announcing for the Giants—Huff became a beloved broadcaster in Washington for the next five decades.

But when he first learned of the deal?

He held a grudge against Mara, feeling betrayed. "What happens to owners, unfortunately, is they listen to their coach," Huff said. "Wellington had to listen to Allie Sherman, who disliked me from the beginning. He didn't like the fact I played a Tom Landry defense...and I wouldn't play the defense he designed."

"'You're not gonna play that defense anymore,'" Huff remembered Sherman saying.

"'Like hell,'" Huff said he responded.

Sherman has said the deal was nothing personal; it was just a trade to improve the Giants, who received defensive tackle Andy Stynchula and running back Dick James. That opinion was not shared by fans, including one surprising critic. "Daddy, why did you trade Sam Huff?" *Sports Illustrated* quoted Sherman's 5-year-old daughter at the time.

Despite the rough start and bitter ending, Huff's time as the toast of a town surging with excitement left him forever grateful to be a Giant.

"Let's say this: New York to me is the greatest city in the world. Sports city," Huff said. "It was such a great time in sports."

14 Harry Carson: The Captain

They see the creases in Harry Carson's 57-year-old face, and they can imagine the wisdom each one has brought. They hear Carson's soft voice speak harsh words, and the Hall of Fame former captain leaves Giants fans nodding in agreement when he calls a current player to task.

Carson has so entrenched himself as the leader of the Giants' mid-1980s resurgence that current fans might find it difficult to picture him as a young man who had not yet mastered the role—a young man who came surprisingly close to earning a label not as a leader but as a quitter.

Twice Carson prepared to walk away from the Giants.

The first time, a string of losing seasons and his own poor play left Carson so frustrated and ashamed that he prepared to go home to Florence, South Carolina, in 1980. The 27-year-old linebacker was so embarrassed he refused to accept his paycheck because he didn't believe himself worthy of the rate.

"I just sort of fell into football; it really wasn't a goal of mine," Carson said, remembering what led to his decision to quit. "I guess after playing for four years and I saw the futility of the team.... I wanted to leave and basically see different scenery. To sort of keep my juices flowing if I was going to continue to play. I wanted to leave."

Ray Perkins, the Giants head coach at the time, talked Carson into returning. The fans booed him in his first game back, and Carson absorbed the taunts, even as he deemed them wrong.

"I heard people call me a bum," Carson said after a 28–7 loss to the Rams. "I can understand them being frustrated. I'm frustrated, too. But I'm not a bum."

Four years later, Carson walked out on Bill Parcells at training camp without an explanation when the coach was trying to salvage Carson's career after a 3–12–1 rookie season. Parcells barked to the media that Carson should consider spending his time AWOL at the library reading about leadership. Lawrence Taylor—whose path to the team was smoothed by Carson after the rookie's holdout in 1981 angered veterans—praised Carson's leadership and suggested Parcells and management look up "honesty" after several of the linebackers' friends had been traded.

Carson returned in a pair of days, dismissing Parcells' criticism, saying his coach may have taken shots but didn't mean them, even as the coach remained terse in discussing the betrayal with the media.

The incidents are not remembered as much because of what came after them—and what occurred for most of Carson's career. The thoughtful reflective man who hit hard on the field gained enough of Parcells' respect that the coach named him the team's only captain for Super Bowl XXI. Parcells sent Carson out there by himself for the pregame coin toss in Pasadena, California. It was a nod to all the time Carson had spent with the Giants and all the losing he had absorbed before emerging as a player who taught his team how to win.

"I think in Parcells' mind, it was an honor," running back Joe Morris said. "I watched Harry Carson. I watched what he did, and you try to pattern yourself after him."

Even when he considered quitting, Carson showed why fans, players, coaches, and staff have built so much respect for him. The man didn't even want to accept his paycheck that time in 1980. He felt he had not earned it and had to be pushed into taking his own salary.

Ultimately, Carson earned his paycheck and so much more. He became the leader of the Super Bowl championship team that made all the frustration worth it.

"I think things happen for a reason. When I was going through that time, I wanted out; I really wanted out," Carson said. "Had

I not gone through those down years, I don't think I would have appreciated winning a Super Bowl quite as much.

"So when I played and I went through those dark times, much like with all of the fans, I could very much identify with what they were feeling and their frustration. I appreciated winning probably more so than some of the people who hadn't gone through that."

* * *

While Taylor terrorized quarterbacks, Carson battered running backs, stopping the run like few have. He was the inside linebacker to Taylor's outside, the Giants' version of a middle linebacker in Parcells' 3-4 defense that took advantage of an abundance of talented linebackers.

Hall of a Player...Finally

Anyone who's heard Harry Carson in his various roles as a broadcaster knows he is never afraid to speak his mind. So after getting frustrated by years of waiting for election into the Hall of Fame, Carson wrote a letter critiquing the process of allowing only writers to vote and asking not to be considered. The Hall did not honor the request.

In 2006, when Carson again decided to avoid the anticipation by flying to Hawaii, he was notified by a kid at the baggage claim that he finally made it into Canton, Ohio. Having had plenty of false starts before, Carson initially took the news with a grain of salt, but when more folks continued to pass on their congratulations, he couldn't ignore a whole shaker.

The stubborn pride that helped him fire up his Giants teammates almost prompted Carson to turn down the honor. But out of loyalty and respect for the memory of Wellington Mara, who died the previous year, the linebacker took his place among the all-time greats.

"The man I'm happiest for is the late Wellington Mara," Carson said after his election. "It had crossed my mind to turn my back on the honor, but if I did that, I'd be disrespecting something Mr. Mara wanted for me so badly. So that wasn't an option."

The converted defensive lineman out of South Carolina State would go down as one of the greatest linebackers to play the game, being voted *Pro Football Weekly*'s best inside linebacker of all time. He was voted to the Pro Bowl nine times, and he was elected to the Hall of Fame on his seventh try in 2006.

But stats and awards will never define Carson because his true value comes from the reverence with which his teammates speak of him.

"Without good leadership, you can't have a good team," Morris said. "Lawrence was a great, great player, but he didn't lead. That was Harry's job.

"You know what's sad about that? There are times people forget about that. They forget he was a great linebacker before Lawrence got there. Great as a player as he was, he was a better leader."

He showed his leadership early with Taylor, helping the No. 2 overall draft pick and high-priced rookie blend in after his high salary demands alienated veterans.

Carson also helped Parcells adapt from his role as a defensive coordinator to head coach after getting on the same page with him. Parcells has called Carson one of the all-time greats.

Lineman George Martin, another defensive leader who played with Carson through the dark days, once said Carson displayed an unrivaled intensity on game day. "He's like a caged animal," Martin told *Sports Illustrated*. "And he's a leader by example. With him it's not, 'You guys go ahead.' It's, 'Follow me.'"

Taylor thanked the friend who's been like a brother long after their playing days ended. After all of Taylor's various misdeeds, Carson supported the man, not the actions, saying simply that you support family.

At Taylor's Hall of Fame induction in 1999, LT acknowledged there had been a rift with Carson, but his old teammate and friend still showed up. "Harry Carson came out for me today, and that's the classiest thing I've ever seen in my life," Taylor said during his speech. "Harry, thank you, thank you. I love you, man. I love you."

They all loved Carson as a teammate, even if he could be rough on rookies. Morris remembered Carson ordering him to stand on flights as a rite of passage. Carson offered his seat on takeoff and landing.

A small dose of rookie ribbing was a small price to pay for a teammate who would be there for anything you needed. "Harry was incredible as a teammate," said offensive lineman Karl Nelson, who remembered Carson stepping up when Nelson battled cancer. "When I was diagnosed the second time around, my younger daughter was born after my first chemo treatment. Harry told my wife, 'If Karl can't be there, I'll be there.' And he did that with another player, when he did have to be there."

All these years later, Carson's still there for his teammates long after they've finished playing.

* * *

One of the best sports blogs around is rarely updated and not often discussed. But if you want to get a better understanding of the football life—the real one, beyond the dramatic music and testosterone-filled culture of today—check out "Harry's Hits" on www.harrycarson.com. There Carson sporadically but passionately delves into the type of NFL issues gaining more attention with each new incident involving concussions or another tragedy with a former player.

Dave Duerson, the safety who played on the Giants 1990 Super Bowl team as well as the '85 Bears, was the latest. He shot himself in the chest, leaving a note saying he wanted his brain studied to help diagnose the effects of the many concussions he endured on the field and the pain he said prompted his suicide at age 50.

It's an issue Carson has long battled. He suffered from post-concussion syndrome, estimating he sustained more than 10 or

15 concussions in his career but kept quiet and played due to the sport's macho code. Nelson calls it the "dumb jock mode," and he succumbed to it, too. He still suffers memory loss at times.

"Dave's suicide, as well as the NFL finally acknowledging the correlation between concussions and ailments like dementia later in life, should open the eyes of players on every level of football as well as the parents of young players and spouses of professional football players," Carson wrote on his blog. "We all better start asking the very personal question, is the neurological risk of playing the game worth it?"

He will keep looking to see what can be done to help players not just find success but safety. Once again, Carson is doing what he does best. Once more, Carson attempts to lead even all those years removed from any thoughts of quitting.

"I would just say," the Hall of Fame captain said, "if I felt there was something that needed to be done or something that needed to be said, or some action that needed to take place to bring the team together—to bring people into the fold—that was a role I was willing to play."

15 Phil Simms

He entered the game of his life, and he couldn't miss. Phil Simms was in a zone, completing pass after pass. Finally, as Simms brought the Giants back from a deficit in the game he couldn't wait to play, he proved his worth. Then he dropped back for one more pass, and his hand struck the helmet of a rushing defender, getting caught in the face mask of Philadelphia's Dennis Harrison.

Simms looked at his right thumb just long enough to realize he did not want to see it. He walked off the field with the thumb hanging as precariously as his career would once more.

No, this was not Simms setting a record for accuracy in Super Bowl XXI after the treasured 1986 season. This was Simms three years earlier in a scene that defined his injury-plagued career as much as his Super Bowl MVP status did.

The week before he injured his thumb, Simms publicly requested a trade, no longer able to stomach losing the starting job to Scott Brunner. But that Sunday, after Brunner threw an interception, rookie head coach Bill Parcells told Simms to go in. The quarterback completed his first four passes, led the Giants to a touchdown, and rallied them to within a point of the Eagles.

Then, in the middle of the rally, Simms broke his thumb.

"As soon as it happened, I said, 'Damn it, there goes another season,'" Simms said after the game. "Everything I ever wanted was right there in that game, and to see it go was unbelievable.... When Bill told me to play, I was ready. There was nothing inside me to hold me back. I was thankful I had the opportunity. I was pumped up. I was playing with emotion."

* * *

He always played with emotion, didn't he? That's why Giants fans grew to love him.

No matter what injury stole another season, as one did for each of his first four years and several others. No matter that he had to battle Brunner for his job before he helped the Giants win their first Super Bowl and battle Jeff Hostetler for it after, when another injury allowed Hostetler to win the 1990 Super Bowl as well as Simms' job in 1991.

Regardless of what Simms faced, he kept coming. That's what made him the most popular Giants quarterback of all time.

Phil Simms constantly battled injuries and threats to his job, but finally emerged as a Super Bowl MVP and record-holder, and he was one of the most popular players in Giants history. (AP Photo/Paul Spinelli)

The golden-haired kid out of Kentucky was greeted with boos when Giants general manager George Young drafted him in the first round out of tiny Morehead State. "Most people have never heard of me," Simms said good-naturedly after a college stint with less than impressive stats. He added an edgy caveat, "But scouts from roughly 20 NFL teams came to Morehead."

Years later, San Francisco head coach Bill Walsh told *Sports Illustrated* that if the Giants had not selected Simms in the first round, he would have picked him in the third. Instead, Walsh settled for a quarterback out of Notre Dame named Joe Montana. "Not to take anything from Joe," Walsh told *Sports Illustrated*, "but I know Phil could have done the things in our offense that Joe did."

Simms did plenty for the Giants. He accumulated 4,044 yards passing when he led the Giants to the playoffs in 1984 after they traded Brunner. He set the club record of 33,462 career passing yards. He threw for a team-record 513 yards in one game and managed the game when the situation called for it countless other times.

His battles with Parcells were legendary, but the men eventually bonded. The coach knew he could test Simms more than most; the quarterback stubbornly screamed right back.

"He would be chirping in Phil Simms' ear the entire time," center Bart Oates remembered. "Just every little thing. You could see some days—Phil...the steam just rose from his ear."

Said lineman Karl Nelson, "He gave it back to Bill as much as Bill gave it to him."

Then he gave it to his teammates, who absorbed it because Simms earned their respect. "I yelled at Bart so much and he would take it and he'd look at me and he'd say, 'Well Phil, you're right. But about the right tackle...that's not me,'" Simms remembered with a laugh. "I said, 'Bart, I don't have time to go yell at everybody, you go fix it.' And he'd go, 'Okay, okay. I'll get it straightened out.'"

* * *

Simms grew during the 1986 season, leading the Giants to a 14–2 record, a 66–3 trouncing of NFC playoff opponents, and a Super Bowl matchup against Denver's future Hall of Fame quarterback, John Elway.

As usual, Simms was far from intimidated as he prepared for one more challenge.

"Phil was just having the week of his life," former running back Joe Morris recalled. "Trust me. Every day, he was, 'Man, Joe, I just feel good. I just really feel good.'"

He felt even better in the Super Bowl. Simms threw 25 passes and completed all but three of them for a record 88 percent completion rate. "After all the guff I've taken over the years, this makes everything worthwhile," Simms said after the Giants' 39–20 win.

Of course, the "guff" wasn't over. It never was with Simms.

So he led the Giants to an 11–3 record in 1990—only to break his leg against Buffalo and watch Hostetler finish the job, leading the Giants to a stunning Super Bowl win over those same Bills.

Parcells quit for health reasons the next year; the woeful Ray Handley took over—and decided to start Hostetler in 1991. Simms regained his job near the end of the season and was again named the starter the next year...until he injured his arm in Week 4 and lost another season.

Dan Reeves took over as the Giants head coach in 1993 and cut Hostetler, giving Simms his old job yet again.

Simms responded once more. He had a Pro Bowl season, leading the Giants on a surprising playoff run as they finished 11–5. They lost the NFC East in the final week when eventual Super Bowl champ Dallas beat them 16–13 in overtime.

After the game, Cowboys coach Jimmy Johnson joined his predecessors around the league in describing Simms as a "winner." As usual, Simms' chance to savor success was fleeting. He led the

Giants to a playoff win over Minnesota followed by a humiliating 44–3 loss to old rival San Francisco.

An even more humbling reality came the next year. The Giants no longer wanted him. Simms was 39. Lawrence Taylor had just retired. The club faced salary cap concerns and had a pair of young quarterbacks, Dave Brown and Kent Graham, they didn't yet know would prove to be disappointments. At that point, they just didn't think their team would be competitive enough to pay Simms, so they cut him after 15 years.

Devastated, he considered playing for another team but couldn't find the right situation.

The Giants retired Simms' jersey in 1995—a year after he turned down the invitation. He went on to his long career as a broadcaster.

While the fiery temper that worked so well on the field sometimes gets the best of him off it—as was the case in 2011 when he got into an altercation with Desmond Howard while chafing at an on-air comment about his son Matt's play as a college quarterback—Simms has mostly become a soft-spoken voice of the past, one who saw his name go up in the team's inaugural Ring of Honor class in 2010 so many years after his arrival was greeted with contempt.

"It's incredible," Simms said. "Sometimes I think back and I go, 'Wow, I did enough to get my name inside of a stadium.' It's really great."

16 Battle of the Reds: First NFL Title Game

Red Badgro sprinted down field on the final play of the first NFL Championship Game, with only Chicago's Red Grange between him and the end zone—between the Giants and a victory. The

30,000 fans at Wrigley Field, riveted by the Giants and Bears all day, tensed once more.

The first NFL title game, which was played in 1933, surpassed expectations, featuring 11 Hall of Famers who fought bitterly through six lead changes while the fans in Chicago battled the cold. There were trick plays and punishing hits, rattling the players' leather helmets throughout this first meeting between the NFL's two divisions, which had been split before the season.

Now it came down to the Bears' Grange, the league's main attraction, and the Giants' Badgro, legend vs. legend, for one final play. Badgro could see a path to the end zone for his teammate, Dale Burnett, who trailed the play. If only he could get him the ball before Grange tackled him, then the Giants would win this historic game.

* * *

It made sense for the teams to play for the first championship because they had clearly been the league's best. The Bears and Giants had gained the most yards; the Giants had scored the most points. The Giants had gone 11–3 to win the Eastern division; Chicago had won the West with a 10–2–1 record.

Grange, who had saved the Giants in their first season as a visitor by drawing 70,000 fans to the Polo Grounds, was nearing the end of his career. As was the custom, he played on both sides of the ball, rushing for 277 yards on 81 carries while also playing defensive back.

Badgro was in his fourth year with the Giants after playing two seasons with the New York Yankees football team. Before that, he had played pro baseball but didn't fare well, hitting .257 for the St. Louis Browns. He was a fearsome defensive end who also posed a threat as a receiver, teaming with fellow Hall of Famer, fullback Ken Strong, to lead the Giants offense.

It had been a wild day with both teams eschewing the usual ground-oriented attacks that dominated the era as Giants coach

Badgro and a Duke Not Named Wellington

At 78, Red Badgro became the oldest player elected to the Hall of Fame with his selection in 1981. It added another item to a list of diverse accomplishments.

Badgro not only played offensive and defensive end as well as receiver, but he did them well enough that his Giants coach Steve Owen once said, "He could block, tackle, and catch passes equally well, and he could do each with the best of them."

Even before football, Badgro showed versatility. He had gone to the University of Southern California on a basketball scholarship while also playing football there. In 1927, as the Giants won their first NFL title, Badgro played for the New York Yankees football team. When the team folded, Badgro decided to play the third sport he had excelled at—baseball.

Unsuccessful, he decided to return to football, where he became a force for the Giants from 1930–35, leading the run-oriented league in receptions with 16 in 1934.

At USC, Badgro and teammate Marion "Duke" Morrison had flirted with another career. They occasionally worked as movie extras. Morrison eventually found the film industry more rewarding. Of course, he's better known by his stage name—John Wayne.

"Uncle Badge chose football," Badgro's niece, Dorothy Westland, once told *The New York Times*, "and John chose movies."

Steve Owen, known for his reliance on defense and field goals, went against his conservative nature.

The Giants pulled off a hidden ball trick—center Mel Hein was made an eligible receiver and he tucked the ball under his jersey, surprising Chicago for a big gain. With the Giants leading 14–9, Bears coach George Halas got creative, too—calling a fake punt, which resulted in a 67-yard pass.

The Giants, later trailing 16–14, regained the lead on another wild play. Strong took a handoff at the 8-yard line but had nowhere to run. So he flipped the ball back to quarterback Harry Newman who eluded the Bears' pass rush to find Strong open in the end zone.

The Giants led 21–16 late, but the Bears regained the lead. Famed running back Bronko Nagurski threw a pass to Bill Hewitt who flipped to Bill Karr just as the Giants closed in. Karr scored from the 19, and the Bears led 23–21.

That set up the final showdown, Badgro vs. Grange. Badgro, who caught a touchdown pass earlier, prepared to lateral to Burnett. Grange would be defenseless, Badgro recalled in the book, *What a Game They Played: An Inside Look at the Golden Era of Pro Football.*

"But," Badgro remembered, "Grange grabbed me around the arms and upper body and I couldn't."

That was it. The first NFL title game was over.

Grange had won the battle of the Reds.

17 The Sneakers Game... Or Was It?

Ray Flaherty had an idea the day of the Giants' 1934 NFL Championship Game against Chicago. The ice had frozen over the field at the Polo Grounds, and the Giants end and assistant coach remembered a similar situation when he was in college at Gonzaga. Back then, cleats made it difficult to dig into the frozen turf, so the Gonzaga team opted for sneakers, which provided better traction.

Flaherty, the future Redskins Hall of Fame head coach and creator of the screen pass, offered his first famous suggestion to Giants head coach Steve Owen. Why don't we try using sneakers, too?

The Giants needed every edge they could get. The Bears had not only been the league's first perfect team, going 13–0 under George Halas, they had also won 18 straight games, including a

23–21 heartbreaker for the Giants in the NFL's first league championship the previous year.

The Giants? They were 8–5 and considered heavy underdogs.

Owen dispatched equipment manager Abe Cohen to find as many pairs of sneakers as he could, but the sporting goods stores were closed in New York on this December Sunday. So Cohen scrambled around the city for half the game before finally heading to Manhattan College and borrowing eight pairs.

Cohen returned by halftime with the Giants down seven. At the break, then on the sideline, the Giants doled out the few pairs Cohen had found to key players, who hustled into them between plays.

The shoes, the story goes, were as magical as the ruby red slippers Dorothy would wear five years later when *The Wizard of Oz* debuted on the big screen. They helped the Giants glide across the field while the Bears stumbled like Keystone Kops. Shocking Chicago with 27 points in the fourth quarter, the Giants pulled off a 30–13 upset of the undefeated Bears.

The Giants had stunned the NFL and won their first championship game. It would be remembered as the Sneakers Game, with the story passed down from generation to generation about how the sneakers made the difference.

Except for one small problem. The story may not be entirely true.

"Yeah, my dad always told me that story, that people made a big deal out of the sneakers, which he felt was a nice story," said Duke lacrosse coach John Danowski, son of Giants quarterback Ed Danowski. "But it was more really [the Bears'] arrogance when it was fourth-and-1. The Giants ended up on a scoring drive."

Danowski said his dad remembered the Bears going for the fourth down late in the game—a memory supported by comments his father made years later to *The New York Times*. The Giants took advantage of the turnover by scoring on the next drive for a 17–13 lead.

Ken Strong

The 17 points Ken Strong scored in the 1934 title game was a record that stood nearly 30 years—just one more highlight in a Hall of Fame career. Strong did almost everything for the Giants in his three stints with the team. Starring from blocking to running and passing as well as punting, kicking, and defense, Strong retired as the team's all-time leading scorer with 324 points at the time—13 touchdowns, 35 field goals, and 141 extra points.

Versatile as Strong was on the field, he also adapted off it, playing with three teams in New York. He began his career with the Staten Island Stapletons in 1932 before jumping to the Giants. But after the 1935 season, Strong had a contract dispute with the Giants and played for the AFL rival Yankees. He returned in 1939 for one last season. Or so he thought.

With World War II raging and players pressed into military service, the Giants lured Strong back solely as a kicker from 1944–47. He returned on two conditions—he didn't want to wear shoulder pads, and he wanted to wear his wristwatch on the field.

"The key to that game came when the Bears led 13–10," the quarterback told the *Times* in 1962. "They had a yard to go on fourth down."

But Bears legendary fullback Bronko Nagurski was stopped by Ken Strong and Bill Morgan. The Giants had the ball, and soon they had the lead. "And on the next play, Ken veered right, bucked up the middle, and went 40 or 50 yards for a touchdown," the elder Danowski told the *Times*. "So we won, going away 30–13."

John Danowski said a relative of one of his father's former teammates also indicated the effect of the sneakers was exaggerated. "Mel Hein's granddaughter—who's a softball coach—she sent me a nice note once," Danowski said of the Giants' Hall of Fame center. "[It] said the same thing."

There's no way to definitively prove just how much of an effect the sneakers had, of course. Even the Bears said the footwear at least played a role. "I think the sneakers gave them an edge in that last half, for they were able to cut back when they were running with the ball and we couldn't cut with them," Nagurski said.

Regardless of how it happened, the Giants had beaten the mighty Bears with the rookie Danowski at quarterback instead of injured starter Harry Newman and without Hall of Fame defensive end Red Badgro, who was also hurt.

Danowski had gotten a break early in the fourth quarter when he threw a pass that Chicago's Carl Brumbaugh picked off at the Bears' 2-yard line—before the Giants' Ike Frankian wrested the ball from him, taking it in for a touchdown to make it 13–10.

From there, Hall of Famer Strong took over, with his big stop of Nagurski, big run for a score, and extra-point kick—teams did not have specialized kickers at the time. Danowski and Strong both added touchdown runs later, and the Giants had won their first title in shocking fashion.

"I never was so pleased with anything in all my life," Giants owner Tim Mara said after the game. "In all other contests with the Bears I always have hoped the whistle would blow and end the game. Today I was hoping it would last for a couple of hours."

The Giants had left the Bears as shellshocked as the previously perfect New England Patriots would be 74 years later.

"We feel that everyone has to lose some time," Nagurski said in a quiet Bears locker room after the game. "But this is a hard time to start."

18 Michael Strahan

He arrived in the room set aside for the Giants' legends, the folks about to have their name placed in the team's inaugural Ring of

Honor, and Michael Strahan offered one of his wide, gap-toothed grins to the reporters waiting for him. "I didn't used to like answering when I was working for them," Strahan said of the Giants, "so you know I don't like answering now."

It was Strahan's typical combination of charm and arrogance, his sense of humor helping him to straddle the line as always. But for Strahan and Giants fans, the former defensive end now resides over the line he'd always wanted to so desperately cross—the one that separates Super Bowl winners from those who have not earned that title.

He retired the year after helping Big Blue to its stunning Super Bowl triumph over New England—and not the year before, like his long-time offensive counterpart, Tiki Barber. So Strahan laughed when asked about Barber, his old partner in crime who, like Strahan, could stir things up with a microphone when he wasn't earning cheers on the field. They had so often been paired together, Strahan leading the defense, Barber the offense, since the 2000 Super Bowl run that ended with a thud against the Ravens. They sparred publicly, with Barber calling out Strahan for contract negotiations, and they always seemed ready to battle for the post-football spotlight with both players grooming themselves for media careers while they still played.

But now Strahan showed the flip side to Barber's bitter status with Giants fans who were expected to—and did—boo the former running back for his criticism of his old team and coach. "They're gonna do what they're gonna do," Strahan said when asked about the possible reaction. "What, am I gonna get on the microphone, 'Don't boo the next guy?'

"I'm hoping they don't boo me. Everyone else is on their own out there. It's a tough world."

Especially in New York. But it's a world Strahan mastered in his time as a Giant, one he left with the most enjoyable of images. There's the flexing of his mammoth biceps after a key sack of Tom Brady in the Super Bowl. A kiss of the Vince Lombardi Super Bowl

Michael Strahan emerged as one of the Giants' greatest defensive linemen. This Super Bowl XLII sack of New England's Tom Brady helped send him into retirement as a champion. (AP Photo/Stephan Savoia)

trophy as confetti fell. That warm, wide smile was used to pitch everything from Chunky Soup to Subway, displayed at the Giants' Super Bowl parade in New York City.

"I have been very fortunate to have a career where I have been lucky enough to stay healthy, to last this long and last long enough to win a Super Bowl…with one of the most improbable teams that I have been on," Strahan said when he retired in 2008.

He's the lone link between championship icons, arriving when Lawrence Taylor and Phil Simms ended one era in 1993, then departing after helping Eli Manning and company clinch the legacy of another.

In between, Strahan collected a team-record 141½ career sacks, a dubious single-season NFL record of 22½, and countless laughs as well as a few controversies on and off the field.

By the time he ended up on the Giants' Ring of Honor, Strahan couldn't believe how far he had come from the time George Young drafted him as a second-round pick out of Texas Southern. Or really, as far back as those days when he grew up in Germany, a military kid watching football on Tuesday mornings that was televised as *Monday Night Football* back in the states.

"It's phenomenal," he said. "You know, you first come here, you're hoping to just keep a job. Playing with LT, Phil Simms, all those great players. You're just overwhelmed by being in the city and playing for this franchise, to last long enough and play well enough to be included in something like this is nothing I could ever imagine as a young guy."

By the end, he inspired the next generation, leaving them as awestruck as he once was of Taylor, grooming linemen Osi Umenyiora and Justin Tuck even as they helped him storm Brady in the Super Bowl.

"I remember my rookie year, Stray took us all out to dinner—not a lot of fanfare; nobody knew about it," Tuck said. "One of the kindest-hearted people I know. He really gets a bad rap because of some of the things he says in the media, but as far as him to his teammates, he always had our back."

Michael Strahan: Giants Highlights

Years: 15 (1993–2007)
Pro Bowls: 7
Career Sacks: 141.5*
Games: 216*
Single-Season Sack High: 22.5, 2001**
Single-Game Sack High: 3—Three times
Led League in Sacks: Twice (2001, 2003—18.5)
NFC Championships: 2
Super Bowl Titles: 1

*Giants record
**NFL record

Tuck remembered former defensive coordinator Tim Lewis once telling Strahan he needed him to make a play. Strahan responded with two straight sacks. After the second one, Tuck said, Strahan "walked off and when he got back, went up to Coach Lewis and said, 'You're welcome.' And I was like, 'This guy is something else.'

"It was hard to be down around Stray because he had fun all the time. Even when he was talking bad about you, it was in a fun manner. It was kind of a joking manner. So we always had fun around him. He always lightened the load."

The week after Tuck reflected on his ex-teammate in December 2010, the Giants lost the infamous Punt Return game to the Eagles, blowing a 17-point lead in the fourth quarter. Strahan then offered an example of one of the "things he says in the media."

Strahan said the Giants should be "ashamed," and Tuck fired back at him, saying he was wrong to criticize his old team even though he was now a broadcaster. But Strahan's bond was still evident by the end of the conversation, as Tuck managed a smile about his friend "Stray."

* * *

While Strahan's imagination of what he could accomplish on the field once grew, now he thinks about what he could do as a broadcaster. The Fox NFL analyst said in 2011 he was keeping his eyes on Regis Philbin's old seat on the general talk show *Live with Regis and Kelly*, and he was scheduled for a tryout.

To land and maintain mainstream national spotlight jobs like that, Strahan will have to avoid past controversies. His ex-wife accused him of spousal abuse in their bitter 2006 divorce—a charge he repeatedly denied. He was also accused of misogyny in bullying a female reporter who asked him about public criticisms he made that year about teammate Plaxico Burress being a "quitter." Strahan, who loudly barked at the reporter, Kelly Naqi, to move to the front of a media crowd and ask her question by looking him in the eyes, later said he would have done the same to a male reporter. He made a fair point that stories shouldn't have necessarily singled out the reporter as female.

"I don't think anybody wants to be looked at as a male or female, especially in this type of business, such a male-driven business," he said.

There was also a troublesome report in the *New York Post* that Strahan had installed a tracking device on girlfriend Nicole Murphy's car in 2009, but the report relied on anonymous sources and was denied by both Strahan and Murphy.

As he continues to plan his post-football life, Strahan is able to look back at his career with "no regrets."

There are enough memories to sustain him now. The first Super Bowl run and the 41–0 rout of Minnesota in the NFC Championship Game. The constant chattering on the field, in the locker room, and with the media.

There's the 2001 sack record he didn't quite earn since his buddy and fellow future Hall of Famer Brett Favre laid down for him as even some of Strahan's Giants teammates acknowledged at the time. But it still came with one of the best seasons a defensive lineman has had.

There's also the pride he took in his all-around game, as he revealed at his retirement press conference that for all his ability to charge the quarterback, he enjoyed stopping the run even more. Ultimately, Strahan's most enduring image will be the last, with him sacking Brady on third down in the third quarter of the Super Bowl and helping the Giants win a title.

And, of course, there's his typically low-key method of celebration. At the podium after the team's victory parade, Strahan leaped in the air before landing with a stomp, sharing a pregame ritual with fans. "We would like to extend this to every other team in the NFL and particularly for the last team we defeated, the New

England Patriots," he said. "Because you know what we did to you? We stomped you out!"

Strahan almost retired the year before but held on. He almost un-retired in August 2008 when Umenyiora suffered a season-ending injury. But Strahan decided against doing so after "throwing around a million scenarios in my head for the past day," as he told Fox Sports then.

That was it. That's how Strahan went out—stomping on a defeated foe, flexing his arms, and landing on top.

19 Tiki Barber: The Greatest Giant You'll Ever Boo

Here's what you need to know about Tiki Barber if you're a Giants fan. You're not allowed to like him too much, if at all, which is an extremely unfortunate statement for the Giants' greatest all-time running back and the team's fan base.

It would be nice for Giants fans' first thoughts of Barber to be his compact, powerful body pinballing off one tackle, then cutting back to avoid another. Or for his transition to post-football life as a broadcaster as a more modern version of his predecessor, Frank Gifford, who is still admired for his time with the Giants.

Due to a deteriorated relationship that began as early as January 2006 when Barber publicly said "we were out-coached" after a playoff loss to Carolina, it's hard to imagine that happening anytime in the near future. But it would be nice.

It would be nice for the first memory of Barber to be about that underdog story New York loves, a 5'10" supposed third-down back blossoming into the team's greatest rusher of all time, overcoming a fumbling problem that almost derailed his career even after he helped lead the Giants to an NFC title.

If Giants fans could get past the sound of Barber's mouth offering another barb to his ex-teammate Eli Manning or his ex-coach Tom Coughlin, maybe they could remember what they used to love. They would see Barber's eyes scanning the field for a hole, a lane, a place he could exploit a weakness as he did while making some of the biggest runs of the past decade when the Giants needed him most.

"He really had great vision, and I think that's probably one of his best attributes," center Shaun O'Hara said. "Even though he wasn't that tall, he always seemed like he could see the field extremely well."

They would see him cutting on a dime, leaving would-be tacklers reaching for air as Barber sprinted away toward the type of 95-yard run he made against Oakland to set a team record and clinch the 2005 NFC East division title.

"We run a play that's designed to go to the right. He puts his foot in the ground, breaks to the left, and runs down the sideline for a 90-yard run," O'Hara recalled. "That play was designed to go to the right; he just saw an opening, put his foot in the ground, and went. And by the time he cut, he was gone. You'd see it time and again."

You would still see it clearly if so much time hadn't passed and if the Giants hadn't won a Super Bowl the very year Barber retired at the top of his game and began blasting his old team as he began his career in broadcasting.

You would still see him holding the ball the proper way, avoiding the fumbles he used to make, learning the tricks he often credits to running backs coach Jerald Ingram, though most others recognize head coach Tom Coughlin as a key contributor—including former Giant Joe Morris, who was taught not to fumble by Coughlin at Syracuse.

Tiki Barber: Giants Highlights

Years: 10 (1997–2006)
Pro Bowls: 3
Yards Per Carry: 4.7
Career Yards: 10,449
Career Yards from Scrimmage: 15,632
Career Touchdowns: 55
Longest Run: 95 yards, at Oakland, December 31, 2005.
Single-Game Rushing Yards: 234, at Washington, December 30, 2006.
Rushing Yards, Season: 1,860, 2005.
Total Yards, Season: 2,390, 2005.

There's the 203 yards Barber picked up against the Eagles in 2002, despite fumbling three times, to help the Giants earn one playoff berth. There's the team-record 234 yards he earned against Washington to clinch another in 2006 when the playoff berth saved Coughlin's job.

But there were also all those shots of Coughlin, from the time Barber the player stood at the postgame podium after the playoff loss to the Panthers in 2005 to so many post-football barbs. Those moments helped alienate fans, even if the criticism was echoed elsewhere.

When Barber wrote in his 2007 autobiography that Coughlin's dictatorial style sapped some of his joy and led to his retirement, Giants management had already talked to Coughlin about lightening up. When Barber criticized Coughlin as possibly losing his team early in 2010, the timing was poor since it was right before the Ring of Honor ceremony in which Barber was booed, but the sentiment was mirrored by many griping fans.

It was different to a degree, of course. Barber appeared to repeatedly betray a man who helped salvage his career. A man who, according to Morris, could have simply washed his hands of Barber instead of trying to help him overcome the fumbling issues.

"They told Tom to get rid of Tiki if you want to, and what Tom said is, 'Look, I'm pretty good with running backs; I had a guy who used to have a problem with fumbling. He became the all-time leading rusher here,'" Morris said a person close to Coughlin told him.

Morris was the former Giants' all-time leading rusher to which Coughlin referred. He said the person close to Coughlin once told him, "Joe, you know he could have gotten rid of him if he wanted to."

"Tom believed in Tiki," Morris said. "I think Tiki's a great player. I respect him as a man, but I think he was out of line. Tiki should have the same indebtedness [I have] because of all the stories I've been told."

The memories of Barber's 10,449 rushing yards with the Giants and his 15,632 yards from scrimmage get pushed to the back of Giants' fans minds. They are buried under an avalanche of words from Barber the broadcaster's mouth, an early retirement—before a decision to un-retire four years later—and a sense of betrayal that permeates the Giants fan base.

It's understandable in some ways, perplexing in others. Barber brings a lot of the grief on himself, with an outspoken persona that goes beyond the bounds of football. And he helped justify the disdain, perhaps kicking it to another level, when he reportedly had an affair with a 23-year-old NBC intern—while his wife was eight months pregnant with twins.

For a man who publicly criticized his father for abandoning his family, it was one more reason for Giants fans to see the player they once loved and admired as a phony and a traitor.

But it can be a little confusing to see fans still revere icons like Lawrence Taylor who, despite much more serious transgressions off the field, received thunderous cheers just as Barber was pelted with boos at the team's Ring of Honor ceremony in 2010.

Yes, Barber had recently criticized Coughlin yet again, sending the fans' reaction into overdrive. But if the rules of the game for fans state you can appreciate what a player does on the field regardless of what he does off it, why are they broken only for crimes against the team but not the rest of society?

You can fairly debate Barber's authenticity. You can fairly cackle at the fact that the year he questioned Manning's "comical" leadership and said Coughlin's dictatorial coaching style helped convince him to retire was also the year they led the Giants to the Super Bowl—even if that requires ignoring the fact that many Giants fans made the same comments.

It made sense to get frustrated that Barber announced his retirement in 2006 in the middle of the season, which, as Manning shot back later, was not the best form of leadership. Barber was outspoken from the beginning, publicly criticizing Michael Strahan's contract negotiations in 2002.

It was more than fair to shake your head, or throw it back with laughter when Barber filed paperwork to un-retire in 2011—and the Giants announced plans to release him as quickly as he pounced on a hole or a microphone.

Four years after saying he wanted to be taken seriously as a journalist and had looked at football as just a "post-college job," Barber wanted back in. Of course, it couldn't hurt that in all that time, he lost his job as a football analyst on NBC and his spot on *The Today Show*, where he once dreamed of replacing Matt Lauer. The network cited a morals clause in dumping Barber, who might not be seen favorably by viewers after dumping his wife a month or so before she went into labor.

You couldn't help but speculate that Barber needed the money.

But for all of those issues, and as teammates and ex-teammates have piled on Barber the way defenders used to after another fumble, O'Hara tried to throw one more block for his old team-mate when asked about him for this book in 2010.

"I think time will eventually kind of heal any of the emotional baggage that fans have toward him," O'Hara said, perhaps in a glimpse of wishful thinking. "It's sad to me for anybody to think anything bad about Tiki, just because when he was a player he gave his heart and soul to the team, and he was a great player. But I know right now there's other things that have happened that people aren't too happy about."

While O'Hara wasn't thrilled to hear Barber blasting off against his ex-team at every turn—and the man did sometimes seem to have either a poor sense of timing or an unhealthy obsession—he did what many fans did not. He recognized Barber was performing in his new job, not his old one. He was no longer a Giant but a member of the media, and his job was to offer critiques.

"You know what? I didn't appreciate some things he said about some of my teammates, but at the same time, he was serving another master," O'Hara said. "He was done. It's not like he was sitting at home calling in radio stations. He was getting paid to analyze and say things. That was his new job. So I didn't take it personally."

But for now at least, being a Giants fan won't allow you to voice that opinion too loudly without ducking. For now, the vision of Barber the player has been buried under the sound of Barber the broadcaster.

So the all-time greatest Giants running back is the subject of boos and derision from the fans he used to thrill. That's at least one thing you should not expect Barber to criticize.

"I don't give people grief for their opinions," Barber said when asked how he thought fans would react to him the week of the Ring of Honor ceremony. "You guys know, I've had plenty of mine. We'll see. Only time will tell."

20 The Debacle at the Meadowlands I

Having long ago completed a career that included five Super Bowl titles and a nod as executive of the year with the San Francisco 49ers, John McVay has had plenty of reasons to sleep soundly. In December 2010, he received a stark reminder of why he still suffered some restless nights.

The Giants had just lost to the Philadelphia Eagles in stunning fashion on a last-second punt return after blowing a 21-point lead in the fourth quarter. The defeat provided a chilling flashback to 1978 and the play known to most of football as the Miracle at the Meadowlands. For Giants' fans it's referred to in a pair of words spoken through gritted teeth: The Fumble.

"You know, I had just gotten down to one nightmare per week," McVay, the head coach of the 1978 Giants, told a *New York Daily News* reporter who had called after the 2010 debacle.

As maddening as it was in 2010 to wonder how punter Matt Dodge could kick the ball to dangerous return man DeSean Jackson with seconds left in a tie game, it could not compare to the disbelief on November 19, 1978. That's when the Giants ran a play they never had to run and fumbled away a game already won.

They just had to take a knee.

The Giants had the ball in their territory on a third-and-2 with 31 seconds left and a 17–12 lead. With the Eagles out of timeouts, the Giants could run out the clock.

Inexplicably, their offensive coordinator Bob Gibson called a running play.

Quarterback Joe Pisarcik—despite his misgivings and the loud resistance his teammates offered—ran the play. Fullback Larry

Csonka barked the loudest. "Don't give me the ball," he said. But Pisarcik remembered Gibson issuing him an ultimatum after he overruled the coach the previous week.

"He told him if he ever changed another play, he would never play quarterback for him again," running back Billy Taylor told the *Daily News* 30 years later.

So Pisarcik ran the play—oh so badly.

He turned to face fullback Larry Csonka, but the pair was not in sync. As Csonka ran past perhaps too quickly, Pisarcik placed the ball not in the aging former Dolphins' hands but on his right hip. The ball bounced off Csonka's hip and Pisarcik stumbled after it, looking progressively worse each step of the way. The ball bounced back toward the quarterback, then off his hands as he fell. Finally, it bounced on a clean hop to Philadelphia defensive back Herman Edwards.

Only a few moments after he had congratulated the Giants on their victory, Edwards scooped up the ball with a clear path to the end zone, running 26 yards for the game-winning touchdown.

"That's the most horrifying ending to a ballgame I've ever seen," McVay said after the 19–17 loss, sounding much like Tom Coughlin would 32 years later.

The play made the 1978 Giants poster boys for the Wilderness Years, when the team went from 1964–80 without a playoff appearance—including several years when they didn't have a true home stadium.

Gibson was fired the next day. The man who had apparently threatened Pisarcik the previous week would never coach again. The move did little to quell fan outrage, which spilled over after too many losing seasons were capped by a humiliating blunder. In the next few weeks, columnists called for Penn State coach Joe Paterno to replace McVay, fans burned tickets in protest, and one man became a symbol of the discontent when he flew over the stadium with a banner that read: "15 Years of Lousy Football—We've Had Enough!"

Even more disturbingly, Giants owner Wellington Mara was hanged in effigy.

Pisarcik was so distraught after the loss that McVay allowed him to go home to Florida for a couple of days. The refuge was fleeting. On the beach, according to a report in *The New York Times*, a man approached the quarterback and said, "Aren't you Joe Pisarcik? Hey, what happened on that play?"

It's the question Pisarcik has heard for the past 32 years, and he doesn't usually bother answering anymore. The last time he talked about the play was with the *Daily News* in 2008. "Quarterback falls down and we would have been out of there," he said. "Time goes on, brother."

Pisarcik, ironically, eventually moved on to join the Eagles to be their backup quarterback. The team greeted him by throwing a football on the floor of the locker room, Edwards recalled. It was an unfortunate turn for Pisarcik, who had led the Giants to some improvement heading into the game and a 14–0 lead on two touchdown passes early.

The Giants had improved from 3–11 in 1976 to 5–9 in '77 and were 5–6 heading into the Eagles' game. But much like the 2010 Giants, they followed their debacle with a rout, losing to Buffalo 41–17 the next week on their way to a 6–10 finish.

The 1978 Giants did at least learn one thing the week after their historic loss. With seconds remaining in the first half against Buffalo, Pisarcik took the snap, then took a knee. As he did, the Giants lined up a player seven yards behind him as a "safety" in the event of a fumble.

"We call that," Pisarcik told reporters after the game, "our Philly play."

21 No Holds Bahr-ed: Giants Win NFC Title Fight

They exchanged blows all day, as they had for the past decade, the Giants and 49ers were locked in a classic playoff game to cap their battles of the past nine years.

The Giants' backup quarterback, Jeff Hostetler, couldn't match 49ers Hall of Famer Joe Montana in talent or experience. But he had waited seven years for the chance to finally start and made the most of it following Phil Simms' injury a few weeks before. Hostetler would not forfeit it easily.

Matt Bahr, the Giants kicker, couldn't guarantee he would play after injuring his neck making a tackle the previous week in a 31–3 win over the Bears to reach the 1990 NFC Championship Game. He considered himself not just a kicker but a player, so he was ready to go.

So were the rest of the Giants, the underdogs who watched the 49ers win the past two Super Bowls as well as the teams' last four meetings. That included the classic 7–3 game in San Francisco that left both teams battered when they met on *Monday Night Football* several weeks earlier.

Now they managed to play an even better game, just one point separating the teams with 4 seconds left on the clock at a sunny Candlestick Park. The teams traded field goals, leads, knock-out blows of their quarterbacks, and finally nervous glances and huddled prayers as Bahr set up for a game-winning field goal try.

Bahr had hit four already as the Giants proved they could move the ball and hold on to it for long stretches, but they could not get into the end zone. That would not matter if Bahr could kick an NFC-playoff-record fifth field goal and erase the 49ers'

1-point lead in one of the greatest contests in championship game history.

He set up for the 42-yard kick, grateful for the timeout 49ers coach George Seifert called to freeze him; it allowed the 12-year veteran extra time to prepare. The snap went to Hostetler, who placed it perfectly for Bahr. He struck the ball and immediately knew what broadcaster Pat Summerall soon told CBS' national television audience:

And the kick…is good! There will be no three-peat. The Giants win it 15–13.

From sofas, bar stools, and anywhere Giants fans gathered, the words elicited as much shock as they did joy. The Giants defeated the seemingly invincible 49ers without their starting quarterback—and without their rookie running back, Rodney Hampton, who broke his leg against Chicago the previous week.

They celebrated all over the field and headed to the Super Bowl in Tampa having secured a victory that would go down in franchise lore as one of the most revered. "We left our heart here last time," said a jubilant Leonard Marshall, who knocked Montana out of the game with a vicious hit in the fourth quarter. "But we knew we'd be back to recapture it."

Marshall exemplified the Giants' heart, crawling on his hands and knees before finding a way to get up, race to Montana's blind side, and wallop him with a sack. He had been aided by Lawrence Taylor, who rushed to Montana's other side, leaving him easy prey for Marshall. Montana, already battling the flu the past few days, left the game with a broken finger and bruised sternum.

The play happened on the series after ex-Giant Jim Burt—who so famously knocked Montana out with a vicious hit for the 1986 Giants—sent Hostetler to the sideline with a diving tackle at his knees.

* * *

The teams punished each other all day. Montana's 49ers drove down the field quickly, and Giants coordinator Bill Belichick's defense was unable to stop the quarterback's razor-sharp passes for most of the game. He missed just four of his first 20.

But the 49ers' running game stalled, and the closer San Francisco got to the end zone, the more the Giants defense stiffened.

The only touchdown it allowed came in the third quarter when cornerback Everson Walls aggressively went for an interception and missed, leaving John Taylor to sprint down the left sideline untouched for a 61-yard score. It was a haunting feeling for Walls, infamously burned as a Dallas Cowboy by a leaping Dwight Clark for The Catch nine years earlier. That famous play sent Montana to his first Super Bowl; now Walls could be responsible for sending him to his fifth.

The touchdown gave the 49ers a 13–6 lead and could have deflated Hostetler and the Giants, who controlled the ball for most of the game, finishing with 39 minutes of possession to San Francisco's 21.

But the Giants knew Hostetler could lead them back. They added more bootlegs and roll-outs to utilize Hostetler's mobility when he replaced Simms weeks earlier, and he took advantage the previous week when he passed for two touchdowns and added 43 rushing yards against the Bears.

The quarterback sustained long drives with clutch passes throughout the NFC Championship Game even if he couldn't get the Giants in the end zone. The closest they came was when Maurice Carthon dropped a sure touchdown on a pass from half-back Dave Meggett earlier in the game.

So when Burt knocked out Hostetler with a hyperextended knee, forcing backup Matt Cavanaugh in, the quarterback knew he would fight the pain. On the sideline, Parcells, the coach who once wouldn't let Hostetler get on the field, pleaded with him.

"Can you go?" Parcells asked time and again, ignoring Hostetler's feverish nods.

"I'm going!" Hostetler finally snapped.

* * *

The Giants still trailed 13–9, but on his first play back, Hostetler ducked under pressure and scrambled for 6 yards, his knee looking as if nothing had happened.

A few plays later, the Giants faced a fourth-and-2 from their 46-yard line.

Parcells, who gambled so often in big spots during the 1986 Super Bowl run, took one of his biggest risks. He called for a direct snap to linebacker Gary Reasons, who was on the punt unit as part of his regular duty as a blocking back. Reasons, who later said he saw a hole big enough "for a Mack truck to drive through," took off for a 30-yard gain. The Giants remained alive even if they were forced to settle for yet another field goal by Bahr to make it 13–12.

Even without Montana, it seemed the 49ers were ready to run out the clock on the Giants' noble upset attempt. Backup Steve Young showed a glimpse of the form that helped him eventually force out Montana and go on to his own Super Bowl glory, hitting tight end Brent Jones for 25 yards. The 49ers fans roared in anticipation as Roger Craig reeled off a pair of 6-yard runs to reach the Giants' 39-yard line, and the clock counted down less than 3 minutes.

This was a dynasty shedding the threat and preparing for its final march to another championship. "I know I was on the sideline thinking, 'We're not getting back in the game,'" Giants center Bart Oates said of the helpless feeling.

But then Craig carried up the middle and Giants nose guard Erik Howard dropped to one knee, fooling his blocker into dismissing him, as intended. From there, Howard dived at Craig, later saying his helmet knocked the ball loose.

Lawrence Taylor pounced on the fumble, and the Giants had one more chance with 2:36 left. "There's definitely a lot of adrenaline there," Oates said. "We got the chance, and we went out and executed it."

* * *

From his own 43, Hostetler rolled right once again, avoiding another sack before firing to tight end Mark Bavaro for 19 yards. A couple of plays later, Hostetler again rolled right. Once more, he hit a wide-open receiver, this time Stephen Baker, who stepped out of bounds at the 49ers' 30, a yard short of the first down with a little more than a minute to play.

Enter Ottis Anderson, the running back who was facing the end of his career and revived it that season. His 34-year-old legs kept churning until he got the first down at the 28. He ran again for 3 yards, then he ran again as the clock kept running with him.

Finally, with 12 seconds left, Hostetler ran on a sneak for 1 final yard and the Giants called timeout with 4 seconds remaining.

On came Bahr, who ended the Montana dynasty and kicked the Giants into their historic Super Bowl matchup with Buffalo.

"I hit it cleanly," he said later. "I knew it was good."

As Bahr started off the crowded field, a television reporter stopped the kicker. On a day when reports of the Persian Gulf War occasionally interrupted and dwarfed the game's telecast, the first thing Bahr pointed to was the yellow bands the players wore on their arms. "These yellow bands," Bahr screamed over the celebration, "are for the troops over there."

Parcells told his players before the game to decide if they wanted to pack for home or Tampa, since the Super Bowl that year was only a week later. Parcells decided to pack for the Florida trip, he told them. It would be one of the most enjoyable he's taken.

"I would say that NFC championship in San Francisco was one of the best times, and certainly the plane ride to Tampa...was one of the happiest times of my whole life," Parcells said 20 years later. "It was just kind of a euphoric time for all of us, and I think everybody who was on that plane felt a great sense of accomplishment."

22 Ice Bowl II: Tynes Kicks It Through

His coach mulled over the most important decision of his career when Lawrence Tynes made the decision for him. The Giants kicker ran onto the field in Green Bay, which had lived up to its name as the Frozen Tundra.

In a few moments, Tynes would race off that field and straight into the locker room, the freezing cold thrusting him from the pursuit of his gleeful teammates. They all wanted to salute the man who kicked them into a 23–20 overtime win and a trip to the Super Bowl.

But for now, Tynes did not think of the minus–1 degree temperature. Nor did he consider the minus–23 wind chill that left his head coach Tom Coughlin's face as bright red as the two field goals Tynes missed in the fourth quarter.

Throughout the 2008 NFC Championship Game, the Giants and Packers offered glimpses of their iconic past, two legendary NFL teams trading blows on a day as bitterly cold as almost any in Lambeau Field's storied history. It had been a classic game, seemingly Hall of Famer Brett Favre's last, and he traded slings with the quarterback who grew up admiring him, Eli Manning. Now the game went into overtime, 50 years after the Giants and Colts played the first sudden-death championship game.

But Tynes surely had no more reason to think of that bit of ancient history than he had his own recent infamy, missing a kick in the final moments that would have won the game. The Giants faced a fourth down at the Packers' 30-yard line after Corey Webster picked off Favre, the quarterback's weakness as a reckless gunslinger biting him at the worst possible moment.

On the Giants' sideline, Coughlin heard the voice in his headset from an assistant coach telling him not to go back to Tynes, who missed a 43-yarder late in the fourth and a 36-yarder even later—with 3 seconds left.

Back in New York, talk-show host David Letterman later acknowledged a thought surely shared by most of the city. "Please don't send him in again," Letterman said of Tynes. "For the love of God! If there's an ounce of mercy in your soul, don't...send... him...in."

But Tynes sent himself in.

"I didn't want to give him any other chance to pull me off that field," Tynes said of Coughlin, who yelled at him on the sideline after the last miss. "So I just went out there to my spot."

* * *

He knew the ball would feel like a rock in that bitter cold, just as it had for the kicks he missed and the two he made earlier in the game. He later discovered his foot had turned black and blue from striking that rock-like ball. But none of that mattered now.

From the sideline, many of the Giants banded together, looked at Tynes in the biggest moment of the season, and resented the sight of him on the field. Players often dread the concept of a game that has been fought for with bodies left battered for days coming down to a player whose jersey generally remains untouched.

And this was not just a game but a season. A season the Giants fought to salvage from the time they were 0–2 and made one of those sweating, grunting goal-line stands in Washington.

They rewarded the year's work all game. Plaxico Burress, the receiver who had tons of talent but did not always live up to his

How Cold Was It?

The most famous NFL game played in frigid temperatures is the 1967 Ice Bowl in Green Bay when Hall of Fame quarterback Bart Starr beat Dallas with a 1-yard sneak. But the Giants and Packers had their own Ice Bowl in New York the last time the teams played for a championship prior to the 2008 title game.

In 1962, the Giants and Packers faced 13-degree weather and 40-mph winds.

But the 2008 game in Green Bay became the new modern frozen face of the NFL with the minus–23 wind chill factor. How cold was it?

"I still remember the back of David Diehl's head, sweaty, dried up, frozen into icicles inside his helmet," defensive lineman Justin Tuck said in 2010 of his teammate on the offensive line. "I still remember my mouthpiece getting frozen in my helmet and having to play without a mouthpiece for a couple plays.

"I still remember Coach's face," Tuck added of Tom Coughlin, whose face infamously turned an increasingly chapped red.

The freezing cold prompted Tuck to make an odd request of quarterback Eli Manning.

"I remember telling Eli a couple of times, 'Go three-and-out' so we could get back on the football field," Tuck said of his defensive unit. "When you're playing, you don't really [feel it]. But when you're sitting on the sideline, yeah, it's chilly. It's very chilly."

potential, caught 11 passes for 151 yards. Brandon Jacobs and Ahmad Bradshaw, the running backs who succeeded Tiki Barber, combined for 130 yards and two touchdowns. Webster, the defensive back buried on the depth chart after blowing his starting job early in the season, hung around and sneaked back into the starter's role just in time for the postseason where he would make the biggest interception of the year.

The defense, knowing its leader Michael Strahan could be playing his final game, shut down Green Bay running back Ryan Grant, reducing him to 29 yards a week after he had run for more than 200. After all that fighting and grunting and sweating, they could end up losing out on a trip to the Super Bowl "Because of the kicker?" said an incredulous Strahan later in an NFL Films interview.

* * *

As Tynes lined up for the kick, back in Alabama, Larry Blakeney, Tynes' old college coach at Troy State, couldn't stop thinking about that kicker. His kicker. In between monitoring the game, Blakeney addressed high school coaches at a seminar, but his mind returned to the kicks his former player had missed.

Finally, Blakeney made his own decision to punt, gave up on the façade, and leveled with the coaches. He told them he was distracted because one of his old players was having a tough day. One of the coaches in the audience interrupted him with some news. Tynes had just won the game.

"Yeah!" Blakeney said, pumping his fist.

In Green Bay, the Giants pumped fists and howled, and Tynes' current coach was just as jubilant as anyone over his first Super Bowl trip as a head coach in his 38th year of coaching.

Tynes ran off the field following his 47-yarder, away from the teammates who now couldn't wait to celebrate with him. "There's some pretty cool pictures of Strahan…chasing after me," Tynes said with a smile. "I knew the party was gonna be in the locker room so…"

After sprinting into the locker room, Tynes raced into a whirl-wind of publicity in the next week, doing the Letterman show and fielding questions from the media about his brother, who was in jail. Tynes absorbed the attention as smoothly as he did his two misses, eventually letting the reality of what happened hit him.

"You have to sit there and really contemplate what happened," he said, remembering the moment three years later. "You kicked the ball for this franchise, this city to go to the Super Bowl. You know, I think it takes a couple days for it to sink in.

"Regardless of the misses...I was 3-for-5 that day, best day in my career."

It's a day that just might get even better over time.

"I definitely remember the made one," defensive lineman Justin Tuck said. He smiled. "Did he miss a field goal in that game?"

23 NFC Champs '86: Long-Suffering Fans Cheer 17–0 Win

They streamed onto the field at Giants Stadium, none of them needing the 40-mph wind gusts to propel them. The Giants raced out for introductions in the 1986 NFC Championship Game against Washington, sprinting from the devastation that left their fans mute or mutinous for so many years.

They found their footing, starting with Phil McConkey, the receiver and punt returner who doubled as a mascot, thrusting himself out of the tunnel and into the heart of the fans who craved this type of moment in their stadium. It had been 23 years since they had won an Eastern division championship in the old pre-Super Bowl days. Thirty since they had claimed an NFL title.

"First [phrase] I ever heard was 'long-suffering Giants fan,'" running back Joe Morris recalled 25 years later. "I remember that clearly. I remember them saying to us, 'You've got to get a championship.'"

Now they were on the cusp of an NFC championship, the team's first. The Giants' first shot at a Super Bowl. They won playoff games in the last few seasons and had taken steps toward respectability. They squashed San Francisco 49–3 the previous week, little more than a year after beating the Niners 17–3 in the team's first postseason game in Giants Stadium. The Giants finally gave their fans reasons to forget about past traumas like The Fumble.

"As Giant football players, we have to live in the past," quarterback Phil Simms said before the game. "People remind us of that. Not that it bothers us, but we'd kind of like to wipe it out."

Coach Bill Parcells showed faith in his defense after the Giants won the coin toss. The wind hissed all over the field, and he decided to kick off to the Redskins so the Giants would have the wind at their backs, even if it meant giving up the ball. That's how much confidence he had in his 14–2 Giants, who had already defeated Washington twice that season. How much confidence he had in that "bunch of crazed dogs" defense led by linebackers Lawrence Taylor, Harry Carson, and Carl Banks.

"The Washington game was just weird," Morris recalled. "'We're taking the wind.' Trust me. If we run into the wind, we have to run the ball. When we're going the other way, we could pass."

The previous season, the Giants watched their hopes wiped out by the wind in Chicago. Punter Sean Landeta missed a punt in Giants territory after the wind blew it and the Bears returned it for an easy touchdown on the way to a 21–0 win. Chicago went on to the Super Bowl, and the Giants resolved to grow stronger and gain the home-field advantage the next year.

Twice in the first quarter, the Redskins punted. Twice, the wind foiled punter Steve Cox, whose punts traveled 23 and 27 yards, respectively. The Giants took advantage of the field position both times, first on a 47-yard field goal by Raul Allegre, then on an 11-yard touchdown pass from Simms to receiver Lionel Manuel who missed most of the season with an injury. The Giants led 10–0.

Landeta redeemed himself from the previous year, kicking into the wind and averaging 42.3 yards per punt for the day; his teammates later commended him for making the difference.

Morris scored on a 1-yard run in the second quarter, and it was 17–0.

The fans grew more rabid with each play. This was no longer the Yankee Stadium crowd, taking the subway into the city like the old days. This was the first major celebration in New Jersey for the Giants. Instead of celebrations at Toots Shor's in Manhattan, there were songs sung at Manny's in Moonachie, New Jersey. This was the blue-collar Big Blue Wrecking Crew that inspired hardhats with the "GIANTS" logo on them—and the old "NY" removed.

But as the time ticked off and the Giants inched closer to a dominating shutout win—even without Taylor, who was injured for most of the second half—it was a celebration for all of them.

Redskins quarterback Jay Schroeder completed just 20-of-50 passes, the wind turning a longer pass into a "knuckle-ball," he said later, as receivers dropped several balls. The Giants helped that incompletion total, sacking him four times—one each for Leonard Marshall, Eric Dorsey, Gary Reasons, and George Martin, who had been there when the fans burned their tickets in protest.

The fans celebrated now, watching Carson douse Parcells with Gatorade as part of the new tradition. Parcells juked and nearly turned the tables on Carson, but the veteran would not have it, making sure his coach got doused.

Jim Burt, who sent the fans into a frenzy the previous week with his knockout hit on 49ers legend Joe Montana, jumped into the stands to join their party, pouring champagne as fans patted him on the back. Eventually, he returned to the field, hopping and screaming and pumping his fist as he finally made his way to the tunnel. The Giants played Denver in the Super Bowl, but now the fans from Jersey and New York celebrated the end of an anxious era.

"It got on everyone's nerves," Taylor said after the game. "You listen to guys say, 'We've been fans ever since the Polo Grounds.' Now, in 1995, they'll be saying, 'You know what? You guys are almost as good as those guys in 1986.'"

24 The Worst Team to Ever Win the NFC Championship

Confetti fell everywhere as the red, white, and blue streamers floated onto the players who didn't want to budge off the Giants Stadium turf they had just owned. Symbols of Big Blue tradition were all over that field the way the 2000 edition of the team had been all over the Vikings in the most dominant NFC Championship Game performance ever. Now the 41–0 win was over and, still in their old jerseys, former stars Lawrence Taylor and Harry Carson mingled with Michael Strahan and Jessie Armstead on one part of the field.

Kerry Collins, the reclamation project at quarterback, stood on another after throwing five touchdown passes in the game of his life. A game he never thought he'd have a chance to play again a couple of years earlier when alcoholism stole his career before he fought to reclaim it.

Finally the patriarch, who had seen so many championship moments, spoke. Wellington Mara did not know, of course, that this would be the last championship he would see before his death in 2005. Nor did the fans know it would be the last one celebrated on the Giants Stadium field where Taylor and Carson once roamed. But everyone paused from the raucous revelry to hear The Duke salute a team no one expected to earn a Super Bowl trip.

"This is the Giants team that was referred to as the worst team ever to win the home-field advantage in the National Football League," Mara told the towel-waving crowd from the postgame stage on the field. "And today, on this field of painted mud, we proved that we're the worst team to ever win the National Football League conference championship.

"I'm happy to say that in two weeks we're going to try to become the worst team ever to win the Super Bowl." They did

Collins Comes Back

While Kerry Collins reached his full potential as a quarterback in the Giants' dominant win over Minnesota, he also addressed the problems that once threatened to keep him from succeeding. With the national spotlight growing on the Giants, Collins did not avoid questions of his alcoholism.

A first-round draft pick out of Penn State, his career started strong with a playoff run for the Carolina Panthers. But he wore out his welcome in Carolina when teammates said he quit on the team. Even worse, he called teammate Muhsin Muhammad the n-word while drunk.

Collins immediately called the racial slur a huge mistake, saying he meant to use the term the way black teammates sometimes used it. Mistake or not, Collins was out of line and apologized. He acknowledged it was not his place to use a word with such a painful history.

But his bouts with alcohol continued, including an arrest on a DWI charge while with the Saints in 1998. After that, Collins started therapy.

He rebounded with the Giants on the field. More importantly, he appeared to remain sober. He discussed his recovery, hoping to provide an example for others trying to come back from self-inflicted wounds.

"Looking back, I'm proud of what I've accomplished," Collins said during a press conference before the Super Bowl. "On and off the field. I guess my life today shows that if you can change—if you're willing to try to change—then good things can happen."

not accomplish that, of course. The Baltimore Ravens' defense dominated the Giants the way New York's offense had thrashed Minnesota, for a 34–7 rout.

But that disappointment would not yet be revealed, and this gleeful celebration was the best kind—the type you savor because it comes as a surprise.

The Giants rallied behind Jim Fassel's playoff guarantee after stumbling in back-to-back losses that led to finger-pointing at 7–4. They reeled off five wins to finish the regular season as the NFC's top seed, but a relatively soft schedule still led to doubts.

A 20–10 win over the Eagles in the divisional round had been more convincing. But no one imagined the walloping the Giants gave the Vikings. Along with Collins' career day—he went 28-of-39 for a still-standing NFC Championship-record 381 yards—and the team's offensive dominance, the Giants defense stunned the Vikings' high-powered offense.

Led by quarterback Dante Culpepper and receiver Randy Moss, the Vikings offense ranked fifth in points and yards and was coming off a 34–16 win over New Orleans in the divisional round. For the season, Culpepper threw 33 touchdowns and only 16 interceptions, connecting with Moss for 15 scores.

But the Giants defense held Minnesota to 114 yards and nine first downs with Culpepper managing just 78 yards passing—18 to Moss. He threw three interceptions, and the Giants sacked him four times.

The night before the game, Taylor and Carson told the then-current Giants that they were proud of them. But as the game progressed, the old pair of Hall of Famers got greedy, their pride taken to a new level. The voices of the past giddily barked at Strahan, telling him they wanted the shutout. Later, amid the confetti and the celebration of former and present players, the team's patriarch saluted one last championship in a lifetime full of them.

"You realize how much tradition is out on the field," running back Tiki Barber said after the game. "It's not just us."

25 Jack Mara

Wellington Mara fought tears in the part of his Hall of Fame speech where he remembered the brother the passing of time denied some Giants fans a chance to know. "I overwhelmingly feel that I come to you here as a surrogate, someone who takes the place of someone else," Mara said at his induction speech in 1997. "If it hadn't been for his untimely death some 30-odd years ago, Jack Mara would certainly have taken his place beside our father long ago to form the first father and son team in the Hall of Fame."

But Jack Mara died of cancer at age 57 in 1965. So Wellington formed that Hall of Fame duo 47 years after their father, Tim, put the Giants in his sons' names.

Due to the Wall Street stock market crash and ensuing Depression in the 1920s and '30s, Mara handed the team to his sons to protect it from creditors. At that point, Jack was just 22 and Wellington was 14. But within the next decade, the brothers started to really take over the organization.

Jack became the president, using his Fordham law degree to handle the financials. Wellington handled some contract duties, too, but he was more involved in the football operations.

Legendary Giants center Mel Hein once said negotiating with Jack was enough to make him seek Tim the next time. "Tim was easier to deal with as far as a contract was concerned," Hein told author Richard Whittingham in the book *What a Game They Played: An Inside Look at the Golden Era of Pro Football*.

"I think Tim was a little more generous and, needless to say, I preferred to deal with him if I needed a raise or anything like that," Hein added. "He would listen to me longer."

Over time, the Giants who played under Jack Mara would not remember contract negotiations as much as they would a man they said, much like his brother, always offered support. "I never thought of him as my boss," former Giants quarterback Charlie Conerly said after Mara's death. "He was my friend."

Hall of Fame safety Emlen Tunnell buried his head in his hands and cried upon hearing Mara had been stricken with cancer. And Frank Gifford, the team's noted star of the '50s, was forever grateful to Jack Mara for his role in making Gifford a Giant. So

Tim Mara and Wellington Mara (left) became the first father-son duo to reach the Hall of Fame, but Wellington claimed his brother Jack (center, talking to NFL commissioner Bert Bell) would have earned the honor if he did not die young. (AP Photo/Joe Caneva)

much so that when Jack died in 1965, a somber and grateful Gifford interrupted his Hawaiian vacation.

"When he heard that, he got on the next plane back to New York," Wellington Mara once recalled. "He said, 'If it weren't for Jack Mara, I never would have gotten to New York. I never would have gotten to Hawaii in the first place.'"

While Jack Mara may have helped Gifford get to New York, he wasn't as eager for New York to see him—or any of the other Giants—on television. At least not when the team was at home. In the early 1950s, as television grew in popularity, the NFL created a blackout rule to offset dwindling attendance figures. Home games would not be shown within a 75-mile radius..

But a judge ruled the television restriction illegal. Mara used his legal skills to counter the ruling, pointing out the Giants' attendance had dropped to 62.5 percent of stadium capacity in 1950 from 91.5 four years earlier. Eventually, a judge ruled in favor of the NFL, allowing the blackout to stand for home games only—and later forcing Giants fans to rent hotel rooms outside the restricted area to watch big games.

While Mara fought against too much television access in the 1950s, he helped make another precedent-setting decision involving television in the '60s. By then, the Giants had grown in popularity thanks in part to the TV coverage that helped fuel enthusiasm. The increased interest, combined with the large New York market, allowed the Giants to sign a $175,000 contract to have their games televised. The amount was four times what small-market Green Bay secured. Recognizing the danger of pushing small-market teams out of business, NFL commissioner Pete Rozelle nudged the Maras and other large-market owners to share the television revenue equally.

Wellington Mara has largely been credited for making the unselfish decision that allowed the league to prosper and blossom into the monolith it is today. While he must have had a role as co-owner, Wellington once said the true praise should go to his brother, who cast the vote for revenue-sharing along with the Bears' George Halas and the Rams' Dan Reeves.

He called it "the most important vote" ever cast in the NFL.

"You could argue that we deserve a bigger piece of the pie," said John Mara, Wellington's son and the team's current co-owner. "But it's the reason that the NFL is the strongest professional league on the planet."

26 Watch the LT/Theismann Play at Own Risk

They showed it so many times on *Monday Night Football* it is now seared into your mind if you watched it that night in November 1985 or any time since.

There's Lawrence Taylor, charging at Redskins quarterback Joe Theismann, "flying around the field like a lunatic and crashing his body into people," as teammate Karl Nelson said. Theismann, trying to throw a long pass after a flea flicker flip from fullback John Riggins, slipped out of the massive grip of Taylor's teammate, Harry Carson.

But now Taylor's coming even harder.

He attacks Theismann with his trademark pounce, leaping from behind the quarterback. As the pair goes down violently, Taylor's right leg flies into Theismann's right ankle, then the back of his knee, bending it under his body violently.

Awkwardly.

The quarterback's weight falls on the leg as Giants linebacker Gary Reasons adds more pressure, piling on to finish the tackle. Theismann's leg snaps in a way so graphic and chilling it horrifies most everyone watching.

Including the fiercest linebacker in the world, who could hear what everyone else had only seen. In an instant, the player bent on punishing an opponent was gone, replaced by a man horrified at what the violent game made him do. Immediately, Taylor jumped up and waved frantically to the Redskins' sideline, pausing only when his hands instinctively went to his helmet in a fit of anguish.

"Get somebody out here!" he screamed over and over. "Get somebody out here!"

"Sad Thing. Awful. But ..."

Joe Morris scored on a 56-yard touchdown run to tie the game 7–7, and the Redskins wanted to answer in the second quarter when they called for the flea flicker play.

The Giants entered the game with a 7–3 record, the Redskins 5–5. After the immediate shock of Lawrence Taylor's hit and Joe Theismann's exit wore off, the Giants had a chance to finish Washington for the season.

Theismann, one of the league's best quarterbacks, played in 163 straight games. His replacement, Jay Schroeder, threw eight passes all year. Despite two more touchdown runs by Morris, including a 41-yarder, Schroeder rallied the Redskins late, hitting tight end Clint Didier for a 14-yard touchdown and a 23–21 win.

Taylor's humanity touched the nation, and his defensive teammates struggled to regroup. But some offensive players like Morris—who had not witnessed the traumatizing play at the time—were jolted by something else.

"I'm sorry that it happened to Joe. Sad thing. Awful. But it [ticked] me off," Morris said. "You know what [ticked] me off? Our defense wasn't mean the rest of the game.

"I remember he got hurt, but we lost the game. I was sad for Joe, but I'm thinking, 'What the hell?' As a human being, I understand he got hurt. [But] we should have been-re-focused on that game."

The Redskins' trainer, Bubba Tyer, had been attending to a player with a dislocated finger, so he didn't see Taylor or Theismann. Taylor's teammates jumped up and waved as well before Taylor finally rushed to the Washington sideline and grabbed Tyer, who hit the field.

When he arrived, Tyer saw Theismann's leg and bone sticking through his sock. Theismann's career was over due to a compound fracture. In that moment, Taylor's looked as though it might never be the same.

"See Lawrence waving...Lawrence was tough, he was mean, but he wasn't looking to hurt anybody," Taylor's teammate, Joe Morris, said. "They knew he was hurt pretty bad. That may be your job, but I don't think…you never react like that if you want to hurt somebody."

The image provided a modern update on the type of violent pictures that had become embedded in the minds of football fans and players in the past. Only this time, unlike the photograph of Y.A. Tittle befuddled and bloody in 1964 or Frank Gifford lying prone on the ground in 1960, the vision lingered with seemingly endless instant replays.

Gifford, broadcasting the game for ABC, immediately recognized Taylor's desperation and what it indicated. "I don't believe Lawrence Taylor would have reacted that way," Gifford told ABC's national television audience, "unless Theismann is really hurt."

While Taylor's anxiety rose following the violent collision, Theismann offered those attending to him a surprising calm. "Please, call my mom and let her know I'm okay," Theismann told Tyer, as he later remembered on ESPN.

He listened to head coach Joe Gibbs try to lighten the tense moment that silenced the large crowd by telling Theismann, "Joe, this is a heck of a mess you left me in." It worked. The men laughed. Eventually, Theismann was rolled off the field on a stretcher, the Washington fans giving the quarterback who won them a Super Bowl two years earlier a standing ovation.

The next day, Taylor called Theismann to check on him. Already, though, the linebacker started to regain his edge, offering a joking response when the quarterback told him he had broken the two major bones in his leg.

"That's because I don't do anything halfway," Taylor joked, according to *LT: Over the Edge*, his 2003 autobiography. "If I'm gonna break them, I'm gonna break them both."

While the pair attempted to lighten the moment with a laugh, they both have one thing in common about the play that won't leave the mind of almost anyone who's seen it. They have not watched it once.

27 Steve Owen: Setting a Giant Tone

In the 1980s, Giants coach Bill Parcells was known for employing a plodding, conservative strategy focused on defense and rushing that inspired lineman Karl Nelson to say, "TV hated us." Old-time Giants fans, however, recalled the glory of the mid-1950s when they gleefully chanted for their defense full of stars.

But before Parcells and the famed 1956 champions, Steve Owen, the first legendary Giants coach, set that tone. "Steve was the first to stress the importance of defense and the advantage of settling for field goals instead of touchdowns," George Halas, Chicago's legendary "Papa Bear," once said of Owen.

Owen utilized that style to lead the team to eight division titles and the franchise's first two NFL championships in his 23 years as head coach. He worked each year with a handshake for an agreement, not a contract. He took over as head coach in 1931 after owner Tim Mara reportedly joked he no longer had a uniform to fit the talented lineman known as "Stout Steve."

Owen had played with the Giants since 1926 when Mara paid $500 for him—the same amount he supposedly paid to buy the team the previous year. By 1931, the Giants so revered Owen that he won the head coaching job over popular quarterback Benny Friedman, who was his co-coach in 1930. Friedman's passing revolutionized the game and helped the Giants draw fans when they were desperate. Mara so coveted Friedman that he bought the entire Detroit team Friedman was playing for to bring him to New York.

But Mara still chose Owen, prompting Friedman's exit. The move might have forever changed the legacy of Giants football. Friedman could have turned the Giants into an early version of a run 'n gun or wide-open passing offense. Instead, a battle-for-every-inch defense became the Giants' trademark.

Owen was known as a strict disciplinarian who believed in the smash-mouth football from his playing days. He had been a member of the 1927 team that barely let opponents score on the way to an 11–1–1 record. The Giants shut out 10 opponents and allowed just 20 points all year to finish atop the NFL standings in the 12-team league, which did not yet have a playoff or championship format.

"Football is a game played down in the dirt and it always will be," Owen once said in his raspy voice, and through a mouth usually filled with tobacco. "There's no use getting fancy about it."

While Owen believed in minimizing risks, he was far from uncreative. He used rare gadget plays with his most trusted players. Hall of Fame center Mel Hein once gained nearly 30 yards by hiding the ball under his shirt after becoming an eligible receiver in the first NFL championship game in 1933.

In that same game, fellow Hall of Famer Ken Strong, playing halfback, took a pitch from quarterback Harry Newman, then flipped the ball back to the quarterback—an early flea flicker—before catching a pass in the end zone for a touchdown.

Owen also became known for his rare strategy of substituting entire units at a time when most players quickly grew exhausted due to their multi-dimensional roles. But Owen, who was enshrined in the Hall of Fame in 1966, made his biggest impact when he created the Umbrella Defense in 1950.

The Cleveland Browns dominated the All-America Football Conference for the past four years and looked to do the same in the NFL with a pair of dominant offensive games led by Hall of Fame quarterback Otto Graham. The Browns offense was thought to be unstoppable, so Owen tried to get creative and proposed a new formation.

It called for six defensive linemen—including two who would drop back into pass coverage—plus one linebacker and four defensive

Steve Owen: Coaching Highlights

Years: 1931–1953*
Record: 151–100–17 (.602)
Inducted into Hall of Fame: 1966

Division Titles
1933—Eastern Division (11–3)
1934—Eastern Division (8–5)
1935—Eastern Division (9–3)
1938—Eastern Division (8–2–1)
1939—Eastern Division (9–1–1)
1941—Eastern Division (8–3–1)
1943—Eastern Division (6–3–1)**
1944—Eastern Division (8–1–1)
1946—Eastern Division (7–3–1)
1950—American Conference (10–2)***

NFL Championship Games
1933—L—at Chicago, 23–21, December 17
1934—W—vs. Chicago, 30–13, December 9
1935—L—at Detroit, 26–7, December 15
1938—W—vs. Green Bay, 23–17, December 11
1939—L—at Green Bay (Mil.), 27–0, December 10
1941—L—at Chicago, 37–9, December 21
1944—L—Green Bay, 14–7, December 17
1946—L—Chicago, 24–14, December 15

*Coached 10 Hall of Famers
**Lost to Washington in playoff 28–0
***Lost to Cleveland in playoff 8–3

backs who fanned out like the spokes of an umbrella. Owen left it up to his talented 26-year-old defensive back, Tom Landry, to work out some kinks. (A few years later, as the Giants' defensive coach, Landry tweaked it even more to create the 4-3 defense, still the basic defense most teams use six decades later.)

The Giants shut out a shocked Graham and the Browns 6–0 and eventually tied them for the division title, forcing a playoff.

The Giants defense again held down the mighty Cleveland offense but lost 8–3.

Owen won his first championship in 1934 in the famous "Sneakers Game." Four years later, Owen's Giants won their second championship against the Packers 23–17. This time, he added an innovation on offense—the A-Formation, which was a variation of the single wing with three backs lining up on one side.

Like so many coaches in the NFL, Owen's time with the Giants did not end smoothly. After so much success early in his career, he did not adapt well to the next era, butting heads with star running back and defensive back Frank Gifford in the early '50s.

Eventually, the Giants decided to replace Owen with Jim Lee Howell, who would lead a new era of Giants success, most notably by hiring Landry as his defensive coach and a young assistant coach at Army, Vince Lombardi, as his offensive coach.

Wellington Mara, who ran the team by that point, once called his decision to let Owen go one of the toughest he ever made.

"It was like telling your father you're putting him out of your home," he said.

"He was a great guy," said John Johnson, who started as a trainer under Owen in 1948. "Everyone thought he was a tough son of a gun."

28 Mel Hein: The Lou Gehrig of the Giants

Wellington Mara called him the most popular Giant in the club's first half-century, adding he was replaced in status only by Lawrence Taylor. The only thing that made Mel Hein's popularity more impressive was the way he earned it. At least half of the time, Hein played one of the game's most anonymous positions—center.

Sure, back when Hein played in the 1930s and '40s, he had to play on both sides of the ball, filling in as a linebacker, as well. And he gave Giants fans plenty to cheer there, strong enough to shed blockers and quick enough to shut down Green Bay receiver Don Hutson, who eluded almost everyone else in the league.

But Hein's rare ability to snap the ball directly to any of the backs behind him while also providing as strong a protection as any Giants lineman ever would, also endeared him to Giants fans. They knew if they went to the Polo Grounds to see the Giants from 1931–45, they were assured of seeing No. 7 on the field.

Hein's 15 years with the club was equaled only by Phil Simms and Michael Strahan. His feat of playing in 170 straight games and playing the full 60 minutes in all but two of them is unparalleled in Giants history.

He was knocked out for an extended period from only one game—on Pearl Harbor Day, December 7, 1941, when he was hospitalized for a broken nose and a concussion. In the 1938 championship win over Green Bay, he also had broken his nose but returned. That year he won the NFL's first MVP award, the only lineman to do so.

"Mel played longer than any Giant," Coach Steve Owen once said, "and was coached less."

The Giants captain barely missed a play, much less a game. He also came close to never playing a down for New York. He was headed to the Providence Steam Rollers out of Washington State, having just signed and mailed a contract for $125 a game. But then he ran into Giants end Ray Flaherty, who informed him the Giants had also mailed him a contract—for $150 a game.

A plan was hatched. Hein sent a telegram to the Providence postmaster hoping against hope the man would go against his job's instinct and return the contract. It worked. The postmaster mailed

Hubbard: A Hall of Famer Twice

To Mel Hein, Cal Hubbard was the Green Bay defensive tackle who was the toughest lineman he battled and a teammate for all of six games. Four years before Hein arrived, Hubbard helped lead the Giants to their first NFL championship in 1927 before divisions and a title game were created. Hubbard played on the Giants line alongside future coach and Hall of Famer Steve Owen, and he also played linebacker.

But having played for small colleges, New York was too big for Hubbard and the Giants sent him to Green Bay in 1929 where he would win three NFL titles on the way to a Hall of Fame career. Despite his relative discomfort in New York, Hubbard did help the Giants after a slew of injuries. Already retired, Hubbard agreed to play one game in 1936—and ended up playing six.

After he finished playing football, Hubbard became famous as a baseball umpire—joining another ex-Giant, Hank Soar, as players who became umps.

Hubbard stood out on the diamond, as well, working out a positioning system for umpires that led to the one used today. He is now the only person to be enshrined in both the Baseball and Pro Football Halls of Fame.

the contract back, and it arrived almost at the same time as the Giants' offer.

"I signed with the Giants and tore up the contract with Providence," Hein said in the book *What a Game They Played: An Inside Look at the Golden Era of Pro Football.*

Hein helped the Giants to two NFL championships and eight division titles. So valuable was Hein that Owen allowed him to come down to play on Sundays only in his final three years so he could keep his day job teaching physical education to students and soldiers prepping for World War II at Union College in upstate Schenectady. Owner Tim Mara made Hein the NFL's highest paid lineman near the end of his career, paying him $5,000 a season.

Finally, Hein retired and went on to coach at the University of Southern California before taking a job supervising officials in the fledgling American Football League. He was a charter member of the Hall of Fame, inducted in 1963.

"He was truly a football legend and a giant among men," Raiders owner Al Davis—who hired Hein for the AFL job—said upon Hein's death in 1992. "Mel was one of the greatest football players who ever lived."

29 Jim Lee Howell

He helped the Giants win a championship under Coach Steve Owen as a Pro Bowl end. He also fought as a marine in World War II.

In 1954, Jim Lee Howell faced the daunting challenge of replacing Owen—the Giants coach for the previous 23 years and owner of two championships and eight division titles. After all that, Howell helped the Giants not only win their third NFL title along with three more division crowns, but he also ushered in the age of football credited with helping the sport thrust itself into the spotlight.

And for all those accomplishments, this is how Howell described his coaching tenure with the Giants. "I just blow up the footballs," Howell said, "and keep order."

The most amazing thing about one of the most accomplished coaches in Giants history? He wasn't exaggerating...at least not by much. Okay, Howell did make one of the most vital moves of the era by going to Mississippi and convincing quarterback Charlie Conerly not to retire. He did make several other key moves and was the man ultimately in charge. But overall Howell's greatest quality as a head coach came not from any of his strategic decisions but from his recognition that he should not make many.

Jim Lee Howell won an NFL title, but he was best known for deferring to his legendary assistant coaches, Vince Lombardi and Tom Landry. (AP Photo)

Also, his ability to spot talent didn't hurt. It enabled him to hire Vince Lombardi as his offensive coach and Tom Landry full-time to coach the defense. The moves allowed Howell to let two of the NFL's most legendary and creative coaches go to work—and left him all but blowing up footballs.

"He's got to be one of the smartest coaches of all time," said Sam Huff, who helped make those '50s Giants famous with his punishing hits for Landry's defense. "Why? He let Tom Landry coach defense and Vince Lombardi coach offense and told us what time the plane was leaving. I've got to give Jim Lee Howell credit. He knew what he had. He let 'em coach."

In the testosterone-fueled football world, stepping aside is no small feat. As a former player and hard-nosed marine—who still lived up to that reputation by keeping order among the Giants as a strict disciplinarian—it would have been easy for Howell to miss what was in front of him.

But Howell recognized the innovation of Landry's 4-3 defense. Howell gave Lombardi, the former Army college coach, room to breathe while he found his way with the pro players.

"He had enough good sense to stay out of the way," Frank Gifford said of Howell. "I'm not demeaning him with that, either. I don't know how many people would have enough common sense or whatever would be the word—strength—to turn it over to two guys who knew a heck of a lot more than he did.

"He used to kid about it. He said, 'All I do is blow the whistle and pump up the balls.' That's about all he did, so he was right."

Well, not exactly. Howell did make crucial calls, including the one that at first mystified then electrified the Giants in 1958. Fans across the NFL know about the Greatest Game Ever Played. But long-time Giants fans know New York never would have reached that classic overtime NFL title game against the Colts if it did not first beat Jim Brown and Cleveland in back-to-back games.

They also know Pat Summerall won the first one with a field goal no one expected him to kick, much less make on a snow-covered field. Howell made the surprising call to send Summerall in.

"You know you can't kick it that far!" Lombardi gleefully told Summerall after he made what was officially ruled to be a 49-yard kick but thought to be longer.

Two weeks later, after the Giants again beat the Browns to advance to the NFL title game, Howell made another important call against the Colts. This time, the play subjected him to second-guessing instead of slaps on the back. Howell decided to punt after the famed "bad spot" call when Gifford was ruled just short of a first down late in the game.

Despite the Giants' powerful offensive line and running game plus the threat of Baltimore Hall of Fame quarterback Johnny Unitas, Howell didn't want to gamble from his own 44-yard line. Baltimore rallied to tie, sending the game into overtime and the Giants into eventual defeat. Howell stood by the call the next day,

Jim Lee Howell: Coaching Highlights

Years: 1954–60
Record: 53–27–4
NFL Championships: 1
Division Titles: 3

NFL Championship games
1956—W—vs. Chicago, 47–7, December 30, (Regular season record: 8–3–1)
1958—L vs. Baltimore, 23–17 (OT), December 28, (9–3)
1959—L at Baltimore, 16–31, December 27, (10–2)

Division titles
1956—Eastern Conference (Jim Lee Howell, 8–3–1)
1958—Eastern Conference (Howell, 9–3)*
1959—Eastern Conference (Howell, 10–2)

*Tied—Defeated Cleveland in playoff, 10–0.

saying he did not regret it. Despite his *laissez-faire* approach in letting his talented coaches handle the day-to-day routine, he was respected by the Giants' organization.

When Howell began to feel that the stress of the game was affecting his home life, he considered retiring. The Maras created a front office position for him that wouldn't call for travel. He happily accepted and coached his final season in 1960. The timing could have been better for the Giants, who watched Landry depart to Dallas and Lombardi leave for Green Bay in the preceding years. Howell remained with the Giants in various roles, reduced over time, until 1986. Nine years later, he passed away in his home state of Arkansas, where he served in the legislature.

Along with Huff, Gifford, and many other celebrated Giants, the man who would just "blow up the footballs" was inducted into the club's Ring of Honor in 2010.

"In my seven years with the club, the experience has been wonderful," he said on his last day as a coach. "This is no malarkey or soft soap. The Giants have been blessed with great players, and my coaching staff has done all the work. I wish there was some way I could tell the fans how much I appreciate their support."

30 If You Leave Me Now: Lombardi and Landry

One coach played defensive back for the Giants, setting records and settling under the wing of his first head coach Steve Owen. He was a natural coach, having earned respect with players before head coach Jim Lee Howell named him the defensive coach full-time in 1956.

The other coach offered the type of vein-throbbing speeches that look good in Hollywood locker rooms but don't usually play as well in professional ones. Players initially met him with eye rolls, dismissing him as a rah-rah college type out of West Point who couldn't cut it in their professional world. When Howell hired him to coach the offense in 1954, the players weren't sure what to make of him.

All these years later, Giants fans know just what to think of Tom Landry and Vince Lombardi, the legendary coaches who led the Giants defense and offense, respectively, in the glory era of the 1950s.

They're the ones who got away. And all the Giants could do was be grateful they had given two of the game's all-time best coaches their start before they took off for Dallas and Green Bay, respectively.

"I played for the greatest coaches who ever coached in the world—Tom Landry and Vince Lombardi," said Sam Huff, the linebacker who became the focal point of Landry's innovative 4-3 defense. "Landry never did swear, and Lombardi did all the time and yet they were so successful."

They also made Howell successful as the Giants won three division titles and one NFL championship from 1956–59.

Lombardi's legend has grown over the past five decades, revitalizing itself in 2010 when an off-Broadway show *Lombardi* premiered and the coach's old team, Green Bay, went on to win the Super Bowl. The Packers played the game in Dallas, where Landry made his name as a head coach beginning in 1960 one year after Lombardi left the Giants for the Packers.

Landry won 250 games and two Super Bowls in 29 years. Lombardi won 96 games in 10 years (for an astounding .738 winning percentage), three NFL championships (two over his old Giants), and the first two Super Bowls. Later, he was honored by having the Super Bowl trophy named after him.

The Giants could have had either of them with better timing.

Howell let the Giants know he was burned out on coaching after the 1959 season and wanted to spend more time with his family. They responded by offering him a front-office job with no travel after one final year of coaching.

Born in Brooklyn, Lombardi loved New York but couldn't pass up the opportunity when Green Bay offered him a job as head coach and general manager after the 1958 season. The Maras always said they would give Lombardi first chance at their head coaching job if Howell left. But by the time they asked him to come back the next season, Lombardi had won a Western division title and the Packers weren't letting him out of his contract.

So the Giants remember Lombardi not as leading them to championships but as defeating them in two championship games against Howell's replacement, Allie Sherman. And the images of Landry as a head coach find him roaming the sideline in his fedora, leading the Cowboys to a pair of Super Bowl championships in the 1970s while the Giants suffered through a decade of football without a playoff appearance.

The Giants can only take consolation in the powerhouse team the pair of coaches built while they were in New York.

Landry started coaching while still a player for the Giants after initially playing for the New York Yankees of the All-America Football Conference. He intercepted 32 passes in seven years with the Giants and helped implement Owen's Umbrella Defense.

When he became the official defensive coach, Landry updated the defense by turning it into the 4-3 still highly utilized today. He made the most of stars like linemen Rosey Grier, Jim Katcavage, and Dick Modzelewski; Huff at middle linebacker; and Hall of Fame safety Emlen Tunnell.

Mostly, he commanded them to strictly adhere to his schemes, allowing little room for freelancing—other than Tunnell, whose free-wheeling ability to dart for the ball convinced Landry to make an exception.

When the game started, those commands did not need to be spoken. "When you made a mistake on Tom Landry's defense, he wouldn't swear to you," Huff said. "He wouldn't even say anything to you. It was just his look.

"He would just chew his lower lip and shake his head, 'No. I taught you better than that.' When you did something good, he would look at you, [as if to say] 'Thatta way to go.'"

While Landry strictly enforced his philosophies, Lombardi wisely sought input from veterans like Frank Gifford and quarterback Charlie Conerly to help gain the trust of the skeptical players. But quickly Lombardi instilled as much loyalty on offense as Landry did on defense, and the Giants' own intra-squad rivalry was known to motivate both sides.

"You can say we were not blood brothers," Huff said with a laugh. "On Sundays, we played well together."

In the multi-faceted attacks of the time, Lombardi rolled out plenty of option passes by Gifford, his running back. Gifford passed for 12 of his 14 career touchdowns under Lombardi and rushed for 25 of his 34 scores.

Gifford remembered that for all of Lombardi's enthusiasm, he had not yet perfectly honed his "winning isn't everything; it's the only thing" persona that defined him with the Packers.

"He actually developed a lot of the rougher traits when he went to Green Bay," Gifford said. He recalled speaking to fellow Hall of Fame running back Paul Hornung of the Packers. "When Vince went up there, we had quite a conversation about it. I think he changed a great deal when he became head coach."

Gifford then said something about Lombardi as painful as it was obvious, a fact he apparently thought might have somehow gotten lost in ancient history, though it never will.

"He was not," Gifford said, "the head coach here."

31 "You Can't Kick It That Far!"

Pat Summerall walked onto a snow-covered field on which he easily could have slipped, the Giants' season left up to his right foot. They had fought to keep that season alive with two straight wins down the stretch in 1958, chasing the Cleveland Browns, facing them head-on now with just 2:07 remaining at Yankee Stadium.

The teams were tied on the scoreboard 10–10 but not in the standings in the season's final week. The Giants were behind the Browns by a game, and with no overtime session for the regular season, they had to beat them to force a one-game playoff for the Eastern division title.

Quarterback Charlie Conerly hit Alex Webster in the end zone for an apparent 55-yard touchdown—until Webster dropped the ball. Now Conerly prepared for one more try on fourth-and-10 when he saw Summerall approaching him.

"What the hell are you doing here?" Conerly said.

In his future career as one of the game's most eloquent broadcasters, Summerall surely would have succinctly explained the situation, adding a poetic touch. But then?

Summerall offered no explanation. He searched for one. "I couldn't believe they were asking me to try it," he said.

Summerall made a 46-yard kick in the second quarter with the snow still falling, but he missed a 36-yarder just minutes earlier—in an era when kicking was not a specialized or entirely reliable pursuit. Only the week before, the Giants won a game because linebacker Harland Svare blocked a last-minute field goal against Detroit.

Summerall also knew how close he came to not going on the field at all. His injured knee kept him from practicing all week and prompted Summerall to tell punter Don Chandler to warm up before the game because he didn't think he could kick.

Offensive coach Vince Lombardi certainly didn't think Summerall could—or should—at that point in the game. Like Conerly, and most of the stunned Giants, he wanted to run another offensive play. While there was no way to tell for sure since the yard lines were covered in white, the kick seemed out of range, especially given the conditions.

But head coach Jim Lee Howell, so famous for relinquishing authority to Lombardi and defensive coach Tom Landry, took this one himself. He overruled Lombardi, whose offense earlier in the fourth quarter had tied the game on a favorite play—a halfback pass from Frank Gifford, this time to Bob Schnelker.

After a game in which Landry's tenacious defense allowed a 65-yard touchdown to Hall of Famer Jim Brown on the first play and little else, Howell left the Giants' fate up to Summerall, the kicker who just joined the team that year.

Eventually, Summerall earned the league's respect, leading the NFL in field goal percentage by making 69 percent of his kicks the next season. He fielded an odd job offer from Steelers' owner Art Rooney following his playing career, as Summerall detailed in his book, *Giants: What I Learned About Life from Vince Lombardi and Tom Landry*. Rooney asked him to coach his team. (When Summerall turned him down to continue broadcasting, Rooney opted for his second choice—Chuck Noll.) But at this point, Summerall mostly played for the Chicago Cardinals and Detroit Lions before them. He hit more than 50 percent on field goals for the first time in 1958.

So, two years after the Giants of Conerly, Gifford, Sam Huff, and Andy Robustelli won a championship, this first-year Giant would decide if they earned the chance to fight for another one. Even Howell apparently questioned his decision at the time.

"I started to call for a pass to try to get a little closer," he said after the game.

Instead, he opted for Summerall. Resigned, Conerly cleared a spot with his hand as he prepared for the hold.

Summerall later said his mind was clear, thinking that he only had to hit the ball well since it was a long kick. He admitted, though, that "I could have cried when I missed the one just before."

Just prior to the snap, Summerall later recalled to reporters, he remembered to "lock my ankle." His ankle locked, Summerall booted the ball, then watched it hook right before soaring through the uprights. The Yankee Stadium crowd roared in approval as did Summerall's stunned coaches and teammates, who held on for the 13–10 win.

"You son of a . . ." Lombardi told Summerall when he returned. "You know you can't kick it that far!"

But he did. And the Giants, winners of three straight games would face the Browns in a rematch the following week.

"Next week? I don't know," Howell told *Sports Illustrated* after the game and amid the Giants' celebration. "This is a great team, emotionally. But how many times emotionally can you do this?"

32 Sam Huff vs. Jim Brown: Winning the East

Jim Brown had rushed for 148 yards in the Giants' last-minute win on Pat Summerall's field goal the previous week. So a look at the stat sheet from the team's Eastern division playoff game in 1958 is an eye-popping endeavor. Brown, arguably the greatest running back in NFL history, rushed seven times—for 8 yards.

How did the Giants defense adjust so quickly in leading the team to its 10–0 win and a trip to face Baltimore in the 1958 NFL championship?

"I knocked him out," Giants linebacker Sam Huff said. "I hit him so hard he couldn't get up. It was the hardest he ever got hit. It was the hardest I ever hit anyone. I told him, 'Stay down, Jim.' And he said, 'I gotta get up. All right, I'm getting up, I'm getting up.... I'm not staying down.'"

While Huff may not have literally knocked Brown out, the Cleveland running back had one of the worst days of his career.

The rivals loved playing each other, but even Huff, for all his tough talk, always knew what he was up against. Brown was the toughest running back the league had seen—known for punishing tacklers more than they punished him. His strength, size, and speed allowed him to average a whopping 5.2 yards per carry, and all this time later he is still widely regarded as the league's best at the position.

"There isn't a linebacker in the league able to play Brown man-to-man," Huff once said after a game in which he didn't fare as well. "It took a team effort."

The respect—and pain—was mutual.

"I don't know if anyone ever hit me harder than Sam Huff," Brown once said. "Especially in that playoff game, he had my number on a couple of plays."

Huff's ability to send Brown stumbling off in disarray led another dominant defensive effort for the Giants. They became the first team to shut out Cleveland since the 1950 Giants, who used coach Steve Owen's Umbrella Defense to foil quarterback Otto Graham.

The Giants offense managed their 10 points thanks to another Summerall field goal—this one from 26 yards out—and a play that left 37-year-old quarterback Charlie Conerly cursing even as he celebrated.

The Giants reached the Cleveland 19-yard line when Conerly opted for a play Vince Lombardi had put in just that week. Right halfback Alex Webster took the handoff and headed left while left halfback Frank Gifford came the other way, taking the ball on a reverse. If the play had continued that way, Conerly would have been fine with it. But Gifford, finding his path blocked, tossed the ball back to his good friend with the graying hair. Conerly stumbled his way to the end zone, causing the Giants to smile—and not just because of their 7–0 lead.

He could have taken it himself, Gifford has joked over the years, but he figured Conerly should get a touchdown.

In the immediate aftermath, Conerly wasn't in agreement.

"Next time I give you the [bleeping] ball," Conerly said according to several accounts, "you keep it."

Regardless of how they got it, the Giants kept the lead thanks to Huff and the Giants defense, which was the most imposing Brown had seen. Of course, Huff lost his share of bouts with his rival and friend, including one time when he taunted him after a tackle.

"You stink!" Huff said.

Brown responded with a long run, then asked Huff how he smelled now.

"When we played you had the highest respect for Jim Brown, Jim Taylor, Gino Marchetti," Huff said, reeling off a trio of Hall of Fame opponents. "You remember their names because you respected them."

33 Andy Robustelli

Around the NFL, he was known as The Enforcer. Giants defensive back Dick Lynch used to call him The Pope. Sam Huff, laughing, said he could be more like a dictator.

And the folks at Robustelli Sporting Goods just called him boss in the 1950s and '60s, when players needed a second job to survive. But when Andy Robustelli arrived in a trade with the Rams in 1956, everyone around the Giants quickly learned to call him something else.

"He was a great leader," Huff said. "He meant a lot to the Giants."

The defensive end won two championships with the Los Angeles Rams. A 19th-round draft pick out of Arnold College, the former navy man grappled and beat the long odds of his late selection the way he did so many offensive linemen. At 31, he made the Pro Bowl twice.

So when the Rams made Robustelli available in a trade after he requested another week before he reported for training camp—his wife was expecting their fourth child in Stamford, Connecticut—Giants GM Wellington Mara pounced. The Giants rejoiced.

"When our coach, Jim Lee Howell, called the team together to announce the trade, Frank Gifford yelled," Mara told the *Hartford Courant* years later. "Frank was so excited. So was the whole team. There has never been a reaction like that for a new player coming here. Not a draft pick like Lawrence Taylor. No one."

Now Robustelli returned to the East, an hour or so from his Stamford home, where he looked to help build a young Giants

One Heck of a Line

Along with Andy Robustelli, the Giants defensive line in the late 1950s and early '60s featured Jim Katcavage, Rosey Grier, and Dick Modzelewski, making it one of football's most imposing lines ever.

Modzelewski came over from Pittsburgh and paired with Grier as the tackles between Robustelli and Katcavage, who had the longest Giants tenure of the group before retiring in 1968. He studied under Robustelli as a rookie and reached the Pro Bowl three times.

Because sacks statistics were not kept then, Katcavage cannot lay claim to a record owned by future Giant Michael Strahan—but unofficial tallies gave him 25 sacks in 1963, which would top Strahan's NFL mark. Wellington Mara once called Katcavage "one of our greatest defensive ends."

Grier, a two-time Pro Bowl pick, was the first major player traded in 1963 as new Giants head coach Allie Sherman and Mara broke up their championship defense, deciding its advancing age merited the moves. Modzelewski departed the next season, and Sam Huff was also dealt in 1964, the first of 18 playoff-free seasons for the Giants.

Grier later achieved the most fame for a variety of reasons, ranging from the peaceful 6'5", 284-pound lineman's book on needlepoint to a musical career as well as later finding a calling as a minister. He also found some controversy at one point for providing spiritual counsel to O.J. Simpson after the former running back was accused of murdering his wife and another man.

Most notably, Grier helped subdue Sirhan Sirhan, the gunman who shot and killed Grier's friend, Senator Robert Kennedy Jr., in 1968.

defense. Mostly Robustelli, much like his counterpart on offense—veteran quarterback Charlie Conerly—set a business-like tone without much fanfare.

In 1956, Robustelli had plenty of younger players to mold, especially on the defensive line. He became part of a group as fierce as any in the league, from Rosey Grier to Jim Katcavage to Dick Modzelewski. They all followed Robustelli's lead because he made the most of his talent and constantly studied the playbook.

"When you analyze Robustelli piecemeal, there's little about him that makes a great end," defensive coach Tom Landry once said. "He seems lacking in size, speed, and other traits. But as soon as you put them all together, you have the best there is."

The folks Robustelli hit didn't seem to notice any lack of size or speed.

"Bobby hits you so hard your bones rattle," Detroit quarterback Bobby Layne said after one game.

Robustelli, 6'1" and 240 pounds at the time, led the talented Giants defense in '56, which held opponents to the fewest yards in the league. New York went 8–3–1 to win the Eastern division a year after finishing 6–5–1.

Then the Giants thrashed Chicago 47–7 in the NFL championship. It was the team's first title in 18 years, and it came 22 years after they shocked the Bears in the Sneakers Game. This was the sequel. The field was icy again in the '56 title game, and the Giants had no problems finding sneakers as Robustelli just brought some from his store, giving the team a possible advantage.

The Giants won six division titles during Robustelli's nine years with them. They won their lone NFL championship in a span of 48 years. It added up to a Hall of Fame induction for Robustelli in 1971, though he often deflected praise.

"I don't know what all the fuss is about," he said upon his retirement. "After all, I'm 36 years old, and I've been playing 13 years. I have to quit sometime."

The Giants weren't quite so eager to see him go, of course. He moved into the front office, where the man who led teams on the field as a seven-time All-Pro didn't fare as well. After contributing to the team's glory years, Robustelli was an all-too-visible part of the Wilderness years in the 1970s when fan outrage over losing boiled over. He resigned his post as director of operations after the 1978 season, several weeks after The Fumble.

But over time, the memory of Robustelli's struggles in the front office faded compared to the memories of the tradition he helped build as a player.

"We were all about winning," he said once. "If I had my way, I would have had my teammates up there on the Hall of Fame stage with me."

34 Charlie Conerly: The Marlboro Man

He had once dreamed of playing for the New York Giants, but now the reality left the quarterback feeling more star-crossed than starry eyed. As a boy in Clarksdale, Mississippi, Charlie Conerly set the improbable goal of playing a sport hardly anyone cared about in a city foreign to his Southern background.

So when the Giants traded for him in 1948—picking him up from the Redskins who already had a quarterback in Sammy Baugh—Conerly couldn't have been happier.

"He was thrilled because he had been a Giants fan," said his wife, Perian Conerly. "He was thrilled, and he never even considered playing for another team after he got started."

He did, however, consider stopping. Year after year, Conerly took hit after hit. On the field and then in the stands. His biggest offensive lineman weighed in the low 200s in the early '50s and they weren't providing enough protection—not that Conerly wouldn't play through pain.

He played with a separated shoulder in 1951 because the other quarterbacks were also hurt. Throughout his career, he fought through injuries that left others wincing. And by the time he arrived in New York, Conerly had been a Marine whose rifle was shot out of his hand in World War II. He also set every college passing record Ole Miss had.

So he was as rugged as the leathery face that drew the Marlboro cigarette folks to come calling, eventually asking him to model as a tough cowboy character, the Marlboro Man.

"He never complained, you know," said former Giants trainer John Johnson, who started with the team the same year Conerly did. "At one time, our offense was 1–2–3, kick; 1–2–3, kick. He would come off the field, never yell at anybody. Just go back in the offense, take his pounding, and do what he had to do."

But Conerly also began to wonder if all those beatings were worth it, especially after the Giants went 3–9 in 1953 and there were no signs his line would improve. The fans were getting worse, too, especially after he threw 25 interceptions that year, making his record-setting 22 touchdowns as a rookie a distant memory.

"Back to the farm, Conerly," fans taunted with signs at the Polo Grounds.

He took their advice. Tired of "looking up at the sky" after too many hits, as the story went in the book *Giants of New York*, Conerly headed back to Mississippi.

* * *

As Vince Lombardi later followed Sam Huff to an airport to save one legendary Giants' career, new head coach Jim Lee Howell traveled to Mississippi. He promised his quarterback he would have a less porous line. Conerly agreed to come back.

Good thing. Just like another former Ole Miss quarterback would some 50 years later, Conerly eventually led the Giants to a championship—leaving the fans who once booed him chanting his name.

The comparison to Eli Manning—the quarterback who later won the Charlie Conerly Award as the top quarterback at Ole Miss—did not stop with Conerly's ability to overcome the fans' skepticism. Much like Manning, Conerly's unflappable mannerisms in the huddle earned his teammates' respect even while fans questioned his passion.

"He's something like our boy here today," Johnson said, comparing Conerly to Manning. "They were easygoing kind of guys."

Conerly calmly assessed play suggestions in the huddle back when quarterbacks called their own plays. He let players offer their ideas before making the final call. He had more options when Howell hired Vince Lombardi to coach the offense and the team gained talent at the end and receiver positions.

He bounced back by throwing 17 touchdowns in 1954 and passing for 1,439 yards—impressive numbers for the time. The Giants grew with Conerly, roommate Frank Gifford improved at left halfback, and the rest of the pieces fell into place.

Conerly was the leader, the man Gifford eventually said made him feel ashamed for being in the Hall of Fame because Conerly was not. Of course, that didn't stop Gifford from trying to steal his old friend's job—three years after Conerly helped the Giants to a 47–7 rout of the Bears in the 1956 NFL Championship Game, Gifford decided he wanted to play quarterback and Howell gave him a shot.

Conerly, showing that even-keel nature and refusal to get swayed by even the most bitter of circumstances, said nothing as the story leaked. Finally, Gifford, wanting to give his friend a chance to lash out, reminded Conerly on the golf course that he might just take his job, according to an account in the book, *Giants of New York*.

As Gifford finished speaking, Conerly completed a successful putt.

"Giff, please," Conerly finally responded, "in the future, don't talk to me when I'm putting."

The next year, in 1959, Conerly answered Gifford's challenge as successfully as Manning later responded to the barbs from his old running back, Tiki Barber.

Conerly won the MVP award.

* * *

The fans by that point roared for Conerly, who received a day in his honor while he was still playing. The Giants feted the quarterback known as Chunkin' Charlie with thousands of dollars of gifts, a pair of cars, and a trip to Europe.

Conerly loved living his dream, rubbing elbows with celebrities he called friends. Actor David Niven visited the Conerlys at their Grand Concourse apartment one night, the Yankees' Whitey Ford the next. Perian, a writer, found gigs writing sports gossip columns, cracking the male-dominated world with the Giants' assistance. She followed that up with a memoir, *Backseat Quarterback*. The whole time Conerly reminded Perian to soak it all in because the wear on his body after years of playing through anything always left him ready to call it a career.

"He would just say, 'You know, you better see all the plays and do all the things you want to do because we're not coming back next year,'" Perian said. "He would just say, 'Well, I think I've had enough.'"

The Giants kept asking him to come back, but then the situation became awkward when they acquired Y.A. Tittle in 1961. Conerly was 40 years old, and Tittle eventually won the job. The old quarterback's pride erupted at times with head coach Allie Sherman, but mostly Conerly said he would do whatever the club needed.

When Tittle faltered in a couple of games, Conerly came roaring back, leading the Giants to one late win with a pair of touchdowns in front of a crowd that saluted everything he endured as their quarterback.

"Imagine a guy who's been [a starter] and then had to sit on the bench, coming back and doing the job Charlie did," Kyle Rote said after Conerly led the Giants to the victory.

Conerly retired after the season, finally living up to his word to make it his last. He outlasted all the beatings and lived out his dream, holding the Giants' major passing records until Phil Simms, another quarterback who struggled through injuries and battles for his job, broke them.

He inspired another kid growing up in Mississippi to root for the Giants. This time it made more sense. Little Archie Manning had a local boy to look up to all the way in New York, one he tried to emulate at Ole Miss and later in the NFL.

Eventually, Manning watched his son, Eli, follow Conerly's path in so many ways. He could only hope his son could say what Conerly did near the end of his career.

"I've had my ups and downs here with the Giants," Conerly said the day his favorite team honored him. "I want to thank you all for sticking by me."

35 Y.A. Tittle: The Giant Who Almost Wasn't One

He grew tired of all those frustrating seasons with San Francisco; there were plenty of finishes in second and third place but not one in first. Y.A. Tittle drew close to the end of a Hall of Fame career as a quarterback and was surrounded by talent with his fellow 49ers, but they could not break through to win the NFL's Western division.

Johnny Unitas' Colts stood in their way one year, Vince Lombardi's Packers the next. So when the news came of a trade to the Giants—who won the NFL's Eastern division three times during Tittle's time in San Francisco—he liked the idea of a shot at first place.

But not as much as he disliked the idea of another result of the trade. He didn't want to disrupt his family's life. So Tittle initially made a decision that would have forever changed Giants' history and likely affected his induction into the Hall of Fame.

He decided to retire. Yes, he wanted the chance to go win in New York—just not enough to inconvenience his family. They had lived in San Francisco for nine years at that point. The kids were in school. He didn't have the heart to tear them from their friends because he'd been taken by another team.

"I almost quit," Tittle said. "I thought about retiring because I had a family and children in school. Different school, it would be difficult."

So how close to retiring was Tittle? "Well, I was pretty close," he remembered four decades later. "Three children, had to take them out of school, put them in another school…"

With Tittle, the Giants went 33–8–1 under Allie Sherman from 1961–63, winning three Eastern division titles. He tied an NFL record with seven touchdowns in a 49–34 win over Washington in 1962. He finished with 10,439 passing yards for the Giants in his four years there, second behind Charlie Conerly on the club's all-time list at that point and sixth by 2011. He set a single-season passing touchdown mark of 36 that stood through the 2010 season.

The Giants celebrated a successful era that did not end until 1964, Tittle's last season. Without Tittle, who knows how the team would have fared?

The Giants have always celebrated Tittle's contributions to their early '60s dominance of the East, but there's someone else they might want to acknowledge—Tittle's mother-in-law. Her decision to pitch in and help his wife by moving from Arizona kept Tittle from retiring. It also allowed him to play without worrying about his kids.

"My wife's mother took care of them," he said. "We brought 'em back here, too [occasionally])…brought them here for 10 days [at a time]. They were young."

* * *

Freed from concerns for his family by his mother-in-law and from worrying about a season-long battle for a division title with the West's Packers, Tittle still had to deal with replacing a Giants icon in Conerly, who played his final season at age 40 in 1961. With Conerly competing for the job, Tittle had to be impressive to win over his teammates, who had admired Conerly's leadership for the past 13 years.

Unlike Conerly, who provided pats on the back, Tittle offered shouts in the ear. He loudly instructed teammates who played poorly. Sometimes he even punctuated his point by throwing his helmet at a lineman to encourage better protection.

Eventually, Tittle's talent won his team over, though the Giants might never have gone as easy on him as they did right before the trade.

Former teammate Sam Huff laughed as he remembered how the Giants learned of the deal before even Tittle knew—right before the team played San Francisco in a preseason game in Portland, Oregon. "'Don't hit Y.A. Tittle. Don't hit him,'" Huff remembers the defensive players getting ordered. "'He belongs to us.' How the hell do you play a preseason game and you're not allowed to hit a quarterback?"

Tittle starred for the Giants, putting up dominating passing numbers in an era that wasn't anywhere near as wide open offensively

Tittle Throws Seven TDs

He hadn't practiced all week because he had hurt his arm the previous week against Detroit. And when Y.A. Tittle started against Washington that fall Sunday at Yankee Stadium, his passes didn't look too healthy.

Early on, he threw seven passes. Six fell incomplete. Not exactly the kind of background you'd expect for an NFL record-setting performance that would stand for at least the next 48 years.

By the time Tittle was done on October 28, 1962, he forgot the first seven passes. The memory was trumped by the seven touchdown passes he threw—tying an NFL mark he now shares with three other quarterbacks.

He might own the record by himself, considering teammates were pushing him to go for the record eighth scoring pass at the end of the Giants' 49–34 win. But, Tittle said, it would be "in bad taste" to show up his opponents with the game already all but over.

Tittle also threw for 505 yards, a team record that wouldn't fall until Phil Simms threw for 513 in 1985. He threw three scores to tight end Joe Walton, the future Jets' head coach, two to Joe Morrison, and one each to Frank Gifford and Del Shofner.

as the modern one. He often hit his favorite target, Del Shofner, who joined the Giants in another trade the same year as Tittle.

Shofner was an All-Pro receiver his first three years with the Giants and became one of the club's best ever. He surpassed 1,100 yards each season and caught 32 touchdowns in that span, leading the league each year. He might have held the title as the team's best overall, but injuries limited him in his final four seasons in New York.

* * *

Along with throwing for more than 3,000 yards in two of his three seasons, Tittle took pride in finally breaking through to win some division titles.

"I had good years in San Francisco, but we didn't win a championship out there...always second place," Tittle said. "Came to

Y.A. Tittle almost didn't accept his trade to New York due to family concerns but things worked out. Under head coach Allie Sherman (right), Tittle set several Giants records and helped them win three straight division titles. (AP Photo/Bob Goldberg)

New York, we won three straight Eastern divisions. That's quite an honor for me. A lot of Hall of Fame players, Robustelli, Frank Gifford, people like that. To play in the biggest city in the world is quite an honor. And for a fine family like the Mara family."

While Tittle avoided second-place division finishes, he couldn't escape the Packers completely.

Green Bay was still too dominant to allow Tittle to win an NFL title. The Packers walloped the Giants 37–0 for the title in 1961 and beat them again the next year 16–7.

Tittle's final shot at a championship was his closest, but the Bears beat the Giants 14–10 in 1963. The quarterback battled serious leg injuries in the second half, and linebacker Sam Huff argued with head coach Allie Sherman to replace him, but Sherman stuck with him. The injured Tittle threw five interceptions.

The next season, Pittsburgh's John Baker knocked Tittle out of a game early in the year. The resulting photo of the 38-year-old quarterback, dazed and bloodied, served as the lingering image of his final year—and the Giants' woeful 2–10–2 season. Tittle recognized his NFL career, which had lasted 17 years, was over.

He lives back in San Francisco now where he still pops in at his insurance company, though he said he mostly leaves the real work to his sons. Yelberton Abraham Tittle is still appreciative of the trade that brought him to New York. There he found that once he solved his own family concerns, he joined a new one.

"They never forget you," Tittle said of the Giants when he returned for their Ring of Honor ceremony in 2010. "They never forget their old ballplayers. This is a family relationship."

36 Ice Bowl I: Lombardi's Return

They wanted him to return to New York so badly, to once again see Vince Lombardi exulting and emoting on the sideline at Yankee Stadium in a late-season game, the frost filling the air like foam. Just not like this. Not on the opposite sideline where Lombardi now led the Green Bay Packers, who wouldn't let him out of his multi-year contract when Giants head coach Jim Lee Howell resigned in 1961.

Lombardi's Packers made the Giants regret letting him go even more at the end of the '61 season when they humiliated New York in a 37–0 rout in Green Bay to clinch their second straight NFL title. But that's how it had gone, so now there would be a rematch in the 1962 title game.

Allie Sherman, the man who took over the Giants, had quarterback Y.A. Tittle and receiver Del Shofner and the offensively infused Giants fresh off another Eastern division title and ready to take another crack at the Pack.

Aside from dealing with quarterback Bart Starr, running backs Paul Hornung and Jim Taylor, linebacker Ray Nitschke and company, the Giants had one more issue with which to deal—a gusting wind that tormented Tittle and the Giants when the Packers did not. Giants fans were so bundled up in assorted hats and scarves wrapped around their chapped lips, they resembled the Invisible Man. Tittle was so bottled up by the 17-degree weather and 30-mph winds, he might have preferred not to be seen.

The Giants, while playing their typical punishing defense, watched their dynamic offense get shut out for the second straight year to Green Bay in a 16–7 loss. Their only touchdown came on a blocked punt recovered in the end zone.

The Giants left the Packers muttering about the punishing hits and saluting New York's pride—but they still did not come close to victory. "They gave everything they had," Sherman said after the game. "We weren't humiliated. There was no humiliation this year." Just the grudging recognition that the Packers were once again better.

The fans in New York were as ravenous as they were cold, eager to swallow up the Packers after last year's rout in Green Bay.

"Beat Green Bay!" they chanted. "Beat Green Bay!" That chant came at a Knicks game the day of the NFL championship, according to several accounts. Fans flocked to hotels outside the 75-mile NFL television blackout radius so they could watch. They also packed the stadium despite the frigid temperature.

All season, the combinations of Tittle-to-Shofner long, and Tittle-to-Alex-Webster short decimated opponents as the Giants ran up a 12–2 record in the East. Tittle finished with a league-record 33 touchdown passes, an astronomical figure at the time. It

A Packers Rout

The Giants' second straight loss to Green Bay in the NFL title game was bad, but the first was worse. Green Bay routed them 37–0, making head coach Allie Sherman and his team look bad in Sherman's first season after replacing Jim Lee Howell.

The Giants felt good about their team with the new passing attack of Pro Bowlers Y.A. Tittle to Del Shofner. They went 10–3–1 to win the East and headed to Green Bay to play the 11–3 Western champion Packers.

The game was a mismatch nearly from the start, though, as Green Bay erupted for 24 points in the second quarter. Bart Starr threw two of his three touchdown passes while Paul Hornung ran for a score and kicked the first of his three field goals.

The Giants offense—without running back Frank Gifford that year after he went into broadcasting before coming back as a flanker—was nearly non-existent. Tittle went 6-of-20 for 65 yards and ended up watching his predecessor at starter, Charlie Conerly, get some time, as well. Conerly managed to complete just 4-of-8 for 54 yards.

would have remained the Giants' club mark if he had not passed it the next season with 36.

But the Packers scouted the Giants well, knowing they needed to take away Mr. Clutch, Webster—the '60s Giants version of Amani Toomer—on third down and short. The wind took away Shofner on long pass plays as the Pro Bowl receiver who averaged 21.4 yards per catch with 12 touchdowns managed only 69 yards on five receptions.

The Packers were so prepared for each of Tittle's tendencies that, along with the wind, they held him to 18-of-41 "aerials" (as *The New York Times* wrote the next day) for 197 yards with an interception.

"Oh, there was never a game so cold," Tittle recalled 48 years later, his teeth all but chattering at the memory. "It was terrible."

Along with the biting winds that felt like they "cut you in two," as Packers defensive end Bill Quinlan said after the game, the team traded blows that might as well have finished the split.

"This was the toughest," a limping Taylor, one of the league's most punishing runners, said after the game. "I can't remember getting hit as hard before." He managed a 7-yard touchdown run in the second quarter to give Green Bay a 10–0 lead. The Packers' only other points came on a trio of field goals by guard Jerry Kramer, more famous for his crucial block in the Packers' Ice Bowl game against Dallas in 1967.

The Giants closed to 10–7 in the third quarter when the speedy cornerback Erich Barnes came racing in to block a punt near the Green Bay goal line and Jim Collier recovered for a touchdown. But they drew no closer, losing a pair of fumbles. Nitschke recovered a big one and also deflected a Tittle pass that turned into an interception.

The Giants were once again a good team that just was not good enough.

"The Packers were always the champs," Tittle remembered. "And they were tough to beat; well-organized, great players, great organization. I enjoyed playing against them—but we didn't win many games against them."

37 No Title for Tittle—Again

The Packers no longer stood in their way, replaced by a Bears team famed for its Monsters of the Midway defense and an offense whose job was to not taint the defense's prowess. The Giants had a match-up they could handle this time—they could battle the Bears' dominant defense with an offense that averaged 32 points a game, a quarterback who threw 36 touchdown passes, and a defense that could surely shut down Chicago's modest offense.

They went to Chicago 11–3 and were favored to win the title that had eluded them the previous two years.

It was obvious what would happen. After getting shut down in back-to-back championship games, quarterback Y.A. Tittle would finally stifle all that talk in the papers about his inability to win the big game. He would hit Del Shofner and Frank Gifford, and the Giants finally would be champions again.

He would do all of those things. Or he would get hurt.

Twice in the first half, Chicago's Larry Morris hit Tittle, injuring the quarterback's left knee. The first time, Tittle left the game for two plays. The second time, when he heard a snap, Tittle vowed not to leave again.

But his game left him. He threw five interceptions, more than a third of his total for the season, and four came in the second half. The last came with the clock ticking down from 10 seconds, the Giants frantically hoping to finish their last drive to keep the 14–10 lead Chicago had from becoming a final score.

But as Tittle flung one more pass toward the end zone, the ball flew toward a group of Bears with no Giant close. It fell into the hands of Chicago's Richie Petitbon, the interception ending another championship loss for the Giants. It was one more defeat that left New York feeling like the Buffalo Bills would three decades later when they lost four straight Super Bowls.

"He was great on one leg," Giants coach Allie Sherman said of Tittle after the game. "I want to make one thing clear. All the writers who had said that Y.A. Tittle does not win the big game don't understand football and don't understand this great athlete, who is the only man around who could have played in the second half with a leg like that. He has won more big games than any quarterback."

Sherman's point about Tittle's ability to play at all seemed reasonable. His choice to let him do so was up for interpretation.

At halftime, with Tittle's left knee wrapped and shot up with Novocaine, linebacker Sam Huff and punter/kicker Don Chandler argued vehemently with Sherman to take out Tittle, according to several accounts. The Giants led 10–7 thanks to a Tittle touchdown pass to Frank Gifford and a stifling defense that had only given up a score after Morris intercepted Tittle's pass and returned it to the Giants' 6-yard line.

Huff, confident as ever, swore the Giants could maintain the lead through their defense and that Tittle was in no shape to play. The injury forced Tittle to throw off his back leg, leaving him in a precarious position as a passer. But the old quarterback, who had the best season of his career, lobbied Sherman to keep him in and it's easy to see why that's the choice the coach made.

Tittle threw for 3,145 yards and completed 60.2 percent of his passes that season. Rookie backup Glynn Griffing played sparingly, completing 40 percent of his passes and throwing four interceptions.

Along with the injury, Tittle battled a Bears defense that held the feared Packers to just one touchdown in two games and allowed just more than 10 points a game. And once again, the Giants played an NFL title game in arctic conditions—it was 11 degrees at game time in Chicago's Wrigley Field, and the temperature later dropped to 6.

(For all the recent clamoring for cold-weather championship games that hearken back to the old days, it's interesting to note they weren't all that popular in some of those old days. *The New York Times* columnist Arthur Daley ripped the "absurdity" of the NFL for playing a four-month season and having it end with bitterly cold weather in which "a true test is impossible.")

Regardless of the weather, the Bears took away two of Tittle's best weapons. For the first time all year, receiver Shofner went without a catch. And Chicago did an exceptional job of scouting the screen pass on which Tittle had not been intercepted all season.

But in the second half, Bears defensive end Ed O'Bradovich read the screen as Morris did in the first half and picked off Tittle's pass. He also returned it nearly the length of the field, getting it to the 14-yard line. From there, Bears quarterback Billy Wade eventually scored on a 1-yard keeper and the Bears had a 14–10 lead.

"We were taught to read screen when Tittle set up then dropped back another two or three yards," O'Bradovich said after the game. "He threw it and I lifted my right arm and hit the ball, and it came down where I could catch it. Tittle acted real well, but he acted just the way we know he acts when he's going to throw the screen."

Tittle, throwing off his back leg, threw three more interceptions. The Giants lost for the third straight time in a title game.

Bears coach George Halas cried in victory, his team's first championship in 17 years. "I don't know what to say about it," Halas said after the game. "It's too much."

The Giants surely agreed.

38 Burress: Making Good on a Super Prediction

As 12 Giants passed by, Brian Lewis, a reporter for the *New York Post*, asked each a variation of the same, simple question. Do you have a prediction for the game?

As they left Giants Stadium and prepared to fly to Arizona for Super Bowl XLII to play the undefeated Patriots, most players said no. They adhered to the motto head coach Tom Coughlin drilled into them: "Talk is cheap. Play the game."

Except for one.

"Do you have a prediction for the game?" Lewis asked Giants receiver Plaxico Burress.

Burress stopped and cocked his head.

"23–17," Burress said.

"23–17?" Lewis repeated, wanting to make sure he heard the Giants receiver correctly so he wouldn't misquote him.

"23–17," Burress said.

It wasn't exactly Joe Namath stuff. Broadway Joe made a bolder proclamation that the Jets would beat the heavily favored Colts in Super Bowl III, "I guarantee it." As Burress later said, he didn't make a guarantee, but a prediction.

But, given the Giants' opponent, Burress' audacity nearly matched that of Namath. The Patriots, preparing to complete their perfect 18–0 season, were 12-point favorites. They scored an NFL-record 589 points, averaging nearly 37 a game. And Tom Brady, the New England quarterback, infamously laughed at the notion the Patriots would be so limited offensively.

Burress' prediction didn't leave Coughlin laughing, though. "That's not what we aspire to do," Coughlin barked. "We want to do our talking on the field. We've had a good theme all year long, which hasn't been that."

The prediction soon became the least of Burress' worries. Five days before the Super Bowl he predicted the Giants would win, Burress slipped in the shower. After already dealing with an injured ankle for most of the season, Burress received potentially devastating news. He had injured the medial collateral ligament in his left knee. He might be out.

"I busted out crying," Burress later told *Sports Illustrated*. "I thought I wasn't going to be able to play in the biggest game of my life."

The injury kept Burress out of practice all week, but his prediction earned attention in interviews. "We want to win this game," he said on Super Bowl media day at a podium on the field in Arizona. "It's interesting. You think of some things in life…and it's okay to want to win, think big, and dream."

Burress looked past the reporters at one point, peering from behind his sunglasses, and located a pair of seats in the stands. He knew who should be sitting in them. "My grandmother was my rock," he said. "She had a quiet confidence. She walked with a swagger, though. If my mom was living and my grandmother was living, they'd probably be sitting right there in that section over there. I think I learned from them a quiet confidence is a good thing to have."

Had Burress' relatives been in that section Sunday, they would have wondered where their favorite player was for most of the game.

In the NFC Championship Game, Burress inspired his teammates with his one-on-one battle against talented Packers cornerback Al Harris. The receiver beat Harris repeatedly for 11 catches and 151 yards in the 23–20 win. But in the Super Bowl, Burress considered it an accomplishment to simply run before the game. Entering the Giants' final drive, he had one catch for 14 yards.

By that point, Brady was no longer amused. He was too busy scraping for the Patriots' second touchdown, which gave them a 14–10 lead with 2:39 left.

Eli Manning responded with his own historic drive, including the most impressive play in Super Bowl history—his mad scramble and 32-yard pass to a leaping David Tyree, who caught the ball against his helmet.

As revered as that play is, it did not win the game. That one came a few plays later when Burress feinted right as if on a slant, making the slightest of movements. A pump-fake from Manning froze Patriots cornerback Ellis Hobbs who bit hard, leaving Burress alone as he veered left toward the corner of the end zone.

Manning lobbed the ball with Hobbs in helpless pursuit. The ball floated toward Burress' outstretched hands, and the receiver pleaded with himself to catch it and keep his feet in bounds. He did. Burress scored on a 13-yard catch to give the Giants the lead. He pointed an index finger at the camera, then dropped to one knee as his teammates celebrated all over the field.

Thirty-five seconds later, it was official. The Giants defeated the Patriots, 17–14.

Turns out Burress' 23–17 predicted score didn't fail to give the Patriots' offense enough credit. It offered too much. "Nobody gave us a shot," Burress said after the game. "I put a little pressure on the defense. They came out and performed beautifully."

39 Roosevelt Brown, Hall of Famer

He was as much of a Giant as any of those who helped lead the city into its bond with the club in the '50s and '60s, even if he played in that anonymous role of an offensive lineman. When the Giants stormed into the city's heart, they often came rushing through thanks to the blocks of Roosevelt Brown, who helped clear their path to prominence.

Brown helped star running back Frank Gifford gain enough attention on the field to earn Hall of Fame status. Brown also helped keep quarterback Charlie Conerly safe after Conerly got so fed up with his lack of protection he retired in 1953 before coach Jim Lee Howell assured him things would improve.

One of the biggest guardians was Brown, who fell all the way to the 27th round that year despite his status on the black All-American team for Morgan State. The Giants discovered the honor in *The Pittsburgh Courier*, a black weekly newspaper, and selected him.

The 6'3", 255-pound tackle signed with the Giants for a few thousand dollars and caught Coach Steve Owen's eye in camp. Brown needed work but showed promise. His build, combining upper body strength with a surprisingly small 29" waist, was that rare blend that promised power and speed so many decades before

*Hall of Fame lineman
Roosevelt Brown
cleared a path for the
Giants offensive stars
of the 1950s and '60s.*
(AP Photo)

49ers and Cowboys defensive lineman Charles Haley would do the same.

Along with fellow 1953 rookies, four-time Pro Bowl center Ray Wietecha and three-time Pro Bowler Jack Stroud, Brown helped the line recover from its early growing pains as the Giants eventually built one of the league's strongest units on the way to six division titles and one NFL championship.

Along the way, the player affectionately known as Rosey offered some of the most dominating line play in the Giants' long, proud tradition of power football. Brown earned himself nine Pro Bowl nods, eight straight All-NFL honors, and an induction into the Hall of Fame in 1975.

While most recent Giants fans salute the likes of Shaun O'Hara, Rich Seubert, and Chris Snee, and the previous generation takes pride in Jumbo Elliott, Bart Oates, and Brad Benson, Brown's strength and speed put him ahead of his time. Enough so that

Gifford—not only Brown's teammate but a long-time analyst for *Monday Night Football* who often labels modern players superior—said Brown would be a rarity among players of his generation.

"He was one of the few players, I think, whether he played then, played today, he could be an All-Pro," Gifford said.

When Sam Huff, the Giants Hall of Fame linebacker, first saw Brown, he couldn't imagine trying to shed his blocks. "I wanted to turn around and go back to West Virginia," Huff once recalled.

Known for his versatility in providing strong run-blocking and pass protection, Brown earned a spot on the NFL's 75th anniversary team in 1994.

While Brown dominated defensive linemen on the field, trainer John Johnson remembers him using a sense of humor off the field to deal with the racism he faced during his career.

"He was a great guy," Johnson said. "I liked him. Ready to go. He said, 'I don't understand white people complaining about black people—you're all sitting out in the sun trying to get like me.'"

* * *

On the field, Brown's dominance led to respect among his peers who marveled at his speed for a lineman.

Upon Brown's death in 2004, Gifford recalled to *The New York Times* a play that helped him gain 79 yards—even if his favorite lineman caused him to do a double-take along the way. "I wouldn't be in the Hall of Fame if it weren't for him," Gifford said. "The longest run of my career was on a pitchout against Washington. Rosie made a block at the line of scrimmage. I cut it up, and then I'm running downfield and I look up and I see No. 79 in front of me, and he wiped out another guy."

Brown played 162 games with the Giants from 1953–65, retiring due to phlebitis. The Giants hired him as a line coach and he remained in the organization in different capacities, including as a scout, until his death of a heart attack at 71 in 2004.

Other Giants Offensive Linemen to Know

Mel Hein and Roosevelt Brown are the most accomplished Giants offensive linemen of all time. Here's a look at some other Giants greats.

Brad Benson (1978–87), T, G, C—Known more recently for his wacky Hyundai commercials, Benson was a key contributor to the Giants' 1986 Super Bowl season when he earned his only Pro Bowl nod.

Al Blozis (1942–44), T—Career cut short by his service in World War II, where he was killed in combat. Had one Pro Bowl season and an All-Pro year, inspiring Mel Hein to say he could have been an all-time great. Inducted in the Giants' inaugural Ring of Honor class in 2010.

Jumbo Elliott (1988–95), T—One-time Pro Bowler is a Giants fan favorite and contributed greatly to Super Bowl XXV win.

Chris Snee (2004–present), G—Head coach Tom Coughlin's son-in-law showed worth on field as a contributor to the Super Bowl team and three-time Pro Bowler by 2010.

Jack Stroud (1953–64), T, G—Three-time Pro Bowler helped the Giants line grow into one of league's best.

Bart Oates (1986–93), C—Five-time Pro Bowler is the only regular Giants lineman on both the '86 and '90 Super Bowl teams.

Shaun O'Hara (2004–present), C—Strong locker room presence and three-time Pro Bowler who helped anchor the line for the Giants 2007 Super Bowl team.

Ray Wietecha (1953–62), C—Four-time Pro Bowler during run of six division titles and one NFL championship.

Among the players he scouted was linebacker Harry Carson, a former defensive lineman the Giants converted to the linebacker position, from which Carson eventually earned his own Hall of Fame honor. "Rosey, in his own way, became somewhat of a mentor to me because he did go to Morgan State," said Carson, who went to South Carolina State, a black college that played Morgan State. "And he was a scout; he was a Hall of Famer. I had the opportunity to talk to Rosey about those great Giants teams that he was a part of."

Those teams spread the love of football through the city and eventually the country.

For Brown, the feeling was mutual. "Nobody plays this game for the money," he said at a time when the relatively small salaries made the statement sound more believable. "You have to enjoy it. You have to have the game in your heart."

40 Bednarik/Gifford: "They Thought Frank Was Dead"

Frank Gifford couldn't explain what was happening, but he didn't like it. At some point in the late 1990s, Gifford's fingers and hand occasionally turned numb. The former Giants star and broadcaster tried to explain the condition to friends or family members, but no one had heard of what he described.

Finally, Gifford went to the doctor who ordered a CT scan. As the technician examined the results, he made a curious discovery. "Have you ever been in an automobile accident?" he asked Gifford.

Gifford all but laughs at the memory now, knowing of only one major wreck in which he had been involved. "I didn't tell them that Bednarik was the model of the car, but that's the only thing I could think of," Gifford said.

Gifford, of course, spoke of Chuck Bednarik, the Philadelphia Eagles' legendary linebacker who knocked Gifford out cold nearly 40 years before that doctor visit.

"What I had was a spinal concussion," Gifford said of the result of the 1960 hit widely considered the most brutal in NFL history. Originally diagnosed with a deep brain concussion at the time of the collision, Gifford didn't learn the full extent of the impact until he saw his doctor in the 1990s. "That's probably when I found out I had the multiple fractures in my neck. Fortunately, after that injury, I didn't play anymore that season."

Gifford missed the next year, and anyone who's seen the famous photo of the play's aftermath would consider him fortunate to return. In the picture, Bednarik appears to tower over a prone Gifford, taunting him.

While the initial impression of Bednarik in the frame might appear unseemly, it still beats the first look at Gifford. He looks dead. That's not an exaggeration. Lying there, unconscious, his arms to his sides, Gifford looks as though he might never get up.

To the left, Giants split end Kyle Rote looks on in concern. To Rote's right, on the ground, is Philadelphia's Chuck Weber, who recovered the ball Gifford fumbled when Bednarik drilled him in the chest and pile-drived him into the ground.

The fumble recovery unofficially clinched the Eagles' 17–10 win in a pivotal game between the teams who were fighting for the Eastern division title.

That sight, Bednarik has explained, and not the prone Gifford, is what caused his jubilation. It's a claim believed by Gifford, who has always maintained the vicious hit was clean.

Even if Bednarik's language was not. "The [bleeping] game is over!" Bednarik screamed on the field. "The [bleeping] game is over!"

In between attending to the unconscious Gifford, team doctor Francis Sweeny, all 5'5" of him, bellowed at the 6'3" Bednarik. "He was over there really letting him hear about it," Giants long-time trainer John Johnson said.

They carried Gifford out on a stretcher amid a hushed Yankee Stadium.

The silence had to be eerie for the crowd, which had been abuzz only a few moments before as the Giants drove down the field trying to tie the game in the closing minutes. On third-and-10, quarterback George Shaw—in for an injured Charlie Conerly—connected with Gifford, who scurried toward the right side of the field. Trying to avoid an Eagles defender in front of him, Gifford didn't see Bednarik coming from behind. The future Hall of Famer crashed violently into Gifford, driving him to the ground.

"It sounded like a rifle shot," Philadelphia defensive lineman Riley Gunnels later said in the book, *The 1960 Philadelphia Eagles.*

Gifford was taken to a small training room where he remained unconscious. It might have been just as well for him not to open his eyes at that moment. Next to him lay a police officer, who had suffered a heart attack earlier in the game. The officer had not survived.

"So we put him on a training table, and they put a sheet over him," Johnson said of the policeman. "And some guys passed by, and they thought Frank was dead, too."

Fortunately, Gifford survived. But he would not play the next season, instead opting to take the first step toward a broadcasting career that would lead him to join the popular *Monday Night Football* crew with Howard Cosell and Dan Meredith the following decade.

Gifford returned to the field the following year as a receiver, playing for three more seasons and teaming up with quarterback Y.A. Tittle before retiring. "It didn't terminate me," said Gifford,

Gifford's Gamesmanship

In an odd scheduling move, the Giants played the Eagles again the next week, but without Frank Gifford, they again fell, this time 31–23. Not that Gifford didn't attempt to help—from the hospital.

Chuck Bednarik had felt so bad about his vicious hit that he called Gifford and sent cards all week, according to the book *Giants of New York.* Gifford, though, didn't take the calls. Not because he was upset. Instead, he hoped to leave Bednarik feeling so bad he might struggle to hit his teammates that week.

Gifford's attempt at emotional manipulation didn't work.

The Eagles went on to win the NFL title, their last in 50 years.

who made the Pro Bowl at a third position after previously making it as a defensive back and running back. "When they think and read a lot of things, they thought it was the end of my career, which is not the case as I said. I played three more years and had pretty good years."

Chant "DEE-fense!" (Your Predecessors Did It First)

The Giants defense of the 1950s, coached by Tom Landry and led by linebacker Sam Huff, played a ferocious style that left them sneering at even their offensive counterparts. Never one to downplay his exploits, Huff barked at his offensive teammates as they went on the field, making an order usually reserved for the defense. "Just hold 'em," Huff said with a laugh. "That's all."

Huff might have underestimated the Giants offense a bit back then, considering stars like Frank Gifford, Charlie Conerly, Kyle Rote, and Alex Webster often put up plenty of points. But the defense had room to boast. While Huff and his mates crowed on the field, the fans at Yankee Stadium stirred in the stands.

Sometime during the late '50s, Giants fans began a chant that's now so familiar it's hard to imagine it once had to be created.

"DEE-fense!" they chanted. "DEE-fense!"

"It almost was a distraction," linebacker Harland Svare has said. "You couldn't hear anything." The affection for the defense that created the history-making chant extended beyond the field and throughout the city.

Huff recalled going to the legendary bar, Toots Shor's, where everyone from Joe DiMaggio and Marilyn Monroe to Gifford, Huff, and company mingled with the jovial, barb-filled owner.

There, too, the city's respect for its beloved defense revealed itself.

"Toots would say, 'All right you guys—the offense, you go in the back,'" Huff said. "'You didn't win the game.'"

42 Ernie Accorsi: The Deal of His Career

Aside from his family, the only person rooting harder for Eli Manning as he drove the Giants down the field for the final historic Super Bowl drive was Ernie Accorsi. Who could blame him? Only everything he believed in and attempted to accomplish for his career hung in the balance.

Accorsi staked his career on Manning when he made the 2004 draft-day deal for him with San Diego. He followed a philosophy he had learned decades before from an old Baltimore Colts scout named Milt Davis. When Accorsi was a public relations man for the Colts, who featured aging quarterback Johnny Unitas, he wondered if the Baltimore legend could shake off nagging injuries and his advanced age to win a title.

Davis, as Accorsi has often recalled, told him the key to judging a quarterback. "Can he take the team down the field with the championship on the line and get it in the end zone?" It's the philosophy that drove Accorsi his entire career, even as he watched it painfully tease him.

In 1983, Accorsi lost a quarterback the same way he gained one 21 years later. John Elway had been as adamant against playing for the Colts as Manning later was against going to San Diego. Accorsi still drafted Elway, but owner Robert Irsay traded the quarterback without Accorsi's knowledge, sending him to Denver where the future Hall of Famer led the Broncos to five Super Bowls and two wins.

The double-cross was only the beginning for Irsay, who also moved the Colts out of Baltimore, sneaking off as moving trucks infamously packed up the team and moved out to Indianapolis in the middle of the night.

Accorsi resigned due to the draft-day betrayal, building a potential championship team with the Cleveland Browns around quarterback Bernie Kosar. But Elway again stuck the dagger in deep, twice beating the Browns in the AFC Championship Game, once on The Drive—the famous 98-yard game-ending march to the end zone—and again when the Browns fumbled while going for the winning score.

* * *

Accorsi persisted in his search. He took a job as George Young's assistant with the Giants and replaced Young after he retired in 1998.

In two years, Accorsi watched his team go on a surprising run to the Super Bowl after he took a chance on another quarterback, Kerry Collins. The veteran who battled through alcohol problems enjoyed a resurgence with New York. But Collins' struggles in the Ravens' 34–7 Super Bowl rout led Accorsi to think his search was not over.

When he scouted Manning, Accorsi saw the type of fire and fight he sought. Without many strong complementary pieces around him at Ole Miss, Manning battled a strong Auburn team down to the wire. "Has courage and poise," Accorsi wrote on his scouting report, as revealed in the book *The GM: A Football Life, a Final Season and a Last Laugh.*

"Most of all," Accorsi wrote, "he has that quality that you can't define. Call it magic."

The Chargers drafted a reluctant Manning with the top overall pick in 2004, dashing Accorsi's hopes and leaving him set to take quarterback Ben Roethlisberger at No. 4. But at the last moment, the Chargers called with an offer—Accorsi could select quarterback Philip Rivers at No. 4 and deal several draft picks as well as defensive lineman Osi Umenyiora.

Despite his desire to acquire his dream quarterback, Accorsi declined. He refused to send Umenyiora, a second-round draft pick the previous year. Instead, he sent another first-round pick for the following season, and the deal was done.

For the next few seasons, Manning showed glimpses of the quarterback Accorsi saw with late comebacks, but he struggled overall. Accorsi wondered if he had made the mistake of his career. When Accorsi retired in 2006, Manning led the Giants to a pair of playoff appearances, but both were first-round exits. Rivers, meanwhile, developed into a Pro Bowl quarterback, and the Chargers added Pro Bowl linebacker Shawne Merriman with one of the Giants' draft picks.

As for Roethlisberger? Well, he won the Super Bowl the year Accorsi retired.

Rather than feeling defeated, Accorsi departed the Giants with faith in the team he built.

"I believe," Accorsi told them, "there is a championship in this room."

* * *

The next season, the championship was no longer in the room but on the field, where most of Accori's acquisitions remained when the Giants played the Patriots in the Super Bowl. There Manning drove the Giants for the winning score just the way Accorsi hoped. Better, actually, as it was the most impressive game-winning Super Bowl drive in the game's history.

Not only had the Giants beaten the undefeated Patriots, they did so with Manning scrambling and fighting to inexplicably escape several tackles on The Play, when he finally emerged and hit

David Tyree—or, at least, his helmet. A few plays later, Manning hit Plaxico Burress—a free agent pickup by Accorsi—in the end zone, and the Giants were on their way to finally rewarding the old GM's faith.

His decision to hold on to Umenyiora was another key to the Super Bowl victory, as the defensive end helped lead a massive pass rush that neutralized Patriots quarterback Tom Brady.

All those years later, Accorsi had finally found a quarterback that made his quest worthwhile. "It's amazing. Sometimes I have to tangibly remind myself that it happened," Accorsi said in the book, *Eli Manning: The Making of a Quarterback.*

"You work for your whole career not for a championship but for a quarterback to win a championship—especially me," he said. "And then to win it that way? I can't tell you how many times I fantasized and dreamt that was the way it was going to be."

43 Jerry Reese: Super GM, Pioneer

He started as a scout, and those instincts never left him. So Jerry Reese did not worry as much as his boss did when the rookie general manager declined to push for many free agents before the 2007 season. Not that Giants co-owner John Mara wanted to start throwing cash around, but he didn't see immediately how the Giants could improve without adding players in key spots.

But Reese did. He made a career of seeing what others couldn't because that's what you do when you're a scout. Reese had been a scout for the Giants when he joined them in 1994, eventually working his way up to player personnel director.

In 2007, he wasn't just seeing what others did not. He did what had not been done, becoming the Giants' first African American general manager. "I embrace the opportunity to carry the torch for African Americans," he said in his first year. "If I do well, then people will say, 'Well, if Jerry Reese can do it...'"

Asked if it was disappointing such a standard still needed to be met, Reese said, "It's sad but true. The truth hurts sometimes."

Sometimes, the truth can help heal, too. By the end of his first season as a rookie GM, Reese answered the question he posed. Jerry Reese could do it all right. Better than anyone expected.

Seventy-three years after the Giants shocked an undefeated Bears team for a championship in an unofficially whites-only league, a black man helped build a squad that scored another stunning upset of a previously perfect team. As a rookie, Reese replaced Ernie Accorsi and lost the team's top offensive threat, Tiki Barber, to retirement. Reese knew he might have to lose his head coach, Tom Coughlin, if things remained the same.

One of the Giants' biggest priorities heading into 2007, following another first-round playoff exit in 2006 by Coughlin's team, was working on the coach's demeanor. Privately, Coughlin demonstrated a caring side that was rarely seen through his many tirades on the sidelines and in practice. Management still believed he could lead the team, but recognizing the realities of the modern era, the front office delivered the message to Coughlin that he needed to make sure his players could relate to him.

"We talked about some things that could be changed, and Tom looked at himself," Reese told *The New York Times* later that year. "He set the pace for being a team guy."

Coughlin's transformation impressed media, fans, and most importantly, the players, and the team began to bond.

Reese also had to deal with Michael Strahan, the talented defensive end who could be as indecisive as he was talented, and who sometimes needed to be catered to as much as he could mentor

Reese's Draft Picks

This is New York, so of course fans shouldn't just let Jerry Reese rest on his Super Bowl title, no matter how fond the memory. Three years and a lot of headaches later—from Plaxico Burress' arrest to the DeSean Jackson punt return and just one disappointing playoff appearance—Reese faces the challenge of showing yet again that the Giants can rebound. While the knock on him is his minimal amount of trades and free-agent signings, Reese has one of the best draft records in the NFL in his first few years. Ten of the players he drafted in his first four years started a significant amount of games for the Giants in 2010.

Here's a quick look at some key performers:

2010 stats	Round	Year
Ahmad Bradshaw, RB, 1,235 yds, 8 TD	7	2007
Mario Manningham, WR, 60 rec, 944 yds, 9 TD	3	2008
Hakeem Nicks, WR, 79 rec, 1,052 yds, 11 TD	1	2009
*Steve Smith, WR, 48 rec, 529 yds, 3 TD	2	2007
Kevin Boss, TE, 35 rec, 531 yds, 5 TD	5	2007
Terrell Thomas, CB, 5 INT, 1 sack, 2 Fum rec	2	2008

*Missed time with injury

younger players. Strahan wasn't sure if he wanted to retire or earn more money through a holdout, but Reese put it on the line and Strahan returned.

Reese excelled at acquiring young talent. His eight draft picks that season all ended up contributing to the Giants' surprising Super Bowl run, which ended in the shocking defeat of the unbeaten Patriots.

First-round draft pick Aaron Ross played a significant role at cornerback. Second-round pick Steve Smith made one of the biggest catches in the Super Bowl, keeping the Giants' last drive alive on third down. Defensive tackle Jay Alford, the third-round pick, all but sealed the game with a sack of Tom Brady. Running back and seventh-round pick Ahmad Bradshaw's role grew late in the season, and his 88-yard run against the Bills helped to clinch a playoff berth; his explosive running helped wear out teams through the postseason. And fifth-round pick Kevin Boss stepped in for injured tight end Jeremy Shockey, making the big play that helped awaken the Giants' offense in the second half against the Patriots.

His few non-draft moves?

Reese wanted a kicker with a stronger leg than incumbent Jay Feely—so he brought in Lawrence Tynes, who kicked the Giants into the Super Bowl. He signed Kawika Mitchell, who helped shore up the linebackers' crew.

It added up to a proud moment after the Giants' 17–14 victory over the Patriots.

In 1988, Doug Williams, the first black quarterback to win a Super Bowl, carried the Lombardi Trophy to the stage where Reese was part of the winning team's celebration.

"After the Super Bowl, Doug called me about three different times, emailed me, texted me, and he called me and he just said, 'You made me so proud,'" Reese said. "Those are the kind of calls that mean so much because Doug really kind of paved the way for African Americans, saying, 'You know what? There can be an African American quarterback to win the Super Bowl; there can be an African American general manager who can lead his team to the Super Bowl.'"

44 Check Out the Tittle Photo

The image assaults your senses the way Pittsburgh's John Baker ravaged Y.A. Tittle in 1964. Blood drips down Tittle's face, by his ear, and more disturbingly, into his dazed eyes. Along with the

Chuck Bednarik–Frank Gifford hit four years earlier, it is one of the most famous sports photos of all time.

It is also one used to illustrate the Giants' transition into one of their darkest periods. It represents the season that would be Tittle's last and the first of 18 straight years the Giants failed to reach the playoffs.

Just don't ask Tittle to describe the shot. "Well, I didn't know what they were doing at that time," Tittle said 46 years later. "I wasn't conscious. When they were getting a picture, I was in dreamland."

The photo, taken by Morris Berman of the *Pittsburgh Post-Gazette* during the Steelers' 27–24 victory early in the 1964 season, eventually won several awards as well as a spot in the Pro Football Hall of Fame. It did not, however, get published when he brought it back to his editor that day. The editor wanted more action shots.

Berman ignored his editor's lack of foresight and recognized the quality of the haunting photo, which so aptly captured the sport's violence. He entered it in contests and won a national head-liner honor.

Berman had zeroed in on one player for a series of photos, hoping the focus would help him find something no one else would. He locked in on Tittle, who was mauled by Baker, the Steelers defensive end. The play resulted in an interception that was returned for a touchdown as well as a pair of bruised ribs for Tittle, who missed the second half.

While most other photographers had only the brutal hit, Berman stuck to his plan and kept his lens on Tittle for the play's aftermath. "I thought if I followed somebody at the heart of things, I might be able to get something," Berman once told the *Phoenix New Times*.

For his part, Tittle, then 38, realized by the end of the awful season that it was time for him to retire. The Giants had won the

NFL's Eastern division three straight times but finished the 1964 season 2–10–2. They would not reach the playoffs again until 1981.

Thanks to Berman, Tittle would always remember the parting shot.

"It won all kinds of awards," Tittle said. "I'm not gonna say I'm glad it happened, but it gave me some publicity."

45 Burt, Giants KO Montana, 49ers

There was Jim Burt, the Giants defensive lineman coming out of nowhere, straight through the line and into the great Joe Montana in a shot. Burt barreled in with a brute force that reverberates even as you watch the 1986 playoff clip now, his forearm blasting the 49ers quarterback into seeming oblivion just after he throws the ball.

As Montana lay on the ground, about to go to the hospital with a concussion, Lawrence Taylor headed to the end zone after the interception Burt helped cause. The play, near the end of the second quarter, gave the Giants a 25-point lead and all but ensured San Francisco would not offer another threat in a 49–3 rout.

"Ohhh, yeah," running back Joe Morris said, remembering Burt's shot. "I'm watching that; I say, 'Oh, my Lord.' Trust me; that was a lick. It was nothing cheap. It just was what it was."

Burt said after the game, "It was clean, but I don't feel good about it."

The Giants had plenty to feel good about after dispatching the 49ers in the playoffs for the second straight season. While the Giants dominated the 49ers in the 17–3 win in 1985 with Morris rushing for 141 yards and Phil Simms throwing two touchdowns, they decimated them in '86.

The first hint came when Hall of Famer Jerry Rice fumbled on his way to a touchdown in the first quarter. Giants' safety Kenny Hill recovered, and New York averted an early disaster.

Simms threw his first of four touchdown passes to Mark Bavaro on the Giants' subsequent 80-yard drive. The drive was led in part by Morris, who topped his previous year's total against the Niners, amassing 159 yards and scoring two touchdowns, including a 45-yard run that gave the Giants a 14–3 lead.

Morris and the Giants gained 216 yards rushing against San Francisco just weeks after totaling 13 in a regular season bout. Of course, Giants coach Bill Parcells offered his customary gentle reminders following that game.

"Every freaking week after that game, [he] started calling it 'Club 13.' Every day," Morris said. "We played them in the playoff game…. Every one of our offensive linemen knew what they had to do."

"'Joe, run as hard as you can,'" Morris remembered the linemen telling him. "'After you get over 13 yards, you can look over there and tell him to shut up.'"

Parcells later called a fake field goal with holder and backup quarterback Jeff Rutledge throwing a 23-yard pass for a first down to Bavaro on fourth-and-6 from the San Francisco 28-yard line.

Another Simms touchdown pass, this time a 15-yarder to Bobby Johnson, made it 21–3. Then Burt knocked out Montana, Taylor took the interception back 34 yards, and the rout was on.

Just weeks after the Giants needed to rally from a 17–0 deficit for a 21–17 win in San Francisco, they humbled the 49ers, winners of two Super Bowls so far that decade.

"They played a perfect game," Niners coach Bill Walsh said after the game. "We were shattered by a great team. I believe they will go all the way."

46 Celebrate with Gatorade (Your Team Did So First)

While Giants fans introduced the world to the tradition of cheering on their team's "DEE-fense" in the 1950s, three decades later the players themselves sparked their own fun custom that's still standing—the celebratory Gatorade dousing of a coach after a big win.

While two legendary Giants linebackers are at the heart of both traditions—with Sam Huff's ball-hawking style inspiring the defense chants and Harry Carson's Hall of Fame skills giving him license for his mischievous postgame missions—don't expect them to compare notes.

"I thought that was stupid," the old-school Huff said to rain on the Gatorade parade. "I don't think anybody would ever pour that on Vince Lombardi."

A fair point considering Lombardi once barked at his running back Alex Webster for the tiniest of leaps in the end zone after a touchdown. Carson made another one in rebuttal.

"Sam's still bitter," he said playfully, referring to Huff's acknowledged harsh feelings over his trade from the Giants. "Sam's still bitter."

That said, the Gatorade tradition was born from the Giants' respect for each other and their grudging respect for their occasional dictator of a coach, Bill Parcells, more than it was by any disrespect for an opponent. "Sports should be fun, and that's what this is," Carson has said.

While Carson wasn't the first to dunk Parcells—that would be Jim Burt in 1985—Carson had the most fun. Once a game was in hand, Carson would go undercover, donning anything from a yellow security slicker to an overcoat and hat to dump the contents of the Gatorade bucket on his coach.

By the time the Giants celebrated their first Super Bowl with a splash, the practice had caught on enough that President Ronald Reagan dunked Carson at the team's White House visit—with a tub of popcorn. Carson, despite the fixed eyes of the secret service, returned the favor. The president laughed.

Gatorade also grew fond of the practice and ended up signing Carson and the Giants to an endorsement deal.

Of course, there is an art to both the execution and the timing. It can be embarrassing to allow the coach to catch you or to dump the drink on yourself. And it can be even worse if you follow the fate of the 2002 Kentucky Wildcats. They dumped a vat on Coach Guy Morriss—then lost the game to LSU on a Hail Mary.

47 Forgive Trey Junkin

That snap will haunt me until the day I die.

—Trey Junkin

To fully understand the depth of the pain Trey Junkin felt on January 5, 2003, it's important to recognize one thing. The above quote from him did not refer to one of the most infamous losses in Giants history. It did not refer to the day Junkin came out of retirement at 41 to provide insurance after a rag-tag assembly of long snappers led to botched kicks all year. It did not come after Junkin capped the second-worst playoff collapse in NFL history when the Giants lost 39–38 to the 49ers after leading 38–14 with more than 17 minutes remaining.

The quote did not come from a stunned Junkin in the locker room after the game when the man renowned for his long-snapping ability somberly discussed how he botched not one but two snaps as the game wound down—the last with six seconds left, which helped cost the Giants a chance at a game-winning field goal.

The final snap and the subsequent fire drill act by holder Matt Allen, who tried to complete a pass when he should have thrown the ball out of bounds, was the final scene in an agonizingly torturous sequence.

For Giants fans, the images are burned into their minds, from Jeremy Shockey skipping around the end zone early to dropping a touchdown pass late. From Tiki Barber blowing a kiss to the San Francisco fans to Michael Strahan directing 49ers receiver Terrell Owens' attention to a scoreboard the Giants would not be able to stomach by game's end.

But as much as Giants fans endure these images, you can only wonder how Junkin copes with this memory all these years later. Especially when you learn which snap Junkin imagined would haunt him until the day he died.

It was one that came six years earlier that he referenced in a 2001 *Sports Illustrated* article, a rare feature on a long snapper so successful at his craft that the magazine tore away the usual anonymity of the position not because of a miscue but because of Junkin's unrivaled skill.

The snap he mentioned?

Some meaningless regular-season botch.

He sent it into a swirling wind for punter Jeff Feagles while both players were with Arizona. The ball was low, but Feagles still managed to get off a punt without incident. Regardless, according to the *SI* article, Junkin was so upset, the only thing that kept him from retiring right after the mistake was a replay indicating the wind altered the ball's course.

If that snap could haunt Junkin until the day he died, what the heck must the one that still angers Giants fans do?

"I'd give anything in the world at this point to have stayed retired so these guys could have a chance," Junkin said after the game at the end of his 19-year career. "They deserved a chance. Quite honestly, I screwed it up."

Quite honestly, he was far from alone.

* * *

In the immediate aftermath of the play, you can add Allen to the list. He fielded the low snap from Junkin with six seconds left and opted to try to make a play.

He rolled right and actually threw a decent pass to lineman Rich Seubert, an eligible receiver on the play. But Allen's better option on the third-down play was to throw the ball out of bounds and give Giants kicker Matt Bryant another shot at the 42-yard field goal. He also could have simply called a timeout, which would have backed up the Giants a few yards but still given them a better shot.

Allen chafed at criticism after the game, saying he made the best play he could in the situation. His argument had at least a touch of validity. He threw on target to Seubert who remarkably appeared poised to catch the pass.

And that's where the other major culprits came in—the officials. Another Giants lineman, who was an ineligible receiver, drew a penalty. But a flag was not thrown on the blatant interference on Seubert by 49ers defensive end Chike Okeafor—a non-call the league admitted was a mistake the next day.

Had the call been made, it would have resulted in offsetting penalties and the down would have been replayed, giving the Giants another chance.

"Let's send the field-goal team back out there and finish this," Strahan said upon hearing the news amid an angry Giants' chorus. For all their anger—whether it was directed at Junkin, Allen, or the officials, it should have been more widespread.

The Giants entered the playoffs on a roll. They looked even more impressive as Amani Toomer caught three touchdown passes from Kerry Collins, Shockey caught another, and Barber ran for one along the way to the 38–14 lead.

But it all fell apart in little more than a quarter as 49ers quarterback Jeff Garcia scampered all over the field, throwing for a pair of touchdowns and rushing for another in the final frenzied 17 minutes. When he threw a 13-yard pass to Tai Streets in the final minute, the scoreboard Strahan pointed to earlier read 49ers 39, Giants 38.

Despite one more big catch for Toomer with 6 seconds left to give the Giants a shot at a field goal, it remained that way. The Giants left their season in San Francisco. And a 41-year-old snapper, once haunted by a bad snap that did no damage, ended his career on one worthier of such anguish.

"On TV, all anybody should ever see of me is my [butt]," Junkin told *Sports Illustrated* in 2001. "Ideally, my name should never come up. If it does, I've made a mistake."

48 Eli Manning: Easy E, Easy Target

Of all the love-hate relationships Giants fans have had with their quarterbacks over the years, the one with Eli Manning currently ranks as the most compelling. Mostly because we don't know how it will end.

Manning's career has followed the path of predecessors Phil Simms and Charlie Conerly, the fellow alum at Ole Miss, and an idol of Manning's father, Archie. There's been the requisite rough start with fans trying to boo the quarterback off the field. Then there's an eventual love-fest as said quarterback comes back from unrealistic expectations, injuries, poor performances, or a combination of all three to end a drought and win a championship.

But Manning's legacy is still as open as it is ensured. He led the Giants to what co-owner John Mara called the greatest win in team history in the Giants' stunning upset of the perfect Patriots in Super Bowl XLII. In doing so, he topped a trio of the game's top quarterbacks and teams—Dallas' Tony Romo, Green Bay's Brett Favre, and of course, New England's Tom Brady.

He did it all in a season that had fans and writers ready to run him out of town (including one who may or may not be the author of this book). So he has earned himself a place of affection long after he's retired no matter what happens.

But while he's still playing? Oh, what happens matters.

New York fans are a demanding lot and have even more reason to be thanks to the Personal Seat Licensing fees they fork over along with so many other high-priced items with which they deal on game day. The last few years since the Super Bowl, they've been frustrated with the team's underachievement, especially after the 2010 collapse and the 25 interceptions Manning threw along with his impressive 31 touchdowns.

In fairness, many of Manning's picks were drops. He is definitely no longer that pre-Super Bowl quarterback who earned the doubts he received as much as he later commanded praise. By now the fans should realize they literally have a championship quarterback. One who's shown he can handle the toughest of circumstances and lead the Giants to a title.

But back then? Manning *had* played that poorly in 2007, especially in the Week 11 41–17 loss to Minnesota. He looked confused on the field and maddeningly unaffected off it after throwing four interceptions that day. The Giants dropped to 7–4 and appeared on the verge of yet another disappointing season.

"I didn't play real well," he said matter-of-factly after the game, his typical emotionless response further infuriating one of the country's most fervent fan bases. "When you throw four interceptions, it is never a good day."

No kidding. That wasn't enough for the fans. Not from a guy many felt had asked for the extra scrutiny. After all, unlike Conerly and Simms, Manning had *asked* to come here. He sought the potential success of the Giants—or at least an escape from San

Eli Manning followed the path of previous Giants championship quarterbacks by enduring doubts before delivering a title. (AP Photo/Paul Sancya)

Diego on draft day—and so he should damn well live up to the expectations that came along.

He had forced that draft-day trade to the Giants in 2004, his famous father speaking publicly for him, as well. Manning had refused to play for San Diego, frowning when the Chargers made him the No. 1 overall pick.

So fans felt Manning was more than fair game, especially when the other two quarterbacks the Giants could have had in that year's draft, Philip Rivers (traded to San Diego for Manning) and Ben Roethlisberger, seemed to be developing more quickly.

Adding to the list of pressures on the 23-year-old quarterback was Manning's impressive contract and the long shadow cast by Eli's famous brother, Peyton. Peyton had already earned a place in the argument as one of the game's greatest all-time quarterbacks, but the pair of brothers were a long way from their backyard football games in Mississippi.

Sure, they enjoyed doing some commercials together the way they once had played. Yes, they hugged at midfield after the first "Manning Bowl" in 2006 when Peyton's Colts squeezed out a win over Eli's Giants, the younger brother throwing an interception after a back-and-forth game.

But even Peyton worried about the pressure put on his brother, later telling reporters to lay off his little brother and to remember how big a head start he had on him. Back home growing up, Peyton might have reveled in that head start, playfully tormenting Eli like a lot of big brothers—but in front of millions of people it was a different story.

The Giants, the familiar refrain went among fans, had gotten the wrong Manning.

But an interesting thing happened when big brother Peyton won the 2007 Super Bowl with the Colts, taking home the MVP. Eli didn't feel more pressure due to his brother's accomplishment. He felt envy. He wanted to win a Super Bowl.

* * *

In training camp for the 2007 season, Manning finally showed a glimpse of the fire fans demanded. Former teammate Tiki Barber, who had retired in 2006 and was now a network analyst, questioned Manning's leadership, saying the quarterback's attempts to lead the previous season were "comical" at times.

Manning, showing a rare edge, zipped back, pointing out Barber's penchant for second-guessing head coach Tom Coughlin and his public acknowledgement in the middle of his last season that he did not want to play anymore.

"I'm not going to lose any sleep about what Tiki has to say," Manning told a group of reporters used to receiving colorless clichés from him. "I guess I could have questioned his leadership skills last year about him calling out the coach and having articles about him retiring in the middle of the season, that he's lost the heart. It's tough as a quarterback to read that your running back's lost the heart in playing the game, and it's the 10th week."

The zing was applauded by Giants fans who had come to view Barber, the team's all-time leading rusher, as a traitor due to his outspoken nature. But the truth is that while fans love to see that type of passionate outburst, it is not always an indicator of what makes a player excel.

For Manning, the key lies in the clichés, in the ability to absorb all of what New York City can throw at him and keep coming back for more, sounding like his same old boring self but bubbling underneath his stoic surface.

"No, you had to tune it out," he said when asked whether the criticism he so often received inspired his success. "You can't change your personality based on what the media says. You have to be yourself. You have to go out there and prepare, keep working. Know that you can get better with time and with preparation."

He would not change his personality. He would keep working. He would get better.

* * *

He grew before our eyes in that 2007 postseason, game to game, sometimes even play to play.

By the time the Giants reached the NFC Championship Game in frigid Green Bay against Manning's old idol, Brett Favre, everyone else finally was starting to remember the potential they had seen when Eli first started pulling off game-winning drives early in his NFL career.

"I think his mental toughness is admirable because of where he plays," Favre said the week of the game. "It's no secret to you guys—he's caught a lot of heat from the media and the public. I can remember saying [to Manning]—'You've handled things well.' He's proven to people he is legit."

He became even more legit after appearing more poised in the brutal Green Bay weather than Favre in the Giants' classic 23–20 overtime win. Then it was on to the Super Bowl and the game and drive that sealed his legacy as another championship Giants quarterback who had endured rough times and still came out on top.

Manning capped his rapid growth spurt by leading the most impressive final Super Bowl drive the game has seen. When he did, fans and media were as shocked as the adrenaline-filled look on Manning's face after he hit the game-winning touchdown pass to Plaxico Burress to beat the Patriots.

"I'll tell you what," center Shaun O'Hara said after the game, "Eli is unstoppable."

That, of course, hasn't quite proven to be the case.

* * *

Manning hasn't followed up the Super Bowl season the way Giants fans would like, instead offering a first-round playoff exit and a pair of playoff-free seasons. No, the sight of Manning—the wide-eyed kid who was always just one properly placed tussle of his mop-styled hair from looking 12—raising the Lombardi Trophy will never be forgotten.

It just might take a few years to remember it if Manning doesn't do it again.

It takes time for nostalgia to set in, and the Giants' disappointments that have followed from their first-round exit in 2008 to their collapse at the end of 2010 left some fans again bitterly questioning their leader.

On one hand, it's silly to even question someone who, as former general manager Ernie Accorsi once said, "did what we drafted him to do." But he did it so early that there's still plenty of time to do more—for better or worse. Considering Manning has passed his toughest test in New York, it's hard to imagine him not rising again. Barring injury, he should go down as the team's most accomplished passer. Whether he will ultimately be remembered as the most loved is another question.

Some folks, though—especially those who have traveled this type of road—already have their minds made up about Manning.

"I'm crazy about Eli," said Charlie Conerly's wife, Perian, who was taunted in the stands before her husband eventually won over the fans for good. "He's just really special."

49 Dick Lynch

He was sometimes not as smooth on the air as he had been on the field, where Dick Lynch could pick off a pass and all but glide to the end zone for a touchdown. But for the occasional mispronounced name, the story that might wander from the action and into some type of salutation for his family, friends, or neighbors were all part of what made Giants fans love Lynch as a broadcaster.

They would turn down the sound on their television, turn up the volume on the radio, and listen to the warm voice with the funny stories that made them feel like Lynch was just about to pass them a drink. Old No. 22 was one of them, even if he had plenty to teach them with countless observations and insight into the game that were as on target as some of those mispronunciations were not.

He was one of them. That's what they loved. What they miss.

"Dick might have understood the Giants' fan base better than anybody—whether it be their enthusiasm for the team or their frustration over the way the club was playing," said fellow longtime WFAN announcer Paul Dottino, the station's Giants beat reporter. "Dick made the fans feel like he was sitting in the same room and sharing the moment with them rather than him pontificating about what was happening on the field."

Lynch had plenty of time to get to know that fan base and vice versa. For 40 years, he spent all those Sundays and Monday nights sharing the fans' joy or aggravation as well as a few birthday greetings and stories of his wife of 46 years, Roz.

For almost a decade before that, the handsome young cornerback helped those late 1950s and early '60s Giants to a quartet of division titles, twice leading the league in interceptions. "I grew up here. I played on great teams here," Lynch told the *New York Daily News* in 2008, a week before the Giants' last Super Bowl win and eight months before his death from cancer. "I've spent my whole life as a Giant."

From the beginning, Lynch was always ready to crack a smile—or prompt one. He came to the Giants in 1959 in a trade from Washington, where he hadn't wanted to play. But after Tom Landry personally scouted Lynch, pushing the Giants to make a deal for him with the Redskins, the cornerback happily returned to his native New York.

Lynch quickly dubbed boisterous defensive leader Andy Robustelli "The Pope," and he was always prepared to jokingly kiss Robustelli's ring.

Lynch caught the tail end of the Giants' glory days, playing in four NFL title games before playing another three years as the team's dark era began in 1964.

He intercepted 35 passes in his Giants career, including a league-high nine in 1961 and '63. He picked off three in a 37–14 rout of the Eagles in the latter year when he also led the league with three touchdown returns and 251 yards.

"Dick wasn't the fastest guy in the world, but he was one of the best man-to-man cover guys this league has ever had," Sam Huff said. "Every defensive back gets beat once in a while, but Dick Lynch made plays more than anybody I've ever seen."

He retired in 1966, with the Giants in the midst of a playoff drought that would last until 1981. Lynch would make valuable plays then, too, helping fill the gap from so many painful losses with his charming stories. Reminding fans, if nothing else, that they had one of their own in the broadcast booth, one last glimpse of a time that started to slip away.

"Dick was a significant and visible connection to the legendary Giants' teams of the '50s and '60s," Dottino said. "[He] became increasingly cherished as the years passed, leaving a very proud, tradition-oriented fan base with fewer conduits to the glory days."

The years passed, and Lynch shared all the memories with the fans, emerging from the frustrating period to a new set of glory days when Bill Parcells' teams won two Super Bowls three decades after Lynch's Giants took over the town.

He was never more one of them than in September 2001. The city grieved the terrorist attacks. The nation mourned. And this time Lynch had to share a pain with his fellow New Yorkers he never could have imagined. His son, Richard, had been killed in the attack on the World Trade Center. The father was in agony as were so many fathers and mothers. He comforted his family the best he could, and they did the same for him. But he could barely bear this and when the Giants returned to the field 12 days later in Kansas City, he returned, too.

"We're just one of 3,000 families," Lynch said.

He took his seat in the broadcast booth that day, later calling it "the toughest thing I ever had to do." That day there was no dip to pass in the living room but a group of listeners wishing so very hard they could reach through their radio to comfort one of their own.

Happier times returned. Lynch was ecstatic to chronicle the Giants' 2007 Super Bowl run capped by the upset of the perfect Patriots. "To see them win it made him feel really proud," said Bob Papa, Lynch's final broadcast partner.

The joy masked the suffering Lynch had endured. After Lynch's death on September 24, 2008, his friend Bill Gallo of the *Daily News* revealed Lynch had battled leukemia for some time but did not want to burden those who did not have to know.

Giants fans mourned, but this time Lynch was not there to share their grief. For 40 years, he had spent Sundays with them. For nearly a decade before, they had come to watch him play.

All that time, Dick Lynch had been one of them. They loved him for that. And they would miss him. They still do.

50 Toomer Gets It Right Before He's Done

As he stood in front of his locker at Giants Stadium, Amani Toomer talked about the biggest game of his career. It came seven years after he learned just how much that type of game can hurt. The ache of the Ravens' rout over the Giants in Super Bowl XXXV had been so great that Toomer's initial reaction to making another Super Bowl in 2008 was not as joyful as it was cautious.

"Oh, crap," he thought to himself.

Now the memories returned, the 33-year-old receiver knowing what he did not at 26. He remembered his thoughts the night before the game against Baltimore when the football world watched the Ravens trounce the Giants 34–7.

He was bitter when he learned that the Giants defensive players had been selected to have their names called for pregame introductions instead of the offense. As he remembered, Toomer expressed disgust with his younger self.

"It was so ridiculous," Toomer said the week before Super Bowl XLII, still irked by his ego seven years later. "It really was. When you really look at the big picture, it was foolish. Did [the intros] matter? No."

Toomer used that pain to remind his 2008 teammates that their Super Bowl trip would haunt them if they did not make the most of it against New England. He should have known better than to worry about getting his share of the spotlight. He had become the most productive and beloved receiver in Giants history without that spotlight during most of his career.

* * *

His career with the Giants began as it would eventually end— Toomer uncertain of why he couldn't get the coaches to make him more involved in the game. The veteran Toomer opted to sign with Kansas City before the Chiefs cut him in his final season, feeling the Giants coaches "had an agenda" to play younger receivers.

When he was a rookie second-round pick out of Michigan, though, Toomer thought then-coach Dan Reeves wasn't giving him a chance. He had introduced himself to Giants fans with an 87-yard punt return in his first game in 1996, providing a hint of his breakaway ability.

He scored another one on a 65-yard return but still couldn't get Reeves to give him a shot at receiver. With limited time on offense, Toomer managed just one catch for 12 yards before he tore his ACL and was lost for the year seven games into the season.

Rookie mistakes had sabotaged him, but before his injury, Toomer acknowledged the hit on his pride. "This has been very frustrating," he told *The New York Times.* "I didn't think I was coming to the NFL and to the Giants to be a kick returner; I thought I was coming to be a receiver.... I've been successful in my life at most things, so this is a struggle. But I am confident it will work out."

It took time and more battles through injuries—and the occasional flare-ups of his ego—but Toomer worked his way into the receiving rotation, beating the 13–0 Broncos with a touchdown catch in 1998 in the closing minute. The 6'3", 208-pounder finally earned a starting spot in 1999, immediately setting a team record for receptions with 79 and pairing with Ike Hilliard to offer the Giants an explosive combination they had never seen.

The Giants weren't known for receivers; they had not had this type of playmaker since Homer Jones caught all those long balls some 30 years before.

The more Toomer played, the more he endeared himself to the fans who not only admired the way Toomer maxed out his 6'3" height with leaping grabs, but also how he did not leap around after a big play. He was an old Giant that way. The type who made them look past stats and into an appreciation only a handful of players in New York achieve.

Time and again, fans saw Toomer perfect that tiptoe along the sideline to pick up another clutch catch. He had taken ballet as a boy, and he later compared some of his moves to the lessons he learned in dance.

"When you catch the ball and know you have one foot in bounds, try to kick your heel with the other, that way you know you're in bounds," Michael Strahan remembered Toomer telling him.

On Toomer's website, fans would get more instruction, such as a high school freshman receiving several in-depth tutorials from an NFL star. When the boy later apologized for bugging him, Toomer replied on the website he was not bothering him—and to please write again.

Toomer never made a Pro Bowl, but Giants fans didn't care as they watched him tiptoe his way along the sideline and into one more Giants record after another. He was Mr. Reliable, the receiver everyone knew would come through in a big spot.

Toomer had done that to the point of exhaustion in 2006 when the Giants stunned the hated Eagles with 17 points in the fourth quarter, then won the game 30–24 in overtime. As impressive as Toomer's team-record-tying 12 catches, 137 yards, and two touchdowns were, they were not even the most indelible image.

Toomer collapsed from exhaustion as Plaxico Burress won the game with a touchdown catch. Toomer, who again had grudgingly accepted getting shoved out of the spotlight when Burress' arrival made him the No. 2 receiver, was carried off the field and administered intravenous fluids in the locker room.

"I was going across the middle, and I was thinking, 'I'm open, I'm open,' but then my legs told me, 'Your game is over,' and I just went down," Toomer said after the game, earning more fans. But that season ended in disappointment with another first-round exit in the playoffs.

The next year Toomer helped the Giants on the playoff run of their lives. In the first round, Toomer caught seven passes and one of Eli Manning's two touchdowns in a 24–14 win. As he walked off the field, Toomer offered rare edge, mocking Tampa Bay defensive back Ronde Barber, who had joined his brother, Tiki, in bashing Manning. "He can be had," Toomer said as he walked off, mimicking Ronde's pregame comments about the quarterback.

The next week, Toomer stepped up with two touchdown catches in the win over Dallas. The first was a 52-yarder in the first half that stunned the favored Cowboys. The second kept the Giants from getting run out of the building at the end of the first half when they tied the score.

Against Green Bay? Well there Toomer was again, leaping for the ball, dragging that foot—Mr. Reliable coming through in one of the biggest spots of all. His 23-yard catch in the fourth quarter helped set up a Giants touchdown in the 23–20 win that sent his team to the Super Bowl.

But he knew going to the Super Bowl was no longer enough. He remembered the feeling that came when he partied with a friend from the Ravens at a club, enjoying himself until the man flashed his Super Bowl ring.

"I want that," Toomer thought then. Now he had the chance to get it.

In his biggest game, Toomer both commanded attention and fell out of the spotlight all at once. David Tyree made the catch no one would ever forget. Burress made the game-winner.

Mr. Reliable? He just led the Giants receivers with six catches for 84 yards, including one last big one on third down on their final drive in the 17–14 win.

As the Giants celebrated in their locker room, team spokesman Pat Hanlon smiled and pointed to Toomer a couple of lockers over. This had been a long time coming for the Giants receiver who battled for everything.

"I see you, A–1," Hanlon shouted, calling Toomer by his nickname. "It took seven years to get it right, and we got it right."

"*Boy*, did we get it right," Toomer said.

51 Leemans, Danowski, Hein, Cuff, and Co. Win '38 Title

They used to all live around the same area in a cluster of hotels near the Polo Grounds so the 1930s-era Giants would be as close as their successors in the '50s were. Mel Hein once remembered how the bond helped them win.

John Danowski, the Duke lacrosse coach and son of former Giants quarterback Ed Danowski, remembered how, even years later, the men who won the 1938 NFL championship kept in touch. "He would just tell stories about the guys—Mel Hein, Tuffy Leemans, the coach [Steve Owen]," Danowski said of his father. "The neatest thing about every Christmas when I was growing up in the '60s, we'd get Christmas cards from all over the country—Hank Soar, Mel Hein, of course, Wellington Mara."

Many of the Giants who beat Green Bay 23–17 for the title in '38 had already been around to win the team's first NFL Championship Game in 1934, but some were not.

In 1936, the NFL had its first college draft, and a high school boy who happened to be on vacation caught a game between George Washington College and Alabama. The running back for George Washington was especially impressive, so the high school kid, Wellington Mara, reported back to his father that Tuffy Leemans looked like a strong player.

He became the No. 2 pick in the NFL draft, which made him the league's second pick in its history. He lived up to the status, leading the league in rushing his rookie year with 830 yards and getting named either first- or second-team All-NFL in the first seven seasons of his eight-year career.

Leemans tossed 25 career touchdown passes at a time when running backs frequently threw option passes or took direct snaps. The Hall of Famer also averaged 13.8 yards on punt returns.

In the 1938 championship game, Leemans scored on a 6-yard run in the first quarter to give the Giants a 9–0 lead. It followed a 14-yard field goal by Ward Cuff, another of the running backs in Owen's A-Formation, which was a variation of the single wing and featured three backs.

Cuff played nine years with the Giants as a wingback, kicker, and punter, twice leading the league in yards per carry with 6.5 and 5.6 in 1943 and '44.

Danowski was a rookie in 1934, pressed into championship duty against the heavily favored Bears. After leading the Giants to that upset, he returned to the championship game in '35 after leading the league in passing, but the Giants lost to the Lions. Having again led all passers in '38, Danowski came through— throwing two touchdowns in the title game, the second to Soar in the third quarter for the win.

The unassuming Danowski didn't like to boast about his exploits, his son said. If anything, he always remembered an anecdote that kept him humble. "One of my dad's favorite stories when he was a rookie, from Riverhead out on Long Island," Danowski said. "People were chanting in the upper cheap seats, 'We want Danowski! We want Danowski!'"

His coach quickly called him over. Danowski threw off the cape players wore to combat the cold. He snapped on his chin strap. He ran as soon as he heard his name.

"You hear those people chanting your name?" Owen asked him.

"Yes, coach," the rookie replied.

"Go up there and see what they want," Owen said.

The son laughs at the memory his father enjoyed sharing before his death in 1997.

"Those guys made friends for a lifetime," he said. "Playing for the Giants and the Mara family—when they talk about the Giants being a third- and fourth-generation franchise, that's how it got started."

52 Yankee Stadium: Do Not Invite Mantles and Giffords to Same Event

The Polo Grounds helped the Giants introduce football to New York City. The stadium, beloved for its baseball team as part of a passionate piece of the city's fabric, still leaves fans pining for the imagery of a time they don't want to forget. But for certain Giants, well past the championship years of the 1930s, the stadium was not fondly remembered.

"The Polo Grounds...was a mess," Frank Gifford said of his time there from 1952–55. "It was like a stable, and as a matter of fact they did keep horses in there."

John Johnson, the Giants' trainer from 1948–2008 chuckled when recalling the difference in amenities from his first year at the Polo Grounds to his final season with the Giants. "Of course, the training room at the Polo Grounds wasn't what it is today," he said. "I gotta say, the Polo Grounds was about ready to come down when I was going in there, I guess."

So when the Giants decided to leave their initial home and move up to Yankee Stadium, the palatial land of the city's sporting kings, Gifford felt a surge of excitement. He felt his Giants, still dwarfed by the Yankees' shadow at that point, could slide into at least a share of the spotlight.

"The real turning point was when we went to Yankee Stadium," Gifford said. "And I know for me, I was awestruck when I walked out of the first dugout and walked onto the field at Yankee Stadium.

"Yankee Stadium. I just couldn't believe it, having played in the Polo Grounds. It was a major step up."

The draw of Yankee Stadium combined with the Giants' improving team—which won its first NFL championship in 18 years in 1956—led to an increase in fans interest. For big games, the Giants drew 50,000 to 60,000 fans—a number Gifford's memory short-changed him on.

"There were times we played at the Polo Grounds, we would outnumber the crowd," Gifford said. "Then in '56 we went to Yankee Stadium, we had 30,000-40,000 people."

While Gifford was humbled by Yankee Stadium, he did not apparently feel the same way about his lockermate from the Yankees—a centerfielder named Mickey Mantle. The feel-good story would include a strong bond between Mantle and Gifford—a pair of imported New Yorkers whose exploits on the field and good looks charmed the city. The true story is more of a tabloid writer's dream.

Gifford chafed at the mention of Mantle in author Jane Leavy's critically acclaimed biography on Mantle, *The Last Boy*. "Excuse me, he shared a locker with *me*," Gifford told Leavy when it was mentioned he had shared one with Mantle.

Gifford proceeded to unload on Mantle, one of the most iconic Yankees of all time, who also happened to be known for his drinking problem and a propensity to pursue women other than his wife.

"[He was a] total a------," Gifford said. "Not a nice person. I didn't know him, but I didn't want to know him. The little bit I was around him, I didn't want to be around him.

"We deified somebody who hits the ball a long way 'cause he's got a bad knee. Other than that, what did he do? What did he really do to help society in any way?"

Of course, if you're scoring at home, it could be pointed out that Gifford's status in New York, while not that of Mantle's, was built on his ability to run with and catch a football. Gifford went on to call Mantle a "sexist" and say "he was not my kind of person. We were MVPs the same year. I would hate to think I was even close to what he was."

The diatribe, again, was as curious as it was provocative. As Leavy points out, Gifford was caught in his own extramarital affair in an extremely embarrassing tabloid story in 1997 that humiliated his third wife, talk-show host Kathie Lee.

In any case, at least Gifford was free from the mess of the Polo Grounds.

53 Fourth-and-17

He stood in the huddle in the biggest moment of his career so far, and this time Phil Simms' coach had recently offered an arm around his shoulder instead of another kick in the pants. The Giants faced a fourth-and-17 in Week 11 of the 1986 season, trailing Minnesota 20–19 with 1:12 left. Simms' ears, along with those of his teammates, could have been filled with the raucous taunts of the fans inside the noisy Metrodome, but they maintained their focus.

Earlier in the week, head coach Bill Parcells had thought of the upcoming schedule for the 8–2 Giants, who would play in Minnesota and then host Denver before traveling to San Francisco and Washington.

The series of tough games was the kind of test the Giants had to pass if they wanted to reach the goal they had set after losing in

Chicago to end their 1985 season. They wanted to earn home-field advantage this time. These were the type of obstacles you had to clear to do it, and now they faced the biggest one.

The Giants had rolled to three straight wins, but Simms had struggled, hitting just 14 of his last 32 passes with three interceptions in his last two games before facing Minnesota. Parcells recognized his usual whipping boy's tentativeness as Simms dealt with injuries to receivers Lionel Manuel and Stacy Robinson. Instead of the usual barbs he threw Simms' way, however, Parcells offered comfort.

"I think you're a great quarterback," the coach told Simms earlier in the week. "And you got that way by being daring and fearless, so let's go."

If ever there was a time to heed the message, this was it. The ball was snapped, and Simms had time. Tons of it.

The offensive linemen, especially tackle Karl Nelson, dominated their men, giving Simms enough time to look left, then center, before finally looking right. Even more impressively, Nelson did all this after taking a kick to the head on third down when the Vikings sacked Simms.

"I got up and said I'm seeing double," Nelson recalled. "[Guard] Chris Godfrey said, 'Block the guy on the right.'"

Finally, Simms spotted Bobby Johnson on the right sideline. Finally, a Vikings lineman broke free as Mike Stensrud rushed past Mark Bavaro. Simms fired a perfect spiral with just a touch of air down the right sideline. Stensrud knocked Simms down after the pass left his fingers.

Johnson was open. The pass was perfect, reaching him just before the approaching defensive back. So was the catch. Johnson kept his feet in bounds, then stepped out.

"I used to look at it all the time, trying to see how we got it done," Johnson told *The New York Times* later that season. "My conclusion is that we did everything right, and Phil threw a great pass."

A few moments later, Raul Allegre kicked the game-winning 33-yard field goal for a 22–20 victory. The Giants had passed their test.

When they look back on the team's first Super Bowl season, most of the Giants acknowledge the fourth-down play as the one that showed them what they could do. Even if they didn't see it at the time.

"I've got to be honest with you—I don't remember the play," said Nelson, who had still been reeling from the kick in the head. "Only reason I know it is I saw it on film and read about it. As far as in the big picture, it was a big stepping stone for us. That team just didn't accept defeat."

54 Bavaro Bowls 'Em Over

Bill Parcells recognized the problem, as did anyone else watching the *Monday Night Football* game against San Francisco on national television.

"Their intensity level is way up *here*," Parcells told his team at halftime, speaking of the 49ers. "Yours is way down *there*. If you don't pick it up…"

Two weeks before in the 1986 season, the Giants had converted the fourth-and-17 against Minnesota, a play they were certain showed they could be a Super Bowl team. Just the last week, George Martin had rumbled 78 yards on an interception return for a score, the big defensive lineman showing Denver, too, the Giants were for real—and providing his teammates with a laugh.

But no one was laughing now as the 10–2 Giants trailed the 49ers in San Francisco 17–0 at the half.

"I don't give a (bleep) what you call," Parcells reportedly barked at offensive coordinator Ron Erhardt. "Give us some frickin' points."

They would soon do just that. Not due to a play that was called but because of the player who would take an ordinary play and turn it into an inspirational image that still leaves adrenaline surging through Giants fans 24 years later.

Giants tight end Mark Bavaro caught the ball over the middle on a short pass from Phil Simms. And there was 49ers Hall of Famer Ronnie Lott—the man who loved to hit—getting dragged down the field like a child leaving a toy store. Lott was joined by several of his teammates, the whole group of proud 49ers reduced to holding on for dear life, Bavaro carried them about 20 yards down field for a 31-yard gain, all but emasculating them on national TV every step of the way.

"I remember thinking to myself—'That's just *tough*,'" running back Joe Morris said. "That's just damn toughness."

That's Bavaro.

The play against the 49ers not only sparked the Giants to yet another huge win on the road to their first Super Bowl victory—a 21–17 comeback that humbled San Francisco. It defined Bavaro, a blue-collar player Giants fans related to during their hard-hitting era of 1980s football. It might also have defined the Giants that season.

"I remember standing there going, 'Okay. Wow, Okay. Whoa! Whoa!" Simms once recalled. "It really did something to the team, and it probably was the signature play for the whole football season."

That's why Giants fans loved the tight end out of Notre Dame, who was so eerily silent and imposing he intimidated even his bluster-filled head coach at times. Parcells was shown on the sideline once saying he didn't know what to make of Bavaro, who started for injured starter Zeke Mowatt in 1985 and became the Giants' tight end for the next six years.

Giants tight end Mark Bavaro said little around the team or press, allowing his bruising play to do the talking. He became a fan favorite for his blue-collar work ethic and ability to catch passes like this one against Green Bay. (AP Photo/ Paul Spinelli)

"I think Bill was afraid of him," Morris said, perhaps only half-joking.

Opponents certainly had reason to fear the player intimidating enough to be nicknamed "Rambo" for the popular Sylvester Stallone movie character of the time—but humble enough to ask teammates to drop the label because he felt it wasn't right to be compared to a veteran.

Bavaro, all 6'4", 245 pounds of him, played six weeks with a broken jaw in 1986 and could distribute one of his own to would-be tacklers. In 1990, he played through a season-long knee condition that kept him from practicing and eventually would force his retirement.

"I used to think that no matter who I played with, I was always tougher than [them]," Bavaro once told NFL Films. "If it ever came down to a fight in the parking lot, I felt good about my chances with anybody."

While Bavaro had those thoughts, he was as outwardly quiet as Jeremy Shockey one day would be loud for the Giants, as beloved as Shockey would come to be reviled. While Shockey became known for boisterous boasts, either in the locker room where he griped about not catching enough passes or on the field where he would taunt opponents, Bavaro all but shrugged at his accomplishments.

"It was nothing special; the plays were all the same stuff," Bavaro said after setting a team record with 12 receptions against Cincinnati in 1985. "I just caught a lot of balls. I'd rather win, that's all."

Bavaro helped the Giants do a lot of that, from the 49ers game to the Super Bowl when he caught four passes for 51 yards in the 39–20 win over Denver.

A rugged blocker in the Giants' conservative run-oriented offense, Bavaro still managed to catch 66 passes for 1,001 yards and four touchdowns in the 1986 season.

He won two Super Bowls with the Giants before a degenerative knee condition forced the club to release him in 1991. Despite initially letting him go, though, Giants owner Wellington Mara—as often was the case—signed Bavaro for the year that he was injured at a contract of $310,000.

Ultimately, the Giants decided Bavaro's knee shouldn't be subjected to the punishment he was always willing to give his body for the sake of the game. He signed on with ex-Giants defensive coordinator Bill Belichick and the Browns in 1992 and an Eagles team he once loathed in '93 and '94, but he was never the same.

All these years later, the player known for his stoic exterior showed he had a lot churning on the inside. In 2008, his novel, *Rough and Tumble,* was published. It featured a Giants tight end who played through pain, a linebacker with off-the-field problems, and a team fighting for a Super Bowl berth after their starting quarterback went down with an injury.

Sound familiar?

"While there are parallels with the 1990 team, the biggest one is that it was my last year with the Giants," Bavaro told *The New York Times*. "That team was special to me because I played that season believing it was my last. In fact, with the condition of my knee, every game that year could have been my last."

For Giants fans, the appreciation for Bavaro comes from the fact he played every game as if it was his last—whether he thought it could be or not.

55 Giants Stadium: Leaving New York

For all of the Giants' wonderful memories in New York, they eventually left to head across the river to East Rutherford, New Jersey, and a whole new batch of memories. They would forever be called the New York Giants, but when the Mara family took them to the Meadowlands in 1976, having signed a 30-year lease in 1971, they earned a new nickname as the Jersey Giants.

The fans on both sides of the border have bickered somewhat ever since.

When the Giants won their first Super Bowl in 1986, New York City Mayor Ed Koch initially refused to honor them with a parade because he said they were now foreigners to him. After American Express provided sponsorship money, Koch acquiesced. But Giants co-owner Tim Mara said the only proper place for a celebration was at Giants Stadium.

"This is our house," Giants coach Bill Parcells told the crowd that had assembled to celebrate.

It would become that and so much more, and the Giants were especially appreciative of having a place to call their own because they never had one before. They were always sharing something or never quite at home, from the Polo Grounds to Yankee Stadium to the nomad period from 1973–76 when they waited for their stadium to be constructed as Yankee Stadium was renovated.

They started off at the Yale Bowl in New Haven, Connecticut— only after Congress helped alter the NFL TV blackout policy, allowing fans to watch at home if a game was a sellout. That prompted the people in charge of the Yale Bowl to relent after resisting the idea. That didn't feel like home though as the Giants went 1–11 in their two years there.

After construction delays left the Giants without their new state-of-the-art stadium in Jersey in 1975, they spent a year going against their instinct and sharing Shea Stadium with the Jets. Of course, nine years later, the Jets joined the Giants in the Meadowlands.

Adding to their little brother complex, the Jets were forced to play in a building known as Giants Stadium. The best the Jets could do was drape banners with their team's green covers as they attempted to play dress-up in the home of the red and blue.

The Giants' first home game came against Dallas in 1976, but the team was in the midst of its 18-year run without a playoff berth, and the fans' introduction to their new 80,000-seat home was not a pretty one. In the 1980s, as the team grew, the affection for the stadium did, as well, with fans flocking out to New Jersey's Route 3 for one big game after another filled with memories of Lawrence Taylor, Phil Simms, Harry Carson, and company. They eventually gave way to Jim Fassel, Jessie Armstead, Michael Strahan, and Tiki Barber on one Super Bowl run, then Eli Manning, Plaxico Burress, and Osi Umenyiora on another.

Along with the Giants and Jets games, the stadium hosted a variety of other events, from soccer's legendary Pele and the New York Cosmos to the 1994 World Cup to Donald Trump's New Jersey Generals of the USFL featuring Herschel Walker and the short-lived ribald alternative XFL to the NFL's World League of American Football (WLAF).

Rutgers called the stadium home in college football, and Army and Navy had a few of their traditional bouts there, as well.

Yankee Stadium may have been home to the Bronx Bombers' Boss, but Giants Stadium was the unofficial home of New Jersey's Boss, rocker Bruce Springsteen, who naturally performed one of his many Giants Stadium concerts as the final one before the stadium was demolished in preparation for the New Meadowlands Stadium that replaced it.

By the time the new stadium opened in 2010, Giants fans had long grown fond of their Jersey residence, from the wafting aromas of barbecuing tailgaters outside to the practice bubble that served as a towering landmark to the spiraling concourse.

Its most joyful celebrations, of course, came when the Giants won their first NFC Championship Game there in 1986 and their last, in 2000, when the Giants celebrated on that "field of painted mud" as owner Wellington Mara proudly called it from the podium on the field.

Training Camp Sites Through the Years

As the Giants moved around several times during the season, they did the same in the preseason. They have trained in 15 different sites, traveling as far west as Salem, Oregon, when the Giants played exhibitions against teams in the West. Albany has been the team's training camp home for the past 15 years, the longest stretch for a site in club history.

If you can make the trip, training camp is a great time to try to get a little closer to the players than would be possible during an actual game, in a more relaxed setting. Here's a look at Giants' training camps through the years:

Site	Years
University of Albany	1996–2010
Fairleigh Dickinson University	1988–95
Pace University	1975–87
Fairfield University	1974, 1961–69
Monmouth College	1972–73
C.W. Post	1970–71
St. Michael's College (Winooski, Vermont)	1959–60, 1956–57
Willamette University (Salem, Oregon)	1958
Gustavus-Adolphus	1952–53
Saranac, New York	1950–51
Pearl River, New York	1947–49, 1934–38
Superior, Wisconsin	1946, 1941–42, 1939
Bear Mountain	1943–45
Blue Hills Country Club (Pearl River)	1940
Pompton Lakes, New Jersey	1933

There were also the rumors of Jimmy Hoffa buried under one end zone, the wicked winter winds chilling opponents the way the Giants' old defense often did.

All of it eventually became home.

"Like all teams that are pretty good, it becomes part of who you are," former quarterback Phil Simms said. "Just the elements and everything involved with Giants Stadium, not many teams looked forward to coming up here and playing. Just as soon as you came out to warm up, you felt that right away, 'Wow, okay, the fans are definitely into this today.' That was part of it, too. Really, the aura or the environment. It was very unique. Didn't sense it quite like that in other places I went around the league."

56 Tom Coughlin: The Cuddlier Curmudgeon

The player griped, creating a stir by claiming Giants coach Tom Coughlin had taken some of the fun out of football for him and needed to loosen up. Coughlin, after his last season ended in disappointment with rumors of his job being in jeopardy before Giants owners John Mara and Steve Tisch pledged their support, offered a sharp rebuke worthy of the man so often known for his scowl.

Or not.

"He should have seen me a few years ago," Coughlin joked of safety Antrel Rolle after the 2010 season. The line prompted laughter due to the déjà vu feeling caused by Rolle's comments on a Miami radio station that Coughlin needed to relax. The use of humor also validated Coughlin's statement. He had changed, even if the alterations are sometimes subtle.

Four years before, Tiki Barber wrote in his book, *Tiki: My Life in the Game and Beyond*, that he retired the previous season partially because "[Coughlin] robbed me of what had been one of the most important things I had in my life, which was the joy I felt playing football. I had lost that. He had taken it away."

Barber was far from alone in his criticism, and Coughlin underwent a slight shift in personality that was credited as the key to the Giants' Super Bowl run. The result was a (slightly) cuddlier curmudgeon, one who would not be confused for bombastic players coach Rex Ryan—as Rolle attested four years later when he favorably compared the Jets' loosey-goosey coach to his more restrictive one.

But Coughlin amended the old-school ways he had followed from his first college coaching job at the Rochester Institute of Technology to his time under the Bill Parcells Future Head Coaches Academy (otherwise known as the late 1980s Giants).

Mara—showing the same value for continuity as his father, Wellington—and Tisch brought Coughlin back after the first-round playoff loss to Philly in 2006 but asked him to show the gentler side he had displayed away from the field to his players.

As much out of necessity as desire, Coughlin took a practical approach to lightening up. "I don't want to be the story," he told *The New York Times* before the 2007 season. "I want our team to be the story. I've spoken long and hard about distractions. I don't want to be one. I don't want to be one for my own team. I want to hopefully reflect on exactly what I say—talk is cheap, play the game, be evaluated for the job we're doing on the field."

Coughlin did what he could to change the story. He interrupted one of his infamous training camp meetings—the type he deemed players late for if they had not arrived a few minutes early—and made a startling announcement. The team was going bowling. It offered a bonding experience. So did a Casino night.

With reporters, Coughlin no longer barked; he merely growled. The man wasn't about to change every last bit of what he believed in over the years, the things that had helped him and quarterback Doug Flutie spark national interest in his Boston College football team so many years before or helped him lead Jacksonville to an AFC Championship Game in the expansion team's infancy.

But he was trying, and his players met him halfway as he leaned on veterans like Michael Strahan and linebacker Antonio Pierce to form a leadership council.

"He's been getting better, I can tell you that," Pierce said as the Giants started to surge that season. "The [speeches] before were kind of like bedtime stories. There was too much going on. Half the guys couldn't relate to it. Now he's getting up to date to the 2000 era. He's been doing a lot of things different each and every week.

"We've had special people come in there and talk to the people.... He knows what buttons to push with certain guys on our team and I think he understands our mentality right now."

One of those special people spoke to the team in Week 3 and provided one of the most inspirational moments of the season. The 0–2 Giants prepared to travel to play the Washington Redskins, and assistant coach Mike Sullivan visited his old Army football teammate, Lt. Col. Greg Gadson, at nearby Walter Reed Hospital.

Gadson had lost both of his legs to a roadside bomb in Baghdad. When he told his old friend he would like to attend

Tom Coughlin's ability to adjust by showing a little more of his jovial side helped the Giants make a run to a stunning Super Bowl upset in 2008.
(AP Photo/Evan Vucci)

the game, Sullivan provided tickets. Later, Sullivan asked him to address the team.

"I just spoke from the heart, as a soldier and as a former football player," Gadson told the *New York Daily News* that year. "I talked to them about the power of sports in people's lives, especially soldiers' lives, how many times I'd watched soldiers get up in the middle of the night after a 12-hour shift if there is a chance to watch a game.

"I told them that of course after all the exteriors had been stripped away, they played the game for themselves. But that they had to play the game for each other."

Humbled by the war hero's words, the Giants beat the Redskins that day, making a goal-line stand that helped turn their season. They credited Gadson for his courage and powerful words, and when they reached the postseason they invited him back out, with Corey Webster giving him his game ball after his interception in the NFC Championship Game against Green Bay.

While Gadson spoke to a much greater purpose than football, the concept of bonding and team-building followed Coughlin's basic tenets. He had built such a strong bond among his former players that members of his first team at RIT, many of whom hadn't spoken to each other in three decades, arranged an impromptu reunion to cheer on their old coach in the Super Bowl.

One player after the other told stories about how Coughlin cracked down on them, from ensuring that they kept their grades up to ordering them to complete a play properly. The men chafed at the orders then but grew grateful over time. As ex-player, Bob Burns, said, "I would be dead" if it wasn't for Coughlin because the coach stuck with him through many issues.

Relayed word of his ex-players' plans by a reporter the day before the Super Bowl and after his media sessions were complete, Coughlin was touched. The coach passed a message back that it was "very meaningful" that his old players would share in the moment.

"I'm getting emotional, which I don't do," Mark McCabe, who helped organize the reunion, said at the time. He paused until he could resume speaking. "I don't think he realizes the influence he had on people, that...that lasts a lifetime, you know?

"You've gotta be kidding me," McCabe said later, when told Coughlin had taken a moment the day before the biggest game of his career to acknowledge his old team. "Unbelievable. That's him. That's him. Unbelievable. That gives me goosebumps."

After the Giants shocked the Patriots with their 17–14 win, Coughlin took a picture of himself in a RIT reunion T-shirt made for the event. In it he held the Lombardi Trophy. It's that kind of behavior that lurks beneath Coughlin's gruff exterior that inspires players who have been around him a while to recognize his value, even when he starts barking again.

"Being with him for four years, I think my picture of Coughlin is competitive," kicker Lawrence Tynes said after Coughlin caught heat for publicly dressing down punter Matt Dodge in the Giants' infamous collapse against the Eagles in 2010. "He's one of the most competitive men that I've played for. That's what drives him still to this day. Whether he yells at you or not, you've got to be able to handle it. He wants to win. He's not yelling at you, he's yelling at the problem. It's fine. You either can deal with it or you can't play in this league.

"He cares about you. For me, I got traded here in '07. I missed mini-camp because my wife was pregnant. The first batch of flowers I got was from Tom Coughlin. A man I barely knew."

Rolle apparently doesn't quite yet know that man as much, or at least he's too concerned with the other side of Coughlin to appreciate it.

Granted, it's easy to say that Coughlin's other side still frustrates those close and far. His crass message, telling his critics they could "kiss my a--" after the Giants finished a disappointing

Playing to Win

As much as Tom Coughlin's ability to adapt helped lead his resurgence and the Giants' run to their Super Bowl XLII win over New England, his old-school mentality played a large part, as well.

The game that the Giants later largely credited for giving them confidence in the playoffs after a 10–6 season was the one in which Coughlin was again widely second-guessed. With the Giants already in the playoffs, recent tradition had made it seem irresponsible to risk injuring starters in the regular season finale against the Patriots.

But Coughlin rejected the scoffing, his hawk's eyes narrowing under his wire-rimmed glasses and insisting that he would play his starters and give his team a chance to get the adrenaline of competition. The result was a classic battle that left New England barely escaping with its perfect season intact 38–35, and the Giants were ready to make a run at a rematch.

"It had a big effect," running back Brandon Jacobs recalled. "We came out, we played with an undefeated team, and we should have beat 'em then. That really gave us confidence in knowing that we could play with anybody. We got into the playoffs the week before that, showed that we could play with them, and ended up beating everybody else and them again."

season by blowing the Eagles game to miss the playoffs was out of line if it was directed in any way at fans, especially considering the Giants had just moved into their new stadium, burning decades of goodwill by charging expensive Personal Seat Licenses during a recession, betraying fans who could no longer afford or justify paying for their family heirloom of season tickets.

As many NFL coaches are, Coughlin can be good at creating an us-against-the-world mentality in his locker room. That may not be appealing to the outside world, but for his own purposes at the very least, it's better than the us-against-him mentality his players used to have.

57 Flipper's Still Running

They were finally back in the playoffs, three long years since they had ended the championship drought with their Super Bowl run in 1986. One thing after another had claimed the past two seasons that were filled with disappointment on the field and problems off it.

The strike had stolen the 1987 season, and the Giants' replacement players were apparently the worst of the lot as they went 0–3 before the strike ended. Lawrence Taylor admitted to drug problems. Offensive lineman Karl Nelson missed a year due to cancer before coming back triumphantly in 1988—only to retire a little while later to go successfully fight the cancer's return.

And just about a year before, there had been one more indignity for the Giants, who felt so sure they were playoff-bound when they played the Jets in the season finale at Giants Stadium. They had watched the Jets—their little brothers on the football field for so long—stun them with a last-second touchdown catch by Al Toon that cost them the division and helped shut them out of the postseason once more.

Now they were back in a playoff game at Giants Stadium after going 12–4 to win the NFC East in 1989. And they were finally done with all the misery as they prepared to play Jim Everett, Flipper Anderson, and the Los Angeles Rams. Or not.

Just 1:06 into sudden-death overtime, Anderson caught a pass from Everett and raced into the end zone and through the tunnel, taking the Giants' season with him. He never broke stride, barreling over a bystander on the field who looked as battered and shell-shocked as Anderson had left the Giants.

The scene is burned into Giants fans minds much like Herman Edwards picking up Joe Pisarcik's fumble, Trey Junkin botching a snap in San Francisco, and DeSean Jackson running back a misguided punt.

Misery finally over? No. Another season was instead.

"I don't think anybody here was ready for the season to be over," Carl Banks said after the game.

The Giants led 13–7 in the third quarter after an Ottis Anderson touchdown run. Led by cornerback Mark Collins, New York had shut down the Rams' proficient passing attack.

Anderson, a second-year receiver, had few catches all season, but his speed led to big plays on the receptions he did make. And in Week 12, he provided an eye-popping example of just how dangerous he could be with an NFL-record-setting 336 yards on 15 catches against the Saints.

But the Giants limited him to one catch for 21 yards in a 31–10 regular-season loss, and now Collins had allowed him just one 20-yard touchdown catch. He thwarted another one with an interception at the Giants' 1-yard line.

Rams kicker Mike Lansford hit two fourth-quarter field goals, and the Giants were headed for their first postseason overtime since the classic 1958 NFL title game against the Colts. It was sudden death with the first team to score winning, so groans came when the Rams won the toss. They got much louder a few plays later when Giants defensive back Sheldon White was called for a 27-yard pass interference penalty on Anderson, giving the Rams the ball at the Giants' 25-yard line.

Replays showed White on Anderson's back as the ball arrived just out of reach of the receiver. Depending on the angle—or the perspective of the person viewing it—it was either the right call or a ridiculous one because Anderson couldn't have caught the ball anyway.

"Superman couldn't have caught that ball," White said after the game.

"I touched it—was that catchable?" Anderson said.

The Giants were livid, including head coach Bill Parcells, who barely contained his opinion at the time, saying only, "You saw the play; that's all I'm going to say about it." (Ten years later, Parcells admitted to *The New York Times* columnist Dave Anderson that it was the only time he felt an official cost his team a game.)

The game-winner came two plays later. By that point, Collins, who felt all but invincible most of the day, had repeatedly motioned to the Giants' sideline for a sub. On the first play of overtime, he heard his ankle snap after a collision.

After the game, he said no one saw him.

So he stayed in as defensive coordinator Bill Belichick called for a bump-and-run on Anderson, the idea being he would pressure the receiver coming off the line. Anderson later told reporters Collins didn't get in a good enough hit, which left him free to use his best asset.

"They can only bump me for five yards, and then it's a foot race after that," Anderson said. "I'm going to win most of those."

With the Giants blitzing, Collins was in single coverage. So Everett took a couple of steps back then floated the ball toward Anderson, who was streaking down the right sideline. He slowed just enough to reach back for the ball past a desperate diving Collins.

"I got a good bump on him. I saw the ball. I couldn't get over enough to get it," Collins said. "I was right there. It was a great catch and a great throw. End of story."

Not quite. Anderson, who had made a pact with teammate Aaron Cox before the game to run straight through the tunnel if given the chance on a game-ending play, stuck to his word.

After sprinting for the end zone, Anderson kept running.

For Giants fans, he is forever doing that.

58 For Calloway, No Place to Hidey-Hidey-Hidey-Hide

The ball bounced toward Chris Calloway just as the Giants had planned. Much of the game had done just that, bounding toward a Giants team that wasn't expected to be in this 1997 playoff game, much less host it at Giants Stadium.

So now, even after Minnesota scored with 1:30 left to make what had once been a 16-point lead just 2 points, the Giants knew they would survive this scare. They had survived so much more, thriving in head coach Jim Fassel's rookie year when they stunned everyone by winning the NFC East following a pair of woeful seasons.

Calloway recovered the onside kick. The Giants won and headed to Green Bay, celebrating their first playoff victory since 1993. The Giants gave up 10 points in 90 seconds to lose 23–22.

"It's like a bad dream and you wish you would wake up," said quarterback Danny Kanell, who threw a first-half touchdown pass. "We had victory right there. I think we all thought we had things in pretty good shape."

They led Minnesota 22–20 with 1:30 left, even after blowing most of that 19–3 halftime lead and after allowing Vikings quarterback Randall Cunningham to threaten the type of torment he used to inflict while with the Eagles.

Calloway was part of the Giants' "hands team," the receiver selected to take the prime spot on the onside kick coverage because he had been so sure-handed in catching 58 passes that year—one of four in a row in which he would snag at least 50 receptions. The Vikings were down to their last timeout.

Despite the scare Cunningham had just put into them with a 30-yard touchdown pass to Jake Reed, the Giants would be fine.

"I figured all we had to do was cover that onside kick," linebacker Corey Miller said after the game. "When that ball started popping out and bouncing around, I got kind of a sick feeling."

Calloway had it. Then he lost it. The ball bounced off his usually reliable hands, and the Vikings recovered. "No excuse," Calloway said later. "It came off low, it came to me, I went down, but it took a funny bounce, hit my chest, and went away."

Okay, Giants cornerback Jason Sehorn told himself. It would be okay. "I still thought they had to go at least 40 yards for a field goal," Sehorn told reporters later. "I didn't think they could do it."

Why would he? Sehorn, who had picked off six passes that year, had kept Vikings star Cris Carter in check most of the game and intercepted a Cunningham pass. The Giants defensive line, led by Michael Strahan and Keith Hamilton, had applied pressure again, each player getting a sack. They had helped compensate for the offense, which had been shut down in the second half with rookie Tiki Barber managing just 29 yards rushing for the game and fumbling at his 4-yard line to set up the Vikings' first touchdown in the third quarter.

Still, the Giants had showed their youth in the second half as the Vikings began to cut into the lead. Defensive backs Phillippi Sparks and Conrad Hamilton got into an argument on the field that turned physical. Future defensive leader Jessie Armstead tried to settle the situation but was dragged into it. Strahan and Keith Hamilton had their own issue on the sidelines.

"The thing this year was that we always played together," Strahan later said. "But the thing that kept us together [all season] tore us apart."

Cunningham would pull at the seams before ripping them off. He hit Carter for 21 yards to the Giants' 34 before a pass interference penalty on Sparks moved Minnesota to the 21. Robert Smith burst up the middle to the 5, and veteran kicker Eddie Murray hit the chip shot with 10 seconds left.

A season full of surprises ended with one more.

"I told them I feel extremely bad for all of us," Fassel said of the Giants, who had gone 11–21 under Dan Reeves the previous two seasons. "But I'm very proud of this team. They've made dramatic strides. I'm just sorry it ended this way."

59 Marshall, Martin, and a Giant Journey for 9/11

They were teammates and bookends on the line and in Giants history. George Martin knew how sweet the Giants' Super Bowl victory was in 1986 because, like Harry Carson, he struggled for so long to even sniff the idea of playing in that game.

The former 11th-round draft pick out of Oregon joined the Giants in 1975, the year matching his jersey number. He retired 13 years, a lot of headaches and frustration, four playoff appearances, and one Super Bowl victory later.

But as Martin prepared for one of his final seasons during that 1986 Super Bowl run—one for which he had to be lobbied by coach Bill Parcells to return—Leonard Marshall was just getting started.

Marshall enjoyed a lot more winning during his time with the Giants, playing a pivotal role in their second Super Bowl run in 1990. When he was done, Marshall earned two Pro Bowl nods and set a Giants career sacks record for defensive linemen with 79.5. (He would later be passed by Michael Strahan, and could also watch Osi Umenyiora knock him down a notch in the future. The sack statistic was not officially recorded until 1982, Martin's eighth season.)

For three years, the pair overlapped, playing opposite ends around nose tackle Jim Burt. They combined for 25.5 sacks in 1985, and Marshall led the way with 12 in '86.

Like many Giants, Marshall clashed with Parcells' successor, Ray Handley, and eventually left the Giants to spend a year each with the Jets and Redskins. But he came back to sign a one-day contract before he retired so he could go out the way he entered. Once a Giant, always a Giant.

"I wanted to retire as a Giant because it's where my career began," Marshall said when he announced his decision in 1996. "They were people who believed in my talents and helped mold me into the man I am today, and I wanted to thank them for that."

Marshall and Martin each had their signature plays.

Marshall knocked Joe Montana out of the classic 1990 NFC Championship Game that sent him and the Giants to their second Super Bowl. The play, in which Marshall crawled to his knees in relentless pursuit before walloping Montana, is regarded as one of the most legendary in NFL postseason history.

Martin owns one of the most beloved Giants plays of all time—an amazingly athletic bat of a John Elway pass followed by a 78-yard obstacle-filled run to the end zone for one of Martin's seven career touchdowns.

In a Super Bowl preview game, Martin helped spark a win that would give the growing Giants confidence during a stretch of games that helped lead them to their eventual title.

Denver led by a field goal and was at the Giants' 13 when Martin, the 6'4", 245-pound former college basketball player, stretched behind him to bat the ball before managing to catch it for the interception. The ensuing runback was as impressive as it was comical at times, with Martin preparing to lateral to a waiting Lawrence Taylor before pulling the ball back to nimbly dodge and leap over tacklers before making it all the way to the end zone.

Taylor later joked he had been ready to offer relief, and Martin acknowledged he might have needed it after a ploddingly exhausting play Parcells called, "One of the greatest plays I ever saw."

Defensive Linemen to Know

Here's a look at some Giants defensive linemen who stood out but were not mentioned prominently in other sections of the book.

Keith Hamilton (1992–2003), DE—63 career sacks, including 10 in 2000, the season he teamed with Michael Strahan to help lead the Giants to the Super Bowl.

Erik Howard (1986–1994), NT, DT, DE—Pro Bowl player for Giants in their 1990 Super Bowl season and backup on 1986 champions. Caused key fumble in '90 NFC title game.

John Mendenhall (1972–1979), DT, NT—Overlooked but well-respected lineman who played during the Giants' dark era and also at a time before sacks were kept as official records.

"When I caught it, it was a bright, sunny day. When I got to the end zone, it was cloudy," joked Martin, who also sacked Elway for a safety in the Giants' Super Bowl win. "The weather had changed considerably."

It would be far from Martin's most impressive journey.

* * *

In 2007, having earned fans with his leadership on the field during his 13-year career, Martin looked to support those who had inspired him off the field. As the Giants of that season earned the nickname "Road Warriors" for their impressive play away from home on the way to another Super Bowl, Martin gave the term new meaning, walking across the country at 54 with the hope of raising awareness and funds for the first-responders to the September 11, 2001, terrorist attacks.

Martin had lost a neighbor, and a co-worker had lost his son in the attack on the Twin Towers. Martin decided to combine his wish to literally walk across the country with his desire to honor the memory of his neighbor, Christian DeSimone, and his co-worker's son, Tyler Ugolyn.

The Giants' old leader, who would later take charge of the NFL Alumni Association with the goal of looking out for players debilitated by injuries, also wanted his walk to benefit the first responders who struggled with medical issues and bills.

"The thing that motivated me was the people who were heroes," Martin said. "They really deserve that kind of attention, that kind of recognition. In the midst of [the tragedy] you have these heroic people rushing down to this disaster, not knowing what they were putting themselves into, risking their health…their very lives.

"And you talk to them and you realize they would have done it all over again. It's much deeper [than a Super Bowl win]. The simple truth of it is, this is a matter of life and death."

By the time Martin's incredible journey from the George Washington Bridge to San Diego was over nine months later, he had traveled 3,003 miles through 13 states and 27 pairs of shoes. He was celebrated across the country he had just traveled, earning recognition as one of ABC News' Persons of the Year.

At a time when the nation often struggles for common ground, Martin found it all over, greeted by diverse people who each saluted his journey. He also discovered the serenity that came from tuning out the modern world at times.

"I've got 4,000 songs in my iPod," Martin said during the journey. "I haven't put it on once, and I won't. It's like going out with a beautiful girl and putting blinders on. I'm seeing this beautiful country face to face…. I don't want to pollute it. I want the flavor of it. I want the personality of this country to seep into my soul. I want to hear the crickets chirping, hear the leaves rustling.

"People said it's a once in a lifetime opportunity. I said, 'No, I don't think it comes that often. I don't think in two or 10 lifetimes.'"

Martin, for so long the leader and captain of the Giants defense, maintains that leadership by calling on his former teammates, fans, and neighbors to take part in his annual fund-raising walk (at a much shorter distance than his own), Giant Steps for 9/11 which takes place in the fall.

60 Sell PCLs at New Meadowlands Stadium

It was part of a trend in the New York sporting landscape where the places that contained so many memories were torn down within a couple of years of each other. Yankee Stadium and Shea Stadium gave way to their new homes in 2009. A year later, the Giants and Jets said good-bye to Giants Stadium and hello to the initially generically named New Meadowlands Stadium.

They hadn't yet found a suitable naming rights sponsor for the $1.6 billion state-of-the-art facility, so the name was subject to change. So were far too many of the loyal Giants fans who enjoyed all those Sundays with their family, thanks to season tickets passed down as family heirlooms.

Apparently the team's famed credo of "Once a Giant, Always a Giant" didn't extend to the fans. With the new stadium—financed privately but like many new arenas still benefitting from tax breaks and generous infrastructure assistance—came the advent of Personal Seat Licenses. The insidious device to hold fans hostage to their memories by making them pay thousands of dollars merely for the *right* to buy season tickets started long ago, but had not reached New York.

You couldn't help but feel for the Giants fans who, in the midst of the country's greatest economic crisis since the Great Depression, were told to pay between $1,000 and $20,000 for the

PSLs—and then the cost of the season ticket prices—if they wanted to hold onto the seats handed down from generation to generation.

You couldn't blame them for all the frustrated cries that went up against John Mara and Steve Tisch, especially when they wondered if Mara's father, Wellington, would have allowed this to happen.

From a business standpoint, John Mara said the Giants could not have built their new palace without the PSLs. "It would have been impossible," Mara said after the announcement, adding that 90 percent of seats would be available for $1,000 PSLs. "We wanted to have a plan that we thought was reasonable and fair and gave us the opportunity to keep everybody from Giants Stadium in the new building and meet our payment requirements. We didn't do this to maximize the proceeds."

While there was some validity to Mara's statements, fans still questioned why the stadium needed to be funded for that much, surpassing the costs of most stadiums. The decades-long waiting list was erased as many Giants fans either refused or couldn't afford to pay.

But Mara raised a fair point. There are times when the old-fashioned affection for sports gives way to the practical realities of finding a way to afford the things you need. Which is why it should be with great reluctance that you introduce the Giants to the new PCLs you have no choice but to charge them.

Personal Cheering Licenses.

Hey, if it's fair for sports teams to exploit their customers' passion with reasonable business explanations, maybe it's time for fans to come up with some of their own. Given the long list of evidence demonstrating how much Giants fans are valued by the franchise—from the loving words offered from management to the pleas by players like Antrel Rolle that the Giants need their fans to support the team instead of boo—it's obvious the fans have a premium service to offer the team.

Their voices.

New Meadowlands Stadium

The Giants and Jets opened their new stadium in 2010 and it was appreciated for its modern amenities. But it didn't quite draw rave reviews for the design. It was often panned for its dull, gray exterior. Once inside, there's more than double the space of Giants Stadium and almost quadruple the concession choices.

There's also that fantastic treasure trove of memories at the Legacy Club Hall of Fame. For those who can afford it, the vast array of increased suite seating offers everything from wet bars to lounges featuring brick pizza ovens. For the players, the locker room and private areas feature the usual amusement-park sized places to relax.

The Giants opened their new stadium with a win over the Carolina Panthers—who had spoiled the closing of Giants Stadium with a rout. Within a few minutes fans provided a familiar greeting that Giants players said made it feel like home.

"It felt like the old place," defensive tackle Barry Cofield said after the game. "They booed us."

How often have you been told you helped make the difference? That a rabid New York crowd helped the Giants swallow up an intimidated opponent and inspired the home team? Sure, you'll show up no matter what. You'll pay too much not to do that if you're fortunate to afford the PSLs. But if they want you to cheer and help affect the outcome? Now it's time to start charging the Giants for the service you have so graciously provided for free all these years.

You don't want to, of course. You wish there was another way. But face it. It would have been impossible for you to afford your tickets without some funding. So go ahead and let the Giants know that you will be more than happy to offer all the lung-busting support you can every Sunday. Then show them the pricelist.

Polite applause goes for $1,000. Clapping added for $5,000. And if they want all that passion that came from decades of feeling connected to a team you loved, complete with the frenzy you always provided...well, that will cost them the big bucks.

You've earned it.

61 The Linebackers: Brad Van Pelt and Carl Banks

As impressive as Hall of Famers Lawrence Taylor and Harry Carson were, the Giants featured a rare combination of quality *and* quantity with a pair of legendary linebacker groups. Carson, Brian Kelley, and Brad Van Pelt formed an impressive unit during the unimpressive 1970s era. When Taylor joined them as a rookie in 1981, they became known as the "Crunch Bunch" and were regarded as the game's best linebackers. Bill Parcells, then the defensive coordinator, made use of their talent by switching to a 3-4 defense, Taylor and Van Pelt on the outside, Kelley and Carson inside.

The quartet earned its nickname with jarring hits, and the players created a poster with the four of them standing ominously on a bulldozer while wearing hard hats, a fond memory for Giants fans of that time.

Van Pelt was to the Giants what Don Mattingly was to the Yankees in some ways—a five-time Pro Bowler and fan favorite during a dark era whose misfortune came in departing right before his team became successful. Even when Van Pelt played in the Giants' one playoff season in his 11 years there (1981), the veteran missed the game that clinched a postseason trip and the two playoff games the Giants played. Rookie Byron Hunt filled in, making a big play to help send the Giants to the postseason.

Van Pelt literally stood out thanks to his No. 10 jersey as a linebacker. (The Giants listed him as a backup kicker, which allowed him to avoid wearing a number in the 50s or 90s as per NFL rules.)

The Crunch Bunch's time on the field together ended in 1984 when Kelley's lack of speed contributed to a decision to trade him to San Diego. Van Pelt, frustrated after years of losing and coming off a 3–12–1 season, demanded a trade. The All-American out of Michigan State who turned down an offer to play pro baseball wanted to go home to Michigan to play for the Lions—or, at least, to California or Florida where he had business interests. Instead, the Giants traded him to Minnesota and he held out before finally getting traded to the Raiders.

"It took me a while to get over the shock and bitterness of the trade, but I told [Wellington Mara] there's too much of the red, white, and blue in my blood," Van Pelt told *The New York Times* later that year. "I feel like I'll always remain a Giant, no matter where I go."

He remained close friends and traveling companions with Taylor, Carson, and Kelley until his shocking death of a heart attack at 57 in 2009.

"One of the greatest players I ever played with," Taylor said after his ex-teammate and friend's death. "I not only liked him as a player, but he was one of my true friends."

Only a few years earlier, they had all built a house together as part of Habitat for Humanity, and Van Pelt had told his old friends he wanted to do more things like that. But Carson recalled with frustration how he wished a man he considered a brother had heeded his advice.

Within the last year of Van Pelt's life, Carson suggested he take up the offer of free cardio screenings for retired NFL players. But Van Pelt told him he had not seen a doctor in more than 20 years; fearful because his father had died of a heart attack at 49, according to Carson. He refused no matter how much Carson persisted.

"It's frustrating; it was painful to lose him when we did because he had something that could have been taken care of," Carson said. "I remember looking at him in his casket. 'You know if you were alive, I'd slap the...out of you.' And I'm sure he would be smiling at me.

"Brad was a big, tough football player, [but] he was still a very vulnerable individual even as an older adult."

* * *

Carl Banks was drafted in the first round in 1984, an All-American out of Michigan State, just like Van Pelt, the man he would replace. But Taylor and Carson—who also had requested a trade but was denied—did not exactly welcome rookies that year as the Giants remade a defense they thought was strong and traded their friends.

Carson left camp at one point. Taylor publicly questioned whether the idea of infusing the defense with youthful speed would work if they didn't have experience.

And Banks got off to a rough start on a team that, after its awful 1983 season, had no way of knowing it was on its way to the first of three straight playoff appearances capped by the eventual Super Bowl.

"Carl, when he first got here, God, he was terrible," former teammate Joe Morris recalled. "I'm thinking, 'This guy sucks. Where did we get this guy from?'

"[But] this guy worked on the game, became a better blitzer, became a great player."

From that challenging inauspicious beginning, Banks became one of the Giants' most beloved players of the 1980s era, helping them win two Super Bowls. In some ways, Banks forever remains in the shadow of his Hall of Fame linebacker mates Taylor and Carson. He was selected to just one Pro Bowl. When the Giants inducted their inaugural Ring of Honor class in 2010, Banks was not listed—although linebacker Jessie Armstead was, a fact that puzzled many despite Armstead's solid contributions.

"I didn't spend much time on it," Banks told *The New York Times*. "I know without a doubt that my contributions have always been greatly appreciated by the organization. In due time, if there's another opportunity, I'm sure they'll consider it. But I didn't feel slighted."

Banks has often said the people within the game have always recognized his skills, a point that was proven when he was named

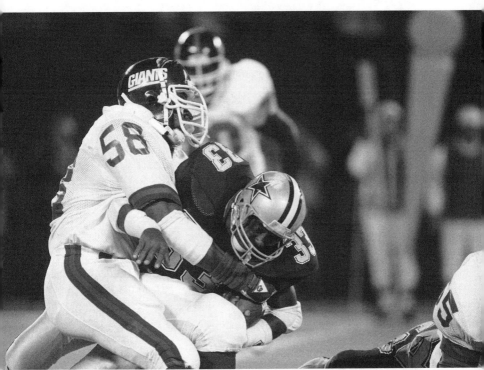

Giants linebacker Carl Banks had big shoes to fill after the "Crunch Bunch" era, but eventually wrapped his arms around enough opponents to earn his own special place in Giants history (AP Photo/Ray Stubblebine)

to the NFL's all-decade team for the 1980s on the second team. In 1989, he was named the NFC Defensive Player of the Year.

Giants fans have always recognized him, too. Whether it was his ability to stop the run or his uncanny ability to neutralize the tight ends he matched up with, Giants fans roared for No. 58.

Banks contributed when he was young and old, from his 14 tackles in Super Bowl XXI in his third year to the greater leadership role he played in helping the Giants to their surprising Super Bowl XXV win over Buffalo.

He's still a familiar voice on WFAN in New York, providing insight on talk shows or handling game analysis with play-by-play man Bob Papa.

Giants Linebackers to Know

Here's a quick look at some Giants linebackers not covered extensively in other sections of the book.

Jessie Armstead (1993–2001)—Five-time Pro Bowler. Led defense with Michael Strahan. Helped lead Giants to Super Bowl XXXV. Versatility allowed him to make 597 tackles, 30 1/2 sacks, and 12 interceptions with the Giants.

Pepper Johnson (1986–1992)—Two-time Super Bowl champ with Giants and part of imposing linebacker crews with Lawrence Taylor, Harry Carson, Carl Banks, and Gary Reasons. Two-time Pro Bowler had 579 tackles, 19 sacks, and 10 interceptions in seven years with the Giants.

Antonio Pierce (2005–2009)—Middle linebacker and confident leader of Giants defense that stunned Tom Brady and the perfect Patriots in Super Bowl XLII. One Pro Bowl, 378 tackles, seven sacks, and four interceptions in five years with Giants.

Gary Reasons (1984–1991)—Two-time Super Bowl champ with Giants; picked off 10 passes in eight years with New York. Most famous for brutal, leaping goal-line hit of Denver's Bobby Humphrey to knock off the Broncos in 1989 and 30-yard run on fake punt that led to game-winning field goal in 1990 NFC Championship Game win over 49ers.

Brian Kelley (1973–83)—Part of the Crunch Bunch crew known as the best in the league with Taylor, Harry Carson, and Brad Van Pelt. Made up for lack of speed with instincts.

As Van Pelt was a member of an intimidating linebacker crew in the early 1980s, Banks helped form a unit that was just as imposing. Along with Taylor, Banks teamed with Gary Reasons and two-time Pro Bowler Pepper Johnson.

By the time they were done, the one-time younger players like Banks and Johnson showed Taylor they could handle replacing one crew of legendary Giants linebackers by adding to the tradition—and helping surpass it.

"When I first got here I wasn't one of the best linebackers we had. I was at the bottom of the barrel," Banks said. "But I worked and worked and worked to be mentioned in the same breath with [the best linebackers of his time]."

62 Good-bye Jim Lee, Hello Allie

For the aging Giants, 1960 marked the end of an era as Coach Jim Lee Howell was gone after six years, one NFL championship, and two Eastern division titles. With assistants Vince Lombardi having left for Green Bay the previous season and Tom Landry going to Dallas that year, the Giants just missed hiring two of the game's most legendary head coaches.

Wellington and Jack Mara brought in Allie Sherman, who had replaced Lombardi as the Giants' offensive coach. At the time, Wellington Mara, at least publicly, said the loss of Lombardi was not that big a disappointment because of the man they hired.

"We had two men in mind from the beginning," Mara said. "When Vinny said no, there was only one man we wanted and that was Allie."

Sherman made sense as a hire for the family-oriented Maras, who lived by their "Once a Giant, Always a Giant" motto. Sherman had been with the Giants as an assistant in the early '50s before moving on to the CFL for a spell. He returned when Lombardi left for Green Bay, replacing him as an offensive coach.

A former quarterback, Sherman opened up the offense, allowing quarterback Charlie Conerly to throw more deep passes—which resulted in Conerly winning the 1959 MVP.

Sherman became a popular Giants head coach, but eventually he became a highly scrutinized one and finally an ex-Giants coach. On the positive side, Sherman's friendly demeanor endeared him to Giants fans as did his input in trades for Y.A. Tittle and receiver Del Shofner, who would form a Pro Bowl duo that connected for many big plays.

The Giants reached the NFL title game three straight times. But they lost all three—the first two to Lombardi's Packers. Along the way, Sherman watched the Giants' popular team age in front of him and helped set up several trades that broke up the team's legendary defense. In the next few years, Rosey Grier and Dick Modzelewski were traded. By 1964, even iconic linebacker Sam Huff was dealt, a move that still leaves him bitter.

According to Huff, Sherman wanted to change former defensive coach Tom Landry's strategy and argued with Sherman about playing with the defense, which had been successful. According to Sherman, he just made deals he thought would help the team. Eventually, after the disappointment of the three NFL title game losses, the Giants began to falter.

An aging roster and poor decisions led to the start of the Giants' 18-year period without a postseason appearance. It also led to Sherman's firing in 1969 following a 37–14 loss to the upstart Jets in the teams' first exhibition game. That was too much to take, and the fans who had offered chants of "Goodbye, Allie" got their wish as he was fired and replaced by former running back Alex Webster.

Sherman later took on another leadership role in the 1990s when New York City Mayor Rudy Giuliani appointed him to head the city's Off-Track Betting agency. That didn't go any better than the end of his time with the Giants, as Sherman was the subject of an expose in the *New York Daily News*, which reported he had mismanaged his job there in many ways.

As for his time with the Giants, Sherman years later recognized that his early '60s teams were good enough to come close to an NFL title but were nearing the end of a dynasty.

"We'd win 12 games a year, but we didn't dominate," Sherman told *The New York Times*. "We did one thing late in the game and we'd win, but we were getting old."

63 Ray Perkins Bridges the Gap

Joe Morris remembered the odd feeling of the NFL scouting combine back in 1982, so many coaches and scouts scrutinizing from afar, leaving players feeling like museum exhibits. He especially recalled Ray Perkins, the Giants head coach, approaching him.

"He walks right up to me, looks me square in the eye," said Morris, the Giants' eventual running back. "I looked him square in the eye, too. He didn't say anything. He just looked at me.

"Joe, you afraid of anything?" Perkins asked.

"My father and God," Morris replied. "That about covers it, coach."

With that, Perkins left.

"One of the strangest things I'd ever seen happen," Morris said nearly 30 years later.

Morris later learned it was not such odd behavior for Perkins, who had been charged with turning the Giants from a ridiculed franchise back into a proud one. He had to make sure he picked the right guys for the job.

After the debacle of The Fumble in 1978, the Mara family made the first big step in hiring general manager George Young.

Young took the next one in '79 by hiring Perkins—whom he had known as a receiver for the Baltimore Colts when Young was an offensive line coach.

Perkins' mission was simple: Win back the fans that burned their tickets in protest after nearly two decades of mediocre-to-awful football.

Perkins succeeded in bridging the gap, helping the Giants earn their first playoff appearance in 18 years in 1981. Just as important, Perkins brought in Bill Parcells as an assistant coach twice—taking him back the second time after Parcells quit to try out the outside world as a realtor. While Parcells went on to win a pair of Super Bowls, Perkins set the foundation for those teams to succeed.

"It was a time in the history of the franchise when they were trying to change the culture," remembered Scott Brunner, the quarterback for the 1981 and '82 team who battled injury-plagued Phil Simms for the job. "[It] had been one of ineptness…[he was] trying to establish an incredible, winning attitude."

Perkins' methods, like his successor Parcells', were not the most endearing. After playing for Bear Bryant at Alabama, Perkins apparently followed his former coach's lead in setting a grueling tone in training camp. It was so grueling that in his first year, players revolted at what they perceived as a dangerous camp excessive even for the highly demanding NFL.

"He was crazy," a member of the Giants who asked not to be named said. "He was nuts."

Perkins backed off—barely. But he continued to work in tandem with Young, who drafted so many key players. Perkins sifted through them regardless of draft status, making sure they were up to the challenge of changing the team's history.

Running back Butch Woolfolk was drafted in the first round in 1982, but Perkins liked Morris enough to push Young to draft him in the second. He gave Morris a chance to fight for—and eventually win—the job. Tight end Dave Young was the team's second-round

Perkins Goes to Alabama

After the success of 1981, Ray Perkins watched his Giants struggle in a strike-shortened '82. There was another quarterback controversy, eventually won by Scott Brunner who held the job after Phil Simms endured yet another injury.

But before the '82 season was complete, Perkins received a call from Alabama. His mentor, Bear Bryant, was retiring, and Perkins was offered the job as his successor. The Giants were 3–3 when Perkins announced that, despite his role in helping the Giants improve, he would take his dream job.

"It's just something I've wanted to do very, very much," he said at a press conference before he left New York.

The Giants reacted quickly, with George Young informing the Maras the best thing for continuity's sake would be to replace Perkins the next season with his right-hand man, defensive coordinator Bill Parcells.

The Giants struggled down the stretch, dropping two of their final three, but Brunner said the coaching move did not catch everyone off guard. "I wasn't surprised," he said. "That was Ray's real love. He went to Alabama [as a student]. We had a couple of Alabama guys on the team, and they would rehash their stories. Roll Tide, all the way.

"It was tough on the team, but we couldn't hold it against him."

pick after Lawrence Taylor in '81, but when he showed up to the '82 camp overweight, Perkins sent him home.

When he returned, Young reportedly had lost some weight but apparently not enough. He collapsed while running one of Perkins' drills. Morris and Woolfolk spotted Young on the ground and attempted to assist him. Perkins saw that and barked out an order.

"You two! You help him up, I'll cut you."

"On command," Morris said, "we drop him, because you have to do what you have to do. I'm thinking, 'Okay, this is gonna be a long process.'"

Young was soon cut from the team.

While Perkins' treatment of players he deemed incapable of helping the Giants could be especially harsh, he offered the players who passed his tests the type of latitude that helped them grow.

The Giants improved to 8–7 in 1981, giving them a shot at the playoffs if they could beat the 12–3 Dallas Cowboys in the final game of the season. In sudden-death overtime, Brunner remembered calling a bootleg as an audible in a big spot. He sprinted for a big gain.

"He came up to me afterward and said, 'Son, if that didn't work, you could have kept on running through the tunnel,'" Brunner recalled with a laugh. "[But] he respected our input. That's what I always appreciated about him. He wasn't locked into his own philosophy."

The Giants won the game and with the Jets' help were back in the playoffs. They even managed to upset the defending NFC champion Eagles in the first round—just three years after the devastating loss to Philly on The Fumble.

The Giants would lose to eventual Super Bowl champ San Francisco the next week, but Perkins' Giants were on the right track. "He was ecstatic," Brunner said. "Everyone in the organization was. He was thrilled. All of a sudden, that was his third year he coached. Kind of validates what he was trying to do."

64 Beating the 'Boys: Crunch Bunch Giants Reach Playoffs

Ray Perkins lifted Joe Danelo onto his shoulders as his way of thanking the Giants kicker for removing the burden from his own, as well as all the Giants who worked so hard to restore this piece of pride. It surged through Giants Stadium where the Giants coach and some players carried Danelo around and the fans roared.

Danelo had just beaten the hated Cowboys with a field goal in overtime on December 19, 1981, giving the Giants a 13–10 win—and, shot at their first playoff appearance since 1963.

Only three years earlier, the noise coming out of the Meadowlands was a steady rage. But now? This was the kind of chaos Giants fans sought.

"It was bedlam at that point when he made it," former quarterback Scott Brunner remembered.

The team would have to wait until the next day to reach the playoffs when the Jets did the neighborly thing and knocked off Green Bay 28–3 to clinch a wild-card spot for the ecstatic 9–7 Giants. The Jets matched their cross-town rival's enthusiasm as the win clinched their first playoff spot since Joe Namath's Jets made it in '69. It marked the first time both teams reached the postseason in the same year, creating a buzz all over New York and New Jersey.

The Giants celebrated with champagne after watching the Jets-Packers game on TV at Giants Stadium.

"Through the efforts of an awful lot of people in our organization," Perkins told the group, "we've got an opportunity to make two toasts—one to the New York Jets and one to our 3:30 start next week in Philadelphia."

The playoff match-up with the Eagles reminded the Giants just how far they had come since The Fumble against Philly three years earlier. So did the cheers of the appreciative crowd as the Giants battled the 12–3 Cowboys in the season finale with their hopes on the line.

Led by the second overall pick, Lawrence Taylor, as well as veterans Harry Carson, Brad Van Pelt, and Brian Kelley, the Giants featured a fearsome quartet of linebackers known as The Crunch Bunch.

While Van Pelt and Kelley would not remain for the team's eventual Super Bowl run, they played a crucial role in making the Giants contenders again.

"Those four guys were as good a group of linebackers as ever played," Brunner said.

An injury cost Van Pelt his shot at the Giants' lone playoff run in his time with the team. But rookie linebacker Byron Hunt would step in and play a crucial role in helping the Giants beat the heavily favored Cowboys.

As often would be the case in his career, second-year quarterback Phil Simms was out with an injury, a separated shoulder forcing him to miss the season's final seven games. Brunner filled in. By his own description, Brunner was "not a great athlete," but his ability to study and read defenses and his conviction in calling audibles helped him lead the Giants to three wins in their last four games before the Dallas contest.

"We were confident," Brunner said. "We were playing at home.... We were on a roll."

Brunner knew the Giants also could rely on bruising running back Rob Carpenter, who the Giants acquired earlier that season. Carpenter was not a flashy All-Pro runner but earned fan favorite status for his ability to grind out tough yards when needed most.

Brunner threw a crucial touchdown pass but also an interception that led to a field goal for the Cowboys. Dallas led 10–7 late when the defense struck.

After Dallas quarterback Danny White pitched to Tony Dorsett, Hunt pounced on the Hall of Fame running back, causing a fumble. George Martin recovered, and the Giants had the ball with about two minutes left.

Five years before a fourth-and-17 play helped define the '86 Giants' season, the '81 Giants faced a fourth-and-13 in the closing moments.

Revenge on the Eagles—And a Big Upset

The Giants didn't waste their return to the playoffs in 1981 with a poor performance. Instead, they shocked the defending NFC champion Eagles 27–21 in the first round before falling to eventual Super Bowl champ San Francisco, 38–24.

New York stunned Philadelphia with a 20–0 lead in the first quarter built largely off Eagles' miscues as well as a key decision by quarterback Scott Brunner and Coach Ray Perkins.

The previous night, Brunner told his coach he wanted to run a play not in the game plan.

"Why you wanna run that?" Perkins asked. "What are you gonna do?"

"I'm gonna hit the halfback in the corner of the end zone," Brunner responded matter-of-factly.

"Okay, okay," Perkins said. "Good play."

Brunner laughed at the memory.

"We got in that situation, and I hit Leon Bright in the end zone," Brunner said of the Giants' first touchdown.

The Eagles eventually came swarming back and seemed set to overtake the Giants. But running back Rob Carpenter did what he did best. He simply ran out the final minutes of the game, rushing left, rushing right, and picking up the necessary first downs one tough yard after the other.

"We knew we could play them," Brunner said of the Eagles. "We knew we could play in their stadium. We just got off to a head start."

Brunner hit John Mistler for 21 yards, keeping the Giants alive.

"Pressure on the right side, had to duck up against the rush," Brunner recalled of the play. "Hit Mistler across the middle. And that kind of got us going, where it got us down the field."

It also got the Giants fans to unleash applause that…well, might have been louder if not for the frigid temperatures.

"It was loud, yeah," Brunner said. "But it was funny because it was so cold everyone's bundled up—it kind of muffled it."

It wasn't as muffled when Danelo kicked a 40-yard field goal to tie the game with 25 seconds left.

In overtime, the Cowboys won the toss, but it didn't matter. The Crunch Bunch was coming.

This time Taylor, who would win Defensive Rookie of the Year honors, attacked Dorsett who fumbled again. The running back appeared to recover, but Taylor offered a hint to one future Hall of Famer that another was in his midst—and on his back.

"I had a chance to pick it up," Dorsett said after the game. "It was a great play by whoever came down on top of me. I had my hand on the ball, and he came down and just took it away."

Like so many Giants kickers through the years in big moments, Danelo missed an important kick before making one.

The Giants got into position for a 33-yard field goal attempt, but Danelo oh-so-painfully bounced it off the upright.

No matter.

Taylor provided another early example of the tenaciousness that marked his career, blitzing White who forced a pass that Hunt intercepted.

The Giants had another chance, and so did Danelo.

He hit a 35-yard field goal to end the game and earn himself a ride around the field.

The Giants were back in the playoffs.

65 Giants Send Romo Back to the Beach

Sixteen seconds remained and Tony Romo prepared for the snap, far removed from the comforting arms of his celebrity girlfriend and their peaceful views on a Mexican beach.

The Dallas Cowboys quarterback found no sand under his feet to kick, only reality slapping him hard in the face.

There were the Giants, the team Romo and the Cowboys had beaten twice in the 2007 season, holding a 21–17 lead in the NFC divisional playoff. There Romo was at the New York 23-yard line on fourth down with one more chance to prove he could finish off the scrappy Giants.

They were known as the Road Warriors now, winners of eight straight games away from home, never packing one bathing suit only an increasingly hard wallop.

The week before while the Giants picked up road win No. 8 in the first round at Tampa Bay, Romo had gone on his own trip during the Cowboys' bye week. He went on a jaunt to Mexico with Jessica Simpson, drawing criticism in Dallas and sparking adrenaline in the Giants' locker room.

There had already been plenty of that.

The Cowboys had gone 13–3 with a squad full of stars and 12 players elected to the Pro Bowl. The Giants, who had allowed Romo to torch them for nearly 600 yards and eight touchdown passes in two games, were not so star-studded.

They sent one player, Osi Umenyiora, to Hawaii for the Pro Bowl after a 10–6 season.

"It is like an all-Pro team vs. an all-Joe team," Giants linebacker Antonio Pierce said in the week before the game. As was often the case with Pierce, a smirk lived beneath the surface. "We are just trying to cover the spread against the all-Pro team. They have seven or eight Pro Bowlers on offense. You can go across the roster and find a Pro Bowler. That is interesting. That is kind of unique in a sense."

The Giants found it even more unique when they learned of Romo's vacation as they prepared for another battle.

New York had no time for frolicking. It had seen cornerback Sam Madison miss the start with an abdominal injury. Cornerback Aaron Ross went out in the third with an injured right shoulder.

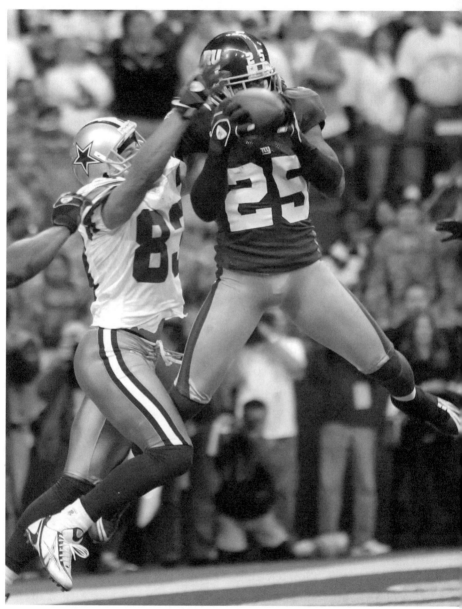

R.W. McQuarters intercepted Dallas quarterback Tony Romo's pass in the final seconds to clinch the Giants' 21–17 win over the Cowboys in the NFC divisional playoff game. The underdog Giants took a big step toward their Super Bowl XLII victory. (AP Photo/Donna McWilliam)

No matter. Corey Webster and R.W. McQuarters stepped in. The Giants had stepped in and up all season since that miserable 0–2 start, blowout losses to Dallas, and Green Bay threatening to take their season before it began.

But now they were in Dallas trying to steal Romo's season. Trying to leave the Cowboys quarterback regretting a trip to one so-called paradise and send him and the 11 other Pro Bowlers to a bittersweet Hawaiian beach trip for the Pro Bowl.

The Giants had come out strong, startling Dallas with a 52-yard touchdown pass from Eli Manning to Amani Toomer for a 7–0 lead. The Cowboys responded with a Romo scoring pass to Terrell Owens, his favorite target in the regular season, to tie the score.

Then the Cowboys went on the type of drive champions do—eating up the clock and beating up the Giants. The Cowboys kept the ball for 10:28 on that second-quarter drive that never seemed to end no matter how many times the Giants pushed Dallas to third down. Finally, Marion Barber ran it in from the 1 and the Cowboys led 14–7.

"I've never been that tired in my life," Pierce admitted later.

But with just 53 seconds left—and the Cowboys threatening to live up to their role as NFC favorites who would finally break an 11-year string without a playoff win—the Giants came back.

Manning, so often maligned throughout his young career for his poor play, drove the Giants down the field, hitting different receivers along the way. Rookie Steve Smith caught a pair. Tight end Kevin Boss, the rookie filling in for an injured Jeremy Shockey, caught a 19-yarder. Finally, Manning found Toomer again, the old Giant scoring from four yards out to tie the game 14–14 with just seven seconds left in the half.

The Cowboys maintained a long drive to open the second half, holding the ball for another eight-plus minutes. But this time the Giants' defense held, and Dallas settled for a field goal.

The Giants did not. Brandon Jacobs scored on a 1-yard run with 13:29 left in the fourth quarter. The all-Joes that had watched the Cowboys run over them in a pair of second halves in the regular season led 21–17.

"What I think you're seeing is the team concept to the Nth degree," Giants coach Tom Coughlin said.

With 16 seconds left, Romo answered with a drive of his own. Unlike his monster games earlier that year, he tossed just 18-of-36 for 201 yards, one touchdown, and one interception. But now he had his chance to send the Cowboys forward.

He stepped back, protected by all those Pro Bowlers on the line, and fired the ball into the end zone. That's where McQuarters stepped in and stepped up for the Giants. His interception all but ended the game, leaving the Giants celebrating and Owens crying for his teammate.

"It's really unfair," a sobbing Owens, usually known for skewering his quarterbacks, said of the criticism Romo received for his Mexican vacation. "That's my teammate. That's my quarterback. You guys do that, it's not fair. We lost as a team."

Fair enough. And the Giants won as one.

They packed for Green Bay and the NFC title game. Bathing suits were certainly not needed.

66 The Debacle at the Meadowlands II

It ended with an image almost as jarring as the one that completed the most infamous loss in Giants history, and it was against the same hated rival. But unlike that sudden nightmare, this one unfolded slowly, and the torment trickled in before it gushed.

Thirty-two years after The Fumble left the Giants speechless, The Punt Return capped a shocking collapse in another devastating loss to Philadelphia for which they had no words.

"You got any?" Giants defensive lineman Justin Tuck said after the Eagles scored 28 points in the final 8½ minutes for a 38–31 defeat of the Giants on December 19, 2010. "I'm searching. I've never been part of anything like this."

Giants fans who remembered a sure victory that became a jaw-dropping loss when Joe Pisarcik fumbled so many years ago knew this feeling all too well. They were almost as stunned to see their rookie punter Matt Dodge kick the ball to dangerous return man DeSean Jackson with just 14 seconds left in regulation.

They were just as heartbroken when Jackson ran back the kick for a game-ending 65-yard touchdown 32 years after Philadelphia's Herman Edwards recovered Pisarcik's fumble and sprinted to the end zone.

In less than nine minutes, the Giants went from being on the verge of clinching the NFC East title and achieving Super Bowl favorite status to a team that would eventually miss the playoffs. "What did I do?" head coach Tom Coughlin said when asked the next day how he had spent the previous night. "I sat in a room with the lights out for about 2½ hours."

When Dodge walked onto the field, the scoreboard at New Meadowlands Stadium revealed a 31–31 tie. The stunned murmurs of the crowd offered a hint that a mere eight minutes earlier, that scoreboard had read Giants 31, Eagles 10.

They had raucously cheered as Eli Manning pumped his fist wildly after his fourth touchdown pass. Having shut down Eagles quarterback Michael Vick as no one had all year, the Giants appeared free to envision a win that would unofficially lock up the NFC East and make them a Super Bowl favorite. But Vick stunned the Giants, passing and running his way all over the field after gaining 157 total yards in the first 3½ quarters. The Giants helped

Vick come back when Coughlin declined to put in a "hands team" for an onside kick, which the Eagles recovered, down 21 with 7:28 left.

"I don't know what was taking place out there," Giants safety Antrel Rolle said. "I really don't. I just know that they were moving the ball, and we weren't stopping them."

With 14 seconds left, amid the silenced crowd, Coughlin and several other Giants scrambled over themselves to bark a specific order to Dodge: Kick the ball out of bounds and away from the speedy Jackson, who had returned two punts for touchdowns the previous season.

"He didn't have to tell me," Dodge said later. "It wasn't rocket science not to kick it to him with [14] seconds left.

"But sometimes," he added, "you don't execute as well as you'd like." The snap from Zak DeOssie came in a tad high, and Dodge hopped up for it slightly. Then he smacked the ball with his right foot, hitting a line drive straight to Jackson.

On the Eagles' sideline, Vick, like everyone else in the stadium, couldn't understand what he was seeing.

"Why would they kick it to DeSean?" he thought to himself.

Jackson, known as a showboating player who had made headlines the previous week for taunting opponents by delaying his trip to the end zone, had begged for a chance to return the kick. Fighting a sprained foot, he had been held in check as a receiver with just three catches. He had little part in the Eagles' comeback, as Vick hit a 65-yard touchdown pass to tight end Brent Celek, scored another on a quarterback draw following the onside kick, and found receiver Jeremy Maclin for the game-tying touchdown.

Due to his injury, Jackson had been held out of return duty, telling coach Andy Reid he would be available only if needed late. Now Jackson got his chance as the line-drive kick came straight at him. But he blew it. Or so it seemed. Jackson fumbled the punt.

Look, Ma! No hands...team

While Tom Coughlin dressed down Matt Dodge for his poor punt, many fans and media felt Coughlin had made his own boneheaded play 7½ minutes earlier. That's when the Eagles, down 21 with 7:43 to play, recovered an onside kick.

Rather than put in his "hands team" (veteran, sure-handed players) to help secure the ball in the event of such a kick, Coughlin said he opted to play for a regular return—because he didn't want to forfeit field position.

The especially head-scratching portion of the strategy was that Coughlin acknowledged anticipating the possibility of the onside kick but still deemed field position was the priority with the Eagles down 21 and running out of time.

"The upside is to try to get field position for your offensive team," Coughlin said. "However, all our people up front, again, were told to watch out for the onside kick."

Granted, the special teams failed in that regard—rookie Duke Calhoun was closest to the ball and was one of several Giants who inexplicably retreated when the ball was kicked despite the warning, making for an easy recovery. Special teams captain Chase Blackburn also later admitted he should have moved some players closer to discourage the kick.

But Coughlin's call was the most confusing.

Even with poor field position, the Giants could have done the most valuable thing possible with a 21-point lead and less than eight minutes left—run off some time.

As the Giants made their way down field, Jackson picked up the ball at his own 34-yard line. He paused for a moment. Then he took a couple of steps back as the Giants rushed. Duke Calhoun, a Giants rookie who had stepped back when he should have moved forward on the onside kick, dived at Jackson, who sidestepped him.

"And when I looked up, I saw a crease and I just shot through that crease," Jackson said.

He shot straight up the middle, leaving a trail of Giants in his wake the way Vick had for most of the final eight minutes. At the Eagles' 37, a desperate Dodge dived at him but missed as Jackson angled right.

DeOssie closed in, but Eagles receiver Jason Avant met him with a violent block that left both men on their back for the remainder of the play—and gave Avant a slight concussion.

From there, Jackson was off to the end zone, pausing only for a taunting stroll along the 1-yard line. The Giants' D.J. Ware, who had passed Jackson when the man cut abruptly to the left for the extra dig at the Giants, could only watch helplessly from the end zone. No matter. Jackson's little show could not make the loss hurt anymore than it already had.

"I've never been around anything like this in my life," said Coughlin who had 41 years of coaching experience to draw on. "It's about as empty as you get to feel in this business, right there."

On the sideline after the game, Coughlin shouted at the rookie Dodge in front of everyone on national TV. But he did not cut Dodge as had been immediately rumored, and the punter himself shook off the criticism and added some of his own.

"There's nothing more you can say," Dodge said after the game. "You can't give the most explosive returner in the game a line drive in a situation like that."

Dodge's teammates, to a man, defended the rookie, rightly pointing out that the game never should have come down to the one play, shocking as it was. They vowed to move on against Green Bay but instead were walloped 45–17 and missed the playoffs despite a 10–6 record.

"Yeah, just shock," Eli Manning said of how he felt walking off the field. "Just kind of, 'How did that happen?'"

67 Tarkenton Scrambles In and Out of Town

He's usually pictured in purple around most of the country, part of the Minnesota Vikings' poster boys for consolation prizes, the 1970s version of the Buffalo Bills. Fran Tarkenton might surely have felt the disappointment and pain of losing three Super Bowls with the Vikings, but he knew just how difficult it was to get there. If nothing else, his time with the Giants taught him that. And in that time, he showed the Giants—and their fans—glimpses of hope during a drought that otherwise provided little.

The Giants were coming off another disastrous season, having gone 1–12–1 in 1966 under head coach Allie Sherman when they managed to deal for Tarkenton—not that the Vikings were that eager to give him up. Known as The Mad Scrambler, Tarkenton's talent was trumped by his clash with head coach Norm Van Brocklin and, apparently, the Vikings in general. His trade demand prompted Van Brocklin's resignation—and Tarkenton still wanted a trade.

Wellington Mara was all too happy to make the deal. And the phrase "too happy" might fit a little too well. The Giants were so desperate to offer their fans a star that they dealt a pair of first- and second-round picks.

Had they not made the trade, the Giants still could have come away with a Hall of Famer that season in eventual Dolphins quarterback Bob Griese. (They also could have foolishly chosen Steve Spurrier, who became a much better college coach than pro quarterback.) They also already had Earl Morrall, who certainly was not as skilled as Tarkenton but had made a habit of connecting deep with Pro Bowl receiver Homer Jones.

62–10: Giants Rout Eagles

Norm Snead, the quarterback who was part of the deal when the Giants sent Fran Tarkenton back to Minnesota, cushioned the blow in 1972. He actually put up better numbers than Tarkenton did that season in leading the Giants to an 8–6 record. Snead and the Giants were especially impressive in setting a club scoring mark with a 62–10 thrashing of the hated—and lowly at that time—Eagles.

Snead threw three touchdown passes—two to Bob Tucker. Ron Johnson, a two-time Pro Bowl running back lost in the vast wasteland that was the Giants in the 1970s, scored twice, and kicker Pete Gogolak set a club record with eight extra points.

Despite the strong start, Snead threw a league-leading 22 interceptions in 1973 and was dealt to San Francisco in the '74 season. Enter veteran Craig Morton—who was all but booed out of town after a pair of bad years but rebounded to take Denver to the Super Bowl in 1977.

The bitterness grew long after Morton left the Giants because they had traded a draft pick to Dallas to acquire him. The Cowboys used that pick to select Randy White—future Hall of Fame defensive lineman.

Not that Tarkenton was a disappointment in his time with the Giants. Far from it, as the Hall of Famer may be the most talented quarterback the team has had. Though his short five-year stay in New York keeps him from being as revered as other top Giants quarterbacks, he held most major NFL passing records when he retired after the 1978 season.

In his five years with the Giants, he threw for 13,905 yards with 103 touchdowns and 72 interceptions. He immediately brought them respect, leading the team back from its awful 1966 effort to a 7–7 season in 1967.

"That was the finest accomplishment of any of my 18 years in professional football," Tarkenton said. "That was a ragamuffin team that played together, played hard, and had soul. That 7–7 team was like being 14–0 with any other team."

The Giants' best year under Tarkenton was 1970 when they went 9–5 and came tantalizingly close to breaking up what would be an 18-year span without a playoff appearance. Tarkenton gave the Yankee Stadium fans some of their best thrills in years—leading the Giants to a 35–33 win over the Redskins when New York outscored Washington 21–0 in the fourth quarter. He also threw a fourth quarter touchdown pass to Ron Johnson to lead the Giants to a come-from-behind 23–20 win over the eventual NFC champion Dallas Cowboys. However, the Giants lost their playoff shot with a loss to the Rams in the season's final week.

Tarkenton had another tiff with management at the end of the 1971 season when he disagreed with the Giants over a business loan and the club traded him back to Minnesota. On their turn in the merry-go-round, the Giants managed just one first- and second-round pick and three other players, including quarterback Norm Snead.

Tarkenton went on to his three Super Bowl losses and eventually starred as a host on a popular 1980s TV show, *That's Incredible.*

68 Spike a Football (Homer Jones Did It First)

The Giants' low-key demeanor through the franchise's history, from Vince Lombardi growling at Alex Webster for taking the slightest of leaps after a long touchdown in the '50s to the team's resistance to cheerleaders even today, is as much a part of the team's tradition as its punishing defense. That's why it's interesting to note the first spike—the very basic celebratory move that eventually led to its sucessors' increasingly creative, attention-grabbing endzone theatrics—originated with the Giants.

It's even more interesting to learn why.

For fans who endured the mid-to-late '60s portion of the Wilderness era of playoff-free football, one of their few joys was watching Homer Jones streak down the field on the receiving end of a long touchdown pass.

Jones put together one of the most impressive stints a Giants receiver has had from 1964–69 for bad to mediocre teams during the lost era for the franchise. In his first year, he caught passes from the retiring Y.A. Tittle. In his final three seasons with the Giants, Jones hooked up with Minnesota Vikings icon Fran Tarkenton, who spent five years in New York. Along the way, Jones led the NFL in touchdown catches with 13 in 1967, had an NFL-long 89-yard reception in 1965, a still-standing team record 98-yard catch in 1966, and averaged 22.6 yards per reception as a Giant.

Jones had plenty of opportunities to slam the ball down in gleeful celebration. Only he didn't thump the ball to the ground with the idea of starting controversy when he introduced the spike in 1965. He did it to avoid one.

Giants icons like Frank Gifford had always thrown the ball in the stands after a touchdown, but in 1965 the NFL banned the practice. The league enforced the new rule with fines that players would chuckle at today, but they intimidated Jones then.

"When I made my first touchdown, I was going to throw the ball in the stands," Jones said in NFL Films' *History of the Giants* video. "In the meantime, I had forgotten they had changed the rules. And I think it was a $500 fine for throwing the ball in the stands.

"And when I crossed the goal line, my ambition was always to throw the ball in the stands, but I thought about that $500 and when it came down to it, I threw it on the ground. So that was the original spike right there. The origin of it."

69 Not-So-Super Bowl XXXV

They returned to the city their predecessors had conquered as Super Bowl underdogs 10 years earlier. The Giants once again had the makings of a feel-good bunch that could pull off a massive upset. Bill Parcells was announced before the Tampa crowd, and memories of the 1990 Giants' ability to slow down the Bills' quick-strike offense filtered through the minds of Giants fans who now hoped to somehow slow down the opposing defense.

Such was the daunting nature of the speedy, ferocious swarm of Baltimore Ravens who set an NFL record for fewest points allowed during the 2000 season.

Jim Fassel's Giants had rallied around his playoff guarantee earlier in the year, and their run inspired a gentle jab from Wellington Mara to the Giants' critics. Mara said the Giants had been the "worst team" to win an NFC title and predicted they would take that back-handed compliment again as Super Bowl champs.

Instead, the Giants succumbed to the Ravens' legendary defense and indeed looked like one of the Super Bowl's worst entries in a 34–7 loss.

"I think Jim nailed it on the head," quarterback Kerry Collins said of his head coach the day after throwing four interceptions in one of the worst games of his career. "It was a great season. It ended with a bad day."

It was as awful a day as the NFC Championship was triumphant. Following a five-touchdown performance in the 41–0 rout of Minnesota, Collins threw the four interceptions and was sacked four times, separating his shoulder in the second half. Collins played through the injury but acknowledged it didn't affect his woeful performance against a Baltimore defense unlike any the Giants had seen.

Led by linebacker Ray Lewis, the Ravens stormed into the game with a defense so speedy, fierce, and dominating, it led to playful questions about the offense's inferiority.

"Both offenses are going to play," Ravens receiver Qadry Ismail joked before the game. "The only controversy is whether [the offenses] get rings. Does the offense share in the championship?"

Ismail earned his share, making a 44-yard catch from quarterback Trent Dilfer, the manage-the-game type of passer who also connected early on a 38-yard touchdown pass to Brandon Stokely. But it was the Ravens defense that often appeared on offense in the sixth-biggest Super Bowl blowout.

Tiki Barber, following a 1,006-yard rushing season, managed just 5 yards on his first four carries and finished with 49 for the game. Collins threw for 112 yards, less than a third of his total against the Vikings.

The Giants' biggest star was punter Brad Maynard, who punted a record 11 times.

The only hints of a chance for the Giants were immediately snuffed out. The first came when Jessie Armstead ran back an interception for a touchdown in the first half—but it was called on a holding penalty. The second came when Ron Dixon returned a Ravens kickoff 97 yards for a touchdown in the third quarter to make it 17–7.

The hope lasted no more than 36 seconds—the time it took for Baltimore's Jermaine Lewis to run back the subsequent kick 83 yards for a 24–7 lead. It was the only time in Super Bowl history teams scored on back-to-back kickoffs.

Ray Lewis made Super Bowl headlines the year before in a much darker way when he was arrested in connection to a murder after the game in Atlanta. Lewis said from the beginning he had nothing to do with the killing and later pled to a misdemeanor charge of obstruction of justice.

A year later, he emerged as the Super Bowl MVP, backing up his bold claim that the Ravens defense was "The best ever! The best ever!" as he shouted on the field after the win.

The Giants could only nod in humble agreement.

70 Tisch, Maras Unite...and Pass Torch

They battled so long, uncle and nephew, not even enjoying two Super Bowl championships together, their feud getting so intense they sat with partitions between their luxury boxes at games. But now Tim Mara had a much bigger battle to fight, facing cancer in 1991, so he decided it was time to give up his half of the New York Football Giants.

With his 1991 sale to Preston Robert Tisch, known more familiarly as Bob, Tim Mara did something that had not been done since his grandfather, Tim Mara, founded the Giants in 1925. He handed over ownership to someone not in the Mara family.

While he and his uncle Wellington were known as opposites—with Wellington's conservative, strict moral code causing him to chafe at some of Tim's less restricted night-life habits—Tim Mara shared some of the older man's thoughts on honoring commitments. He had agreed to the sale for a reported $75 million before the Giants went on their second Super Bowl run, capped by their stunning 20–19 victory over Buffalo. Despite the Giants' sudden increase in prestige, the deal remained the same.

"We agreed on the deal before the Super Bowl and didn't close 'til afterward," Tisch told *The New York Times* upon Tim Mara's death several years later. "He didn't change one word of what we had agreed on even though they became the Super Bowl champions."

The sad family saga of the co-owners and relatives ended with Tim Mara's death in 1995. After a period of years in which they didn't speak at all, the pair did speak in the year before Tim Mara's death, according to a *The New York Times* report.

Tisch fit in smoothly with Wellington Mara as the first non-family member to own a major stake in the team. A former postmaster general and the president of the Loews movie corporation at the time of the sale, Tisch—credited with coining the term "power breakfast"—brought a sharp business-like demeanor to contrast Mara's gentle nature that didn't always consider the bottom line.

"The times have changed," Tisch told *Forbes* in 2003. "The Maras were never businesspeople."

Not that Tisch was a caricature of a soulless business shark. He was also renowned for his philanthropy and his genial nature. Like Giants founder Tim Mara, Tisch said he bought his piece of the team to "keep it in the family."

While Wellington Mara remained the patriarch of the team, and really the league, Tisch stuck to the business end, apparently also affecting how John Mara, Wellington's son and successor, viewed his role.

"One of the first things Bob Tisch told me when he came in was, 'Raise the revenue, cut the expenses,'" John Mara told *Forbes* in 2003. "Everything else in business is bull."

Tisch died just 21 days after Wellington Mara did in 2005. Before Mara passed, Giants players and head coach Tom Coughlin visited him in his Manhattan apartment. By that point, John Mara had taken over the day-to-day operations of the football team. Steve

Tisch, Bob's son and a Hollywood producer who had a hand in classics such as *Forrest Gump* and *The Pursuit of Happyness*, became the club's executive vice president. The family business had spread to two families, with other Mara and Tisch relatives taking on key roles.

71 The USFL and CFL: Keep One Hall of Famer, Lose One

For the briefest of periods, Lawrence Taylor was under contract to play football for Donald Trump. But Taylor never gave Trump the chance to utter the catch phrase he made famous years later on *The Apprentice*. Before Trump could say, "You're fired," to the Giants linebacker—whom he had signed to a contract to play in the NFL's budding rival USFL in 1984, Taylor had two words of his own.

"I quit."

Okay, so it wasn't that simple, and it took some help from the Giants to keep Taylor from intercepting his own legacy with a short-sighted move. Taylor wasn't yet making as much money as he'd like at $190,000 a year. As he wrote in his autobiography, *LT: Over the Edge,* Trump offered him $4 million over five years for a "futures" contract. While Taylor was under contract with the Giants for four more years, Trump signed him to a deal beginning in 1988.

Along with a $1 million payment that Taylor apparently initially recognized as a bonus—but was later labeled a 25-year interest-free loan—the Giants linebacker jumped at the money.

"I got one million in cash, man!" Taylor wrote, recounting what he told his horrified agent. "I don't want to beat this."

The agent explained Taylor could re-negotiate with the Giants, who also expressed shock. Not wanting to lose their talented young linebacker, they hastily renegotiated Taylor's contract—and helped buy him out of the one Trump had offered. Trump would be paid $750,000, and the $1 million would be returned.

"I ended up selling him back to the Giants," Trump said in the LT book. "I did it not because of the money, but because I never felt Lawrence Taylor should be in the USFL. I had too much respect for him as a football player."

Of course, that didn't explain why Trump signed him in the first place, and the buzz his New Jersey Generals got from the idea of adding Taylor to go with Heisman Trophy winner Herschel Walker couldn't have hurt. The push for the extra money Trump offered to play in a less prestigious league came 30 years after another Giants Hall of Famer altered his own legacy.

Arnie Weinmeister is widely considered the greatest Giants defensive lineman of all time. If you're a younger Giants fan, you might now well ask, "Who the heck is Arnie Weinmeister?" If it wasn't for Taylor's agent, George Young, and the Giants, fans might one day have asked the same question about Taylor.

For all of Weinmeister's dominance with the Giants, he left the team to join the Canadian Football League after just four seasons. After playing for the New York Yankees of the All-America Football Conference for two years, Weinmeister joined the Giants. He made the Pro Bowl in each of his years in the league.

As Taylor was for the Giants in the 1980s and '90s, Weinmeister was a pioneer while playing with the Yankees, then the Giants from 1950–53. At 6'4" 235 pounds, he had a size advantage over most players of his era. Making him even more unstoppable, Weinmeister had speed to match. It all allowed him to rush the passer and thrill fans from the defensive side like no one they'd seen before. Sound familiar?

"It was a wonder to see him on the field," Cleveland Browns end Dante Lavelli once told *The New York Times*. "He was one of the first big men who could move that quickly."

But Weinmeister, a Canadian native, returned to his original country to play with British Columbia after a contract dispute with the Giants. The Giants, much like they would 30 years later with Taylor, attempted to block the steal of their game-changing defensive player. But courts ruled against them, saying Weinmeister was now a member of the CFL.

Weinmeister has one of the shortest NFL tenures of any Hall of Famer. And unlike Taylor, his name isn't known among football fans anywhere near as much as it could have been.

72 Landeta, the Wind, and Da Bears: Oh, My!

For the first time since the 1963 championship, the Giants and Bears, two of the NFL's original titans built on testosterone and brute force, were playing in a playoff game. So when they prepared to meet after the 1985 season, throwback coaches Mike Ditka and Bill Parcells were eager to mix it up.

"We were sitting in the steam room saying, 'Wouldn't it be great if the Bears and Giants could meet again in the playoffs?'" Ditka told *The New York Times* the week of the game, recalling a convention meeting between the Giants coach and himself. "I think it's good for football. These are two of the oldest franchises. They have been in the league almost from the beginning. I know I'll get some of the other teams mad at me, but compared to the Bears and the Giants, they're Johnny-come-latelys."

Despite Parcells' old-school style and Ditka's jaw-clenched ode to the past, the Bears especially reminded everyone it was indeed 1985. A cocky bunch, they produced a music video far before the reality TV and Twitter age made attention-grabbing the norm. Along with their traditional gut-pounding defense—led by linebacker Mike Singletary and the aptly named William "The Refrigerator" Perry—and an offense anchored by future Hall of Fame running back Walter Payton, the Bears broke from their old mold. Rambunctious quarterback Jim McMahon flapped his gums and flung the ball for un-Bear-like big plays.

Defensive coordinator Buddy Ryan boasted so many years before his boisterous son Rex took over the Jets. Ryan told reporters one week would not allow the Giants to prepare for his famed "46" defense. The 15–1 Bears were heavy favorites, but the Giants, fresh off a 17–3 win over San Francisco in the first playoff game at Giants Stadium, were not intimidated.

Chicago temperatures were projected to be in the 20s with a nasty wind-chill. But Ditka said the weather would not influence such an important game. Well, except maybe in one way.

"What could be a factor is the wind," he said before the game. "If it comes across the lake, it could be difficult for kicking."

* * *

Twenty-six years and a Super Bowl championship later, former Giants running back Joe Morris tried to be understanding. "Unfortunately the wind in Chicago is a lot different," he said, recalling teammate Sean Landeta's wayward punt fiasco, which became the story of the Giants' 21–0 loss to the Bears.

Morris didn't get too far in his empathy. "I wanted to kill him," he said of his thought immediately after the kick. "Guy shanks a punt—you're looking at him, too. 'What the hell do you do all week?'"

Ah, the infamous players against punters and kickers routine. It's as old as the powerhouse Bears-Giants rivalry. The anger didn't last past the initial sight of watching the wind-blown ball graze off Landeta's foot—and get returned by the Bears' Shaun Gayle for a 5-yard touchdown. It gave the Bears a 7–0 lead in the

Bears-Giants Playoff History

NFL Championship Games

1933—L—at Chicago, 23–21, December 17, (Head coach Steve
  Owen, 11–3 reg. season)
1934—W—vs. Chicago, 30–13, December 9 (Owen, 8–5)
1941—L—at Chicago, 37–9, December 21, (Owen, 8–3)
1946—L—Chicago, 24–14, December 15, (Owen, 7–3–1)
1956—W—vs. Chicago, 47–7, December 30, (Jim Lee Howell, 8–3–1)
1963—L—at Chicago, 14–10, December 29 (Allie Sherman, 11–3)

NFC Playoff Games

1985—L—at Chicago, 21–0, January 5 (Head coach Bill Parcells, 10–6)
1990—W—vs. Chicago, 31–3, January 13 (Parcells, 13–3)

first quarter, and with that wind and their defense, it seemed like a lot more.

But after the initial frustration, Morris and the Giants realized there was no point in bashing the punter. "How many times has Sean dropped the ball on his foot and made a [great] kick?" Morris said. "He was trying to make an effort to kick the damn ball…. Can't do anything about it. Out there playing. If he makes a big kick, guess what? We're glad we've got him."

Landeta would make plenty of big kicks for the Giants, especially the next season in the NFC Championship Game against the Redskins. He would become arguably their greatest punter as part of a 23-year professional football career.

But he will always be remembered for the wind-blown football folly that left him all but helpless. "The wind just blew it," Landeta said after the game. "I did everything normal, but when I dropped the ball, I saw it moving."

He later acknowledged the tedious ordeal of one person after another asking him what happened so many years later. The answer was right there for everyone to see, he figured. The wind moved it, and he muffed it.

The game is remembered for Landeta's (non-)kick, but he can barely be blamed for the loss. In a game so frigid both quarterbacks wore gloves, the Giants were as overmatched against the Bears as Landeta was against the wind.

The Bears, who went on to crush New England in the Super Bowl 46–10, sacked Phil Simms six times and limited Morris to 32 yards rushing. McMahon hit Dennis McKinnon with a pair of touchdown passes in the third quarter to put the game away.

Mostly, the loss served a strong purpose for the Giants, even if it came in the future. Many of them later credited the bitter feeling for giving them increased focus the next season.

"What I remember most about that game, we knew we were a tough team, thought we were a good team, but the Bears were tougher," Morris said. "We knew we had to get our playoff games at home."

73 Take a Look at Your Official NFL Game Ball

On one side of the shiny gold NFL logo and opposite the commissioner's signature is the nickname that has been imprinted on every official ball. It shows just how much of an impact Wellington Mara left on the game.

"The Duke." That's what the football is called in honor of Mara—named by his father for the Duke of Wellington and nicknamed "The Duke" by Giants players when he was a boy. The league's teams unanimously voted to offer Mara that honor in March 2006, five months after his death.

"I can think of no tribute that would have pleased Wellington Mara more," Giants GM Ernie Accorsi said at the time. "Because what Mr. Mara was most passionate about was the game and the playing of the game on the field."

As touching as the honor was, it was trumped only by one small fact. It's the second time the league named the ball for him. Legendary Chicago Bears owner George Halas suggested labeling the ball "The Duke" in 1941 when Halas and Wellington's father, Tim Mara, arranged for Wilson Sporting Goods to become the league's official game-ball supplier. The elder Mara's role in completing the deal inspired Halas to pay tribute to Mara's son, and the NFL agreed.

For almost 30 years, Mara's moniker adorned the ball until the NFL-AFL merger in 1970 prompted the league to opt for a re-design. But "The Duke" returned in 2006 and is expected to remain part of the football for the foreseeable future.

"He loved his relationships with the players, the coaches, the scouts, the equipment people, the trainers; all the people who make our game possible," John Mara, Wellington's oldest son and the current team president said when the move was announced. "'The Duke' football is a fitting acknowledgement of those relationships and my father's devotion to our league and our sport."

74 Simms Goes Down, Hoss Steps Up

Once again an injury derailed Phil Simms' season. Only this time, the misfortune didn't just cost a Giants quarterback a chance he had fought so hard for—it offered one. When Simms broke his foot in the 1990 Giants' Week 15 Super Bowl preview against Buffalo, Jeff Hostetler stepped in and secured his own legacy.

By the time Hostetler was done, the West Virginia University graduate known as Hoss, who had spent a football lifetime waiting for promises to be fulfilled, would lead the Giants to a Super Bowl victory and take Simms' job the next season.

"Yeah," Hostetler said amid the Giants' celebration after their 20–19 win over the Bills in Super Bowl XXV, "it was worth the wait."

The wait started for Hostetler at Penn State where he didn't get to play. He decided to transfer to West Virginia, where he played for Don Nehlen—and ended up marrying the coach's daughter, Vicky. The Giants drafted him in the third round in 1984, but as the third-string quarterback behind Simms and Jeff Rutledge, Hostetler didn't get his first start at quarterback until 1988. He filled in for an injured Simms against New Orleans and made the most of the chance by throwing an 85-yard touchdown to Stephen Baker in the first half. Regardless, Coach Bill Parcells subbed Rutledge in the second half, and a frustrated Hostetler called for a trade in the locker room after the game.

"I couldn't believe it," Hostetler said later.

Regardless, the Giants wouldn't trade him, and all he could do was continue biding his time. Finally, his frustration boiled over in 1990 when, after seven years and two starts, he told his wife he would quit football after that week's game.

The Giants had started the season 11–2, but just like in 1986, he didn't feel a part of it. That's the game in which Simms broke his foot. Suddenly, Hostetler had to take over a playoff-bound Giants team.

"I played behind one of the all-time Giants' best quarterbacks; he holds all the records," Hostetler said later that year. "But I've always believed I could play, and my teammates believed I could play. I'm just thankful to God for the opportunity."

Once he got it, Hostetler didn't let go of it. He passed for two touchdowns and rushed for 43 yards in the playoffs against Chicago. The Giants adapted their offense to suit the quarterback's mobility by implementing more bootlegs and roll-outs.

Quarterback Jeff Hostetler waited his whole career for a chance to play and finally got it when Phil Simms was injured in 1990. The Giants utilized Hostetler's mobility and "Hoss" helped lead them on a surprising Super Bowl run. (AP Photo/Mark Lennihan)

Against San Francisco in the classic NFC Championship Game, Hostetler absorbed a blow by ex-teammate Jim Burt that caused a hyperextended knee, but he returned on the Giants' next series. "It hurt like crazy, but at this point in my season and at this point in the game and, really, at this point in my career," Hostetler said after the Giants' 15–13 win, "I knew I wasn't coming out."

He led the Giants to the final game-winning field-goal drive, then helped them stun Buffalo in the Super Bowl. While the Giants defense shut down the high-scoring Bills, so did Hostetler and the offense with their clock-killing drives. Hostetler finished 20-of-32 for 222 yards and a touchdown.

He had won a Super Bowl and a shot at the starting quarterback job he coveted.

The next season, after Coach Bill Parcells stunned the team with his resignation, Ray Handley took over. One of his first big moves was to create a quarterback competition between Hostetler and Simms, who once again did not take kindly to the idea.

Hostetler brought back good memories by winning the *Monday Night Football* season-opener against the 49ers in 1991 and went 7–5 in his 12 starts. But Hostetler broke his back against Tampa Bay, and Simms finished out the season.

The next year Simms won back his job but eventually was lost to another injury and Hostetler filled in, starting in Week 6 until a concussion ended his season early. When Dan Reeves replaced Handley as head coach, he eliminated the controversy, keeping Simms as Hostetler was let go. Hostetler joined the Raiders and earned a trip to the Pro Bowl and the playoffs, but he never again approached his Super Bowl success.

"I was really excited to be in a Super Bowl, playing," Hostetler said that day. "I didn't have any nerves. I felt good. I just felt good."

75 Joe Morris and Rodney Hampton

Joe Morris sat in the film room as a rookie with the Giants, looking intently on the screen. When he first arrived at Syracuse University, Morris had waved off his head coach's talk that he would make the NFL; he just expected to use his scholarship to get a job and become a teacher. He never imagined he would break the school record for rushing, passing NFL Hall of Famers Jim Brown and Floyd Little and Heisman Trophy winner Ernie Davis in the process.

But now he was doing his best to make the Giants team, wondering why they had drafted him in the second round when they took running back Butch Woolfolk in the first. As he stared at the screen, Morris couldn't help but ask about the player dwarfed by all the others.

"Who's that little guy in the huddle?" Morris remembered asking.

"Joe," the reply came, "that's you."

The 5'7" running back absorbed the laughter of his teammates and coaches but didn't share it.

"Oh, my freaking God," he thought. "I'm going to get killed."

No, he would not. What he would do was become the Giants' leading all-time rusher and an integral part of their resurgence in the '80s as well as their first Super Bowl team in 1986. He endured head coach Ray Perkins' intense training camp his rookie year and hung around long enough in his battles with Woolfolk that when the first-round pick got injured in 1984, Coach Bill Parcells told Morris he was in the game "until I tell you you're out."

Sure, Morris would still have to fend off George Adams the next year when the Giants picked the back in the first round. But by that point, Morris wasn't letting anyone steal his job. This was the chance he had sought since he was a rookie, the one he had patiently waited for the way he would learn to just as patiently anticipate a block that could spring the speedy running back on another big run.

He would have plenty of those, always sure to thank his linemen and especially fullback Maurice Carthon. Without them, Morris said, he wouldn't have helped lead the Giants to that championship. He still gets a tear in his eye when he sees his old linemen and remembers what they accomplished together. There's plenty to recall.

That breakout year in 1985 when Morris rushed for a then-team-record 1,336 yards and 21 touchdowns. The 1,516 rushing yards he recorded to top it the next season. The back-to-back games of 181 yards rushing against Washington and Dallas in '86. The 159 yards rushing against San Francisco in the playoffs that year, the 87 yards in the NFC Championship Game and of course, the 67 yards and a touchdown in Super Bowl XXI when Phil Simms took center stage.

"It's one of those things that, it's the culmination of everything you've ever done in athletics—it's the biggest stage in the world," Morris said. "Nothing else like it. To be honest, to have my name in the program—starting running back for the New York Giants, a team with so much tradition—it was an honor."

Morris finished with one more honor before his time with the Giants ended. The player who never imagined he could have broken the records of Brown, Little, and Davis in college now found himself breaking the records of Alex Webster and Frank Gifford in the NFL. He gained 5,296 yards rushing for the Giants to set the team record.

In 1990, after missing the previous season with a broken foot, Morris faced another challenge. There was another first-round draft pick named Rodney Hampton as well as veteran teammate Ottis Anderson with which to compete.

This time Morris, age 30 at the time, could not hold on to his job, and the Giants released him.

"When you leave, it's very difficult—it's hard," said Morris, who finished his career with a year in Cleveland. "[But] people treat me with a respect and a kindness that's very uncommon. People remember stories and things I have done.… They tell me about a play; they tell me about their dad loving me.… The way I'm treated.… Giants fans are such good people. Giants fans are really good people."

* * *

Morris' exit marked Hampton's entrance. The first-round pick out of Georgia made an immediate impact, scoring on his first play as a Giant—an 89-yard run in the preseason against the Bills.

He spent the year as Anderson's backup while the Giants made another Super Bowl run. Hobbled at times by a sore ankle, Hampton still managed 455 yards and a 4.2 per carry average as a rookie. He did not get a chance to spell eventual Super Bowl MVP Anderson in the Giants' 20–19 win over the Bills, nor did he play in the NFC title game win over San Francisco—Hampton fractured his fibula in the divisional playoff win over Chicago.

During the next eight seasons, Hampton was the face of the transition between eras, the Super Bowl Giants fading and giving way to the Ray Handley/Dan Reeves/Dave Brown Giants who managed a playoff appearance in the last seasons for Lawrence Taylor and Phil Simms.

Before San Francisco humbled the Giants 44–3, Hampton led them to a 17–10 win over Minnesota in the first round, rushing for 161 yards and two third-quarter touchdowns—including a 51-yarder. He rushed for more than 1,000 yards in five straight seasons, made the Pro Bowl twice, and mostly toiled in anonymity as the Giants struggled through a down period. Lacking the cutback ability and speed of Morris, Hampton was more of a grinder known for his grace off the field and his power on it.

Hampton eventually surpassed Morris as the Giants' all-time leading rusher with 6,897 yards.

In 1997, the first-round pick whose presence helped usher out the preceding Giants' all-time leading rusher, found himself in a similar situation. That year, the Giants found a rookie running back, Tiki Barber, who helped the team to another resurgence and a playoff spot. Facing a trade, Hampton retired after the season, leading the way for Barber to pass him on the club's all-time rushing list as he had once passed Morris.

"I have a lot of pride about my career," Hampton once said. "I look back and I feel like I did pretty well. I get respect from the fans, and I get to do a lot of things in the New York area. I've been blessed to have played in New York."

76 Kyle Rote, Alex Webster, and Joe Morrison

The trio of Kyle Rote, Alex Webster, and Joe Morrison helped lead the Giants offense in the 1950s and '60s glory years as the versatile players complemented other stars like quarterbacks Charlie Conerly and Y.A. Tittle and running back Frank Gifford.

They also connected with fans and the Giants organization, as Rote and Webster became deeply embedded in Giants lore, and Morrison, who was one of the longest tenured Giants, playing with them for 14 years, had his number retired—though there's some question as to how that happened.

There was no question about Rote's talent as the All-American tailback from SMU was the No. 1 overall pick in the 1951 draft. Rote was a multi-talented threat for SMU, once rushing for 115 yards and three touchdowns and passing for 146 yards in a game against Notre Dame.

But a leg injury early in his Giants career cost him what could have been an even more impressive career than he had while making four straight Pro Bowls as a running back and split end. "He would have been the greatest player of all time," said Gifford, who was drafted by the Giants the next season. "Unbelievable athlete."

As it was, Rote still managed to help the Giants to their 1956 NFL championship and four division titles while gaining 5,668 yards from scrimmage. He retired as the Giants' team leader in many receiving categories. Amani Toomer, who eventually put his name atop most of Rote's old records, once said it was "an honor" to be compared to the player revered for his class. Many of Rote's teammates offered him an even greater honor. More than a dozen teammates are said to have named their sons after him.

"He was the ultimate captain," teammate Sam Huff said.

Like Huff, Gifford, and so many of his former Giants teammates, Rote became a broadcaster after he retired from the Giants in 1961, working for NBC in the 1960s and '70s.

Rote's own son, Kyle Rote Jr., became a Hall of Fame soccer player, thanking his late father for his influence in his acceptance speech in 2010.

* * *

Webster was known as Big Red and fans loved his bruising, battering style on the field and his genial nature off it. He joined the Giants after a stint in the Canadian Football League with the Montreal Alouettes, where he was named an All-Star in 1954.

Webster began as a right halfback to Gifford's left halfback in the Giants offense of the mid-1950s. The pairing worked well for the Giants, who won the 1956 crown, lost the famed '58 NFL Championship game, and captured six Eastern Division titles in Webster's 10 years with the team.

In 1961, head coach Allie Sherman switched Webster to full-back, and the move paid off. Webster never looked at himself as the type of nimble running back Gifford was. He provided a contrast, one perfectly suited for fullback.

"I was a different style of player," Webster said on the MSG Network show *Giants Chronicles*. "I was a head-on and he was a shifty type of runner. As big as I was, I was the slowest guy in the backfield."

He found enough speed to gain a career-high 928 yards in 1961 when he shifted to fullback. For his career, he gained 4,638 yards rushing and 2,679 yards receiving.

Webster's popularity was immense—maybe too much so. As another example of the Mara way, the owners hired Webster as a backfield coach when he retired after the 1964 season. Which would have been fine, but the Giants began their descent into the Wilderness Era—the period when they went 18 years without a playoff appearance.

Head coach Allie Sherman was fired, and Webster was named the new head coach—a position he admits might not have been his best. He spent five years as the man in charge, but his pride as a two-time Pro Bowler and his 29–40–1 record eventually pushed him to resign. He told Wellington Mara he just wasn't cut out for the job.

"Worst mistake of my life," he said on *Giants Chronicles* of becoming a head coach. "To become head coach, you're more of a disciplinarian, which I was not."

* * *

Webster, according to various reports, made another mistake as coach, though it came off the field. When Morrison retired in 1972 after 14 years, one of the longest stints a Giant has had with the club, Webster, in his duties as coach, apparently misspoke.

He claimed it was "great to retire Joe's number" instead of simply announcing the retirement as planned, according to the reports. Morrison might not have been the Giants' flashiest star, but he was a versatile one who played six positions for the team. That type of utility work surely went over well with Mara, who was been known to appreciate the unsung players, like linemen, the most.

Morrison retired as the Giants' career receptions leader at the time with 395 yards and gained 4,993 yards and 47 touchdowns. He also had 2,474 yards rushing and 18 touchdowns on the ground. He went on to coach in college football before his death in 1989 at 51.

"He was the ultimate team player," Mara told *The New York Times* after Morrison's death. "Run the ball, catch, play on the special teams, anything."

77 Simms to...LT? Icons Say Good-bye

One always has to come when the other is going, such is the routine for players on either side of the ball. So in an odd way, it made sense that two of the Giants' most legendary players, despite playing their last game together, would have their jerseys retired a year apart.

Lawrence Taylor and Phil Simms wrapped up an era that brought the Giants their first two Super Bowl wins, and both players finished their careers with a 44–3 playoff loss to San Francisco on January 15, 1994.

Simms, who had to fight for every inch with the Giants, whether he was battling injury or the team's doubts, fittingly departed after one more scrap. Despite a strong season, the advent of free agency and the salary cap inspired the Giants to cut Simms, who bitterly attempted to find another team for which he could play. He was not successful, but during the search, he initially declined the Giants' offer to retire his jersey.

Taylor, whose fights had always been with his own demons, knew immediately after the 49ers loss that he would no longer battle on a football field.

"I think it's time for me to retire," he said, crying. "I've done everything I can do."

So it turned out that Taylor's No. 56 was retired on October 10, 1994, and Simms' No. 11 was taken out of circulation the following September. On his night, Taylor slipped on his familiar blue No. 56 jersey over his civilian clothes as the fans roared for "LT! LT!"

"This is about me and you, Giants fans," he said. "You've always been there. No matter what was said, no matter what was written, no matter what happened in my personal life, we've always been in this together. Without you, there would've been a Lawrence Taylor, but there wouldn't have been an LT."

Nearly a year later as Simms prepared for his night, he found a way for his defensive counterpart to stay on the field with him instead of criss-crossing as usual. The pair recounted the story to NFL Films, recalling how an image that remains with Giants fans was born.

Simms had not wanted to make a speech. He wanted to say thank you and throw one more pass. So when he saw Taylor in the tunnel before the game, he asked him to come on the field with him.

"Of course," Taylor said. The pair had not spoken for a couple of years before that, Taylor said, but he wanted to be there for his friend, and the hug they shared told him he had done the right thing. Out on the field, Simms told the crowd he wanted to throw one more pass—to Taylor. Taylor, dressed in a sports coat and wearing flip-flops, smiled nervously.

"Man, make sure it's a good pass," Taylor told Simms as he hugged him before going out for the pass.

"All of a sudden, it kind of hit me—I put Lawrence in a really tough spot," Simms said later, laughing.

Taylor thought he was catching a screen. Simms waved for his friend to go out farther.

And farther.

"He looked at me and he said, 'No, no, no, no. Go," Taylor recalled. "'Go?' He wants me to run. And he throws this big old bomb down the field."

Taylor joked he would have had to run out of the stadium if he had dropped it. But he did not. He ran under the pass and caught it, taking a few more steps as Giants fans roared one final time for the end of an era. Simms and Taylor had connected, the offense and defense coming together just this once.

78 Do Not Throw a Snowball

It's one of the most embarrassing days in Giants history, and the most sobering statement is that the humiliation had nothing to do with the 17–3 lead the team blew. It had everything to do with a massive outbreak of behavior that morphed from child-like to childish to outright dangerous, irresponsible, and stupid by the end of a 27–17 loss to San Diego.

The Snowball Game.

It goes down not just in Giants infamy but in awful sports-crowd moments—right up there with Bill Veeck's disco demolition night in Chicago, when fans threw records on the field, and the obviously flawed 10-cent beer night in Cleveland.

Giants fans, disgusted by the team's miserable play in the last week of a 5–11 season and emboldened by snow that hadn't been cleared from the stands at Giants Stadium, took to pelting anyone on the field with icy outrage. The toll for the disastrous day in December 1995: 115 people arrested, 15 injured, and 75 season-ticket holders who were punished by having their tickets revoked.

The Giants took out a full page ad in a San Diego newspaper apologizing to the Chargers—whose 60-year-old equipment manager, Sid Brooks, was knocked to the ground by an iceball—and their fans.

"We don't want this to be a police state, but we also don't want this to be a home for rowdiness," Wellington Mara said in announcing the revocation of season tickets. "Something has to be done. People buy tickets and have every right to feel safe."

While the snowball-throwing might have seemed amusing at first, it became less so as the game wore on and, as many have surmised, the alcohol took effect.

The worst moment came when Brooks was drilled with an iceball in the head. Brooks fell to the ground, his body slowly folding from the impact. "He wasn't moving or anything," Chargers defensive end Chris Mims said after the game. "I couldn't believe the fans were still trying to hit him. From that distance, getting hit in the face with a snowball is like getting hit in the face with a baseball."

The Giants had struggled through another poor season with quarterback Dave Brown leading the way. The Chargers had a playoff spot on the line and were rallying from a 17–3 deficit, cutting the lead to 17–10 early in the fourth quarter.

Given the December 23 game's proximity to Christmas, the cold weather, and the Giants' poor season, many season-ticket holders had given away their seats for the day. Adding to the other factors that caused a large portion of the fans to ignore warnings the Giants could forfeit the game was the simple presence of the snow. The New Jersey Sports and Exposition Authority's decision not to bother shoveling the snow from the stands, though it had fallen two days earlier, reportedly contributed to the bitterness.

Fans had to be especially bitter to see Shaun Gayle—who had scored a touchdown on Sean Landeta's infamous muffed punt 10 years earlier for the Bears—return an interception 99 yards for a 24–17 lead. Regardless, the increasing bombardment of snowballs—which were flung at Gayle as he reached the end zone—brought national shame on Giants' fans.

"And there are still morons throwing snowballs, even through all this," NBC announcer Marv Albert told the audience after Brooks collapsed. "Very ugly scene here at Giants Stadium."

The officials decided to finish the game despite the fans' failure to heed the warning and Giants coach Dan Reeve's admission that he would argue against a forfeit if necessary.

One fan, Jeffrey Lange, became the face of the incident as an Associated Press photographer caught him winding up to throw a snowball, and he was featured on the front page of the *New York Post*. The Giants called for a $1,000 reward for anyone who could identify him and callers managed to do just that, resulting in his arrest on a disorderly conduct charge. Lange, who had a prior record, balked at the attention paid him.

"It's like being thrown out there like a piece of meat to the lions," Lange said at a news conference. "It's absurd. I can't believe I've been singled out." He later said he lost his job because of the incident and claimed he had only thrown snowballs at fellow fans, not toward the field.

Fifteen years later, Giants fans still reminisce about the incident, filling up message boards, some with shame, some with glee. Most agree that it was an odd bit of mob behavior that started off innocently but got out of hand and put a black mark on a fan base usually known for its class.

79 Remember the Giants Service Men

The Giants had clinched the Eastern Division and were playing a relatively meaningless season finale against the Brooklyn Dodgers as they prepared for the next week's NFL title game against Chicago. But there was plenty to celebrate as future Hall of Famer Alphonse "Tuffy" Leemans was getting a day in his honor.

So the fans did not pay much attention when the message came over the public address system shortly after the game started. "Attention please," the announcer said. "Here is an urgent message: Will Col. William J. Donovan call Operator 19 in Washington immediately?"

Only after the game, when all armed personnel were asked to report to their stations, would fans find out why the colonel had been paged on December 7, 1941. The naval base at Pearl Harbor had been bombed by Japanese aircraft.

"At halftime our coach, Steve Owen, told us about Pearl Harbor," Jim Poole, a Giants end then, remembered. "He gave us such a bad account of all the bad things that happened there; it was like we didn't want to go back out on the field." The Giants went back on the field—and did so again two weeks later when just 13,341 fans bothered showing up to see the Bears defeat them for the NFL title.

Today, the concept of a mass exodus of NFL players to the military seems odd despite two current wars going on. Arizona's Pat

Tillman was lauded as a rare symbol of sacrifice when he forfeited a hefty contract to serve his country after the September 11 terrorist attacks in 2001. The symbol became that much more stark when he was killed in Afghanistan by friendly fire.

But after Pearl Harbor, players immediately chose service over sport. The league was left with mostly older players since those in their prime used their strength to fight in World War II. The NFL nearly folded, losing some teams along the way while others merged. The Giants, like many teams, called some old favorites— like Ken Strong, Mel Hein, and Cal Hubbard—out of retirement.

Despite the desperation to fill rosters, not a single NFL team acquired a black player until 1946, continuing what had been considered an unofficial ban since the mid-1930s. The military service of African Americans did help shame the league—and the country—into being more inclusive, and the league began to re-integrate in 1946.

Several Giants responded to the bombing with the desire to defend their country.

"When the Japanese bombed Pearl Harbor, my dad enlisted, like a lot of other men," John Danowski said about his father, Ed, the Giants former quarterback. "That's who those men were. Very selfless."

Jack Lummus, a rookie receiver who had played in nine games and caught one pass for five yards, enlisted, too. Unlike Danowski, he would not return.

Neither would 6'6", 250-pound tackle Al Blozis, who persisted in his attempt to enlist even after he was turned down several times due to a size requirement that deemed him too big. He was not accepted into the armed forces until 1943. Instead, he earned Pro Bowl honors one year and All-Pro status another. On furlough, Blozis played in the 1944 championship loss to Green Bay.

Another Attack 60 Years Later

Sixty years later, the Giants had just flown back from Denver when the nation was attacked on September 11, 2001. Only a couple of hours after the Giants landed at Newark Liberty International Airport, one of the sets of hijackers took off from there. The plane eventually went down in Pennsylvania thanks to the heroic efforts of passengers who had already heard of other planes crashing into the World Trade Center and Pentagon.

Less than a month later, the Giants again played as war broke out; this time President George W. Bush announced to the nation that America had retaliated against al-Qaeda in Afghanistan.

The Giants and the New Jersey Sports and Exposition Authority decided not to make an official announcement at Giants Stadium. The choice upset some fans, who believed they had a right to know. News did travel through some parts of the stands, however. Unlike the case in 1941, fans had access to mini-TVs, radios, and cell phones.

"You see people all in the stands who had radios or TVs," NJSEA president James DiEleuterio said that day. "There's all sorts of ways to get the information."

Six weeks later, Second Lieutenant Blozis was killed in France. He had insisted on combat after being given a desk job. The Giants retired his No. 32 jersey.

"If he hadn't been killed, he could have been the greatest tackle who ever played football," Hein said. "He was good his first year; the second year he was great."

First Lieutenant Lummus died in the famed Battle of Iwo Jima. He had been credited with almost single-handedly wiping out three Japanese strongholds before stepping on a land mine. His legs were blown off, and Lummus died later. Before he did, the 29-year-old former Giants split end managed to let his surgeon know something.

"I guess the New York Giants have lost the services of a damned good end," he said.

80 The Babe Ruth of Football

You may not instantly recognize the name Benny Friedman, but here's what you should know. Without him, there's little chance you would know the names Eli Manning, Phil Simms, Y.A. Tittle, or Charlie Conerly. You might not have even learned the names Dan Marino and Steve Young, the legendary quarterbacks who seemingly overshadowed Friedman's Hall of Fame induction in 2005.

What Babe Ruth did for the home run and baseball, Friedman did for the forward pass and the NFL. The pair of pioneers played at the same time, but as the decades passed, Ruth's legend grew while Friedman's diminished.

A hefty, melon-shaped ball and the game's rules made passing such a disadvantage that an incompletion in certain situations resulted in a turnover. But Friedman's ability to pass so thrilled fans—still tiptoeing toward professional football—that the league loosened the passing restrictions, setting a preliminary stage for future quarterbacks.

"Friedman was the first pro quarterback to recognize the potential of the pass," Chicago Bears player, coach, and owner George Halas said. "Until Friedman came along, the pass had been used as a desperation weapon."

How impressive was Friedman? He inspired Giants owner Tim Mara to acquire an entire team to get him—and he proved to be worth the move. Mara's Giants lost anywhere from $40,000 to $54,000 in 1928, according to various reports. The Giants couldn't even attract fans for free—other than the famed Red Grange's appearance with a visiting team in 1925 when 70,000 folks came to watch.

Mara purchased the Detroit Wolverines mostly to secure Friedman. Such was the legend of Friedman who not only offered football's most dangerous running/passing combination but also attracted more fans than any player not named Grange. At that point, college football's popularity surpassed that of the budding pro game, and Friedman's former status as a two-time All-American at Michigan had made him valuable in the NFL.

The move worked. The Giants turned a profit of $8,500 in 1929—the year of the Wall Street crash and the start of the Great Depression. Friedman led the Giants to a 13–1–1 record a year after they had gone 4–7–2.

His 20 touchdown passes stood as a season record for years. His mark as the only player to lead the league in rushing and passing touchdowns has yet to fall.

Eventually, he commanded $10,000 a year during the country's darkest economic days. He left the Giants after they selected teammate and his co-coach Steve Owen over him as the team's sole head coach in 1931. With the Giants struggling financially, Friedman returned later that season but left again after Mara denied him a piece of ownership. The Giants, Mara told him, were reserved for his sons.

Friedman had faced his own dark times. The son of orthodox Jewish immigrants from Russia, he had battled anti-Semitism at Michigan before getting along better with his second coach there, according to Murray Greenberg's acclaimed book, *Passing Game: Benny Friedman and the Transformation of Football.*

Friedman had a reputation as a braggart, Greenberg wrote. It became a Catch–22 with Friedman's legacy suffering and him trying to remind people of why it should not have. Frustrated by annual Hall of Fame snubs, Friedman pushed harder, crowing about his admittedly impressive resume and frequently writing *The New York Times* to remind voters of his credentials.

The plan might have backfired as voters appeared turned off by the boasting, according to Greenberg. Friedman's induction did not come until 2005, 23 years after he died. His nephew David spoke for him so many years after he led the way for quarterbacks like Marino and Young.

"To know my uncle, you would have to understand that he never sought out the easy way of doing things," Freidman said from the podium. "He enjoyed being able to do things few others could do, or do as well as he. So...my uncle chose the more difficult way to distinguish himself as a quarterback."

81 Gogolak: The Kicker Who Changed the NFL—Twice

He had never seen a football game in Hungary, so when Pete Gogolak watched one as a teenager in upstate New York, he nudged his father and asked why all the kickers struck the ball so strangely. Instead of the sideways motion he had known and loved from soccer fields all over his homeland, these folks kicked the odd, oblong ball head-on. "Hey Dad," he said, "what a funny way to kick a football."

By the next year, recognizing the lack of soccer teams, the teenager grew interested in the new sport where he would eventually become the person getting the strange looks. His high school coaches, then his college coaches, and eventually his pro coaches had no way of knowing at first what Gogolak would end up doing when he applied his soccer-style kicking to football.

He would revolutionize the NFL. Twice. First, he altered the way the sport's kickers approached the ball, becoming the first soccer-style kicker to find success in the NFL. Then, that success became so impressive in the daunting wind-swept winter weather of the Buffalo Bills' War Memorial Stadium that he would tempt Wellington Mara into a bold move that helped changed the course of the NFL.

Mara broke the unwritten rule of poaching a player from the upstart AFL to bring Gogolak to the NFL's Giants. The move

Pete Gogolak revolutionized NFL kicking and helped alter the league in general.
(AP Photo)

momentarily stalled merger talks between the leagues as the AFL's owners balked at Mara's betrayal. But it also led to a battle between the leagues, which started signing each others' players whenever they could. That battle helped facilitate the merger, leading to the unified NFL that exists today and setting the stage for the annual Super Bowl.

"I have never forgotten that Wellington Mara had the guts to pick up a player from the other league," Gogolak said. "And I think it was very courageous of a decision to make, so I'm very happy about it."

A courageous decision? Maybe. A desperate one? Definitely.

Facing rough kicking conditions at Yankee Stadium, the Giants watched Bob Timberlake go 1-for-15 on field-goal attempts in 1965. Knowing Gogolak had scored 115 points and 102 points, respectively, in his two seasons with the Bills, Mara made the deal.

Of course, when Gogolak first started playing football, it was hard to imagine him becoming the subject of a bidding war that would escalate into something that changed the face of pro football. It was hard for most folks to even imagine what he was doing.

"I got really interested in the game, so in my junior year of high school I tried out for the team," Gogolak said. "And nobody ever [just] kicked in those days, and I just said, 'Hey, this is something I can do, and this is an actual way to kick—whether it's a parabola shaped football or a round-shaped soccer ball—his is an actual way to kick a ball.'"

Gogolak kept at it and improved. His brother, Charlie, who would also play in the league, also gained interest. The trickle eventually became a downpour, and as time passed, soccer-style kickers became the majority, leaving the straight-ahead kickers as unknown to the current generation as Gogolak was then.

"I just really worked at it during a couple of summers and I said, 'This is something that can be done,'" Gogolak said. "And I

Giants All-Time Kicking Leaders

Scoring—Career
646—Pete Gogolak (1966–74), (268-pat, 126-fg)
526—Brad Daluiso (1993–2000), (157-pat, 123-fg)
482—Joe Danelo (1976–82), (170-pat, 104-fg)

Most Field Goals—Career
126—Pete Gogolak (1966–74)
123—Brad Daluiso (1993–2000)
104—Joe Danelo (1976–82)

Most Field Goals—Season
35—John Carney (2008)
35—Jay Feely (2005)
35—Ali Haji-Sheikh (1983)

Most Points—Season
148—Jay Feely, 2005 (43-pat, 35-fg)
143—John Carney, 2008 (38-pat, 35-fg)
127—Ali Haji-Sheikh, 1983 (22-pat, 35-fg)

Longest Field Goal
56—Ali Haji-Sheikh, at Detroit, November 7, 1983

Most Field Goals—Game
6—Joe Danelo, at Seattle, October 18, 1991

went to college and then my brother Charlie, two years later, got into this and then a couple of years later…they brought in some kickers from Europe. I always say that I should have patented this kick. I'd be a rich man today."

When he first arrived in Bills camp, Gogolak found players were so stunned by his unorthodox style that he had difficulty finding a holder.

"It was such a new way to kick a football, and the holder was always afraid," Gogolak said. "The holder was afraid that, coming from the side, I would kick him in the butt or kick his hands."

Gogolak helped them adjust, continuing his kicking success for a Giants team that suffered through mediocre seasons but enjoyed some offensive prowess with future Hall of Famer Fran Tarkenton at quarterback from 1967–71. By the time Gogolak retired after his nine years with the Giants, he had scored 646 points, a team record that is still intact and not expected to be challenged in the near future.

Along with his team mark, Gogolak's pioneering status earned him a nod in the Giants' inaugural Ring of Honor class in 2010.

"Yeah, I'm very surprised," Gogolak said when asked if he was surprised his record still stood. "I still really don't know why…so many good kickers came and for some reason kickers just don't stay that long."

82 Odd Cancer Coincidences

Karl Nelson heard the words, another variation of the ones every person dreads. The ones that had become all too sickeningly familiar around the Giants in the 1980s, when young men who played a sport that made them feel invincible kept getting reminded that certainly was not the case.

The Giants lost Doug Kotar in 1983 to an inoperable brain tumor at 32, one year after the running back retired. John Tuggle had earned the team's respect after making the team in 1983 despite getting the "Mr. Irrelevant" tag given to the last player drafted. He played just one year with the Giants and died at 25 in 1986.

A year after Tuggle's death, Nelson, the Giants offensive lineman, was hearing a doctor tell him he had Hodgkin's disease, a form of lymph cancer. Despite the humbling recent history,

Nelson's mind still went to a place of youthful invincibility. "Okay, what do I have to do to get better so I can play football again?" he said.

His then-wife Heidi was incredulous. "You're acting like a dumb jock," she said.

Twenty-four years later, Nelson acknowledges something few people do about an ex-spouse. "She was right," he said. "That was my driving force. She called it my 'dumb jock' mode."

Many of the other Giants were in a mode where they suddenly became concerned about yet another case of cancer afflicting one of their own. Along with Nelson, Kotar, and Tuggle, linebacker Dan Lloyd was diagnosed with lymphoma in 1981, but he was able to recover.

"There were rumors about the problems with the stadium," said Scott Brunner, Giants quarterback from 1980–83. "The high incidences of cancer from players who were living there basically all day. You'd go to the meetings there, go to the locker rooms there, weight train. We did everything. I guess it was in the back of the mind. I didn't necessarily believe it, but the rumors were there that it was a death trap."

After Nelson was diagnosed, though, it jumped to the forefront for several Giants, including Giants captain Harry Carson. "I wanted a trade and considered retiring," Carson told the *Daily News* back then. "I didn't like the things that were happening, starting with Dan Lloyd. When I signed my last contract, I considered it to be hazard pay for where we played."

The New Jersey Sports and Exposition Authority commissioned several studies that cleared the Meadowlands area from a connection to the odd cancer incidences. Doctors said no link to the four cases was found.

Nelson battled through several exhausting processes in fighting the cancer, leaving him with weight loss and scars. As had been the case with Kotar, Tuggle, and Lloyd, Giants owner Wellington Mara did his part to ease Nelson's burden.

Mara reached out to him to make sure he could earn a full paycheck despite a players' strike that went on in 1987—and the players' union agreed to let Nelson accept his checks.

"The Maras were incredible to me when I was going through my health problems," Nelson said. "I was probably the only player in the league that got every game check that year.

"George [Young] called me into the office," Nelson said of the general manager. "'We'd like to do this for you, Karl.' I never saw a deductible. I never saw a co-insurance [payment]. If I was in the hospital in the city, the Giants would send a car for my wife to pick her up and see me, send her home at night."

While the front office provided comfort for Nelson, his return to the team was more awkward. Bill Parcells was supportive during the roughest of times—Nelson called him "incredible"—but when Nelson visited practice before he could play, Parcells and the team went into normal mode for injured players.

"Most of them didn't know how to handle it, so they didn't handle it," Nelson said. "Once I came back practicing, I was fine."

Nelson returned in 1988, amazingly cleared to play. He played nine games, but the cancer came back. That was it. He retired. Fortunately, he was able to beat it again and is cancer free.

"It's a lot of work," he said of his cancer battles, "but you want to get back adjusted as quickly as you can."

The Giants who were not as fortunate in their cancer battles are still remembered by their teammates.

"They were wonderful teammates," Brunner said. "Doug Kotar…he was just a wonderful guy. And then John Tuggle…. It was a shock."

83 From Super Star to Prisoner

Plaxico Burress' game-winning catch in the Super Bowl thrust him into Giants lore, and it also appeared to end concerns about his commitment to the team. After questions about his attitude in Pittsburgh and with the Giants, and a few off-the-field incidents, Burress had started to reach his potential as a big-play receiver who could go down as the team's all-time best.

That would all shockingly change the next year when Burress created a stir as stunning as his success. As the gallows humor has gone, Burress all but literally shot himself in the foot.

The infamous incident in November 2008—when Burress concealed a gun without a permit in New York City and accidently shot himself in the thigh—eventually sent him to prison for two years on a weapons charge. The man who once talked about dreaming big as he wondered where his grandmother and mother would have sat if they were alive for the Super Bowl now had to wonder something more painful.

"What do I tell him?" Burress told the *New York Daily News* in September 2010, speaking of his 3-year-old son, Elijah. The boy had repeatedly asked his daddy why he wasn't home or playing football. "How am I supposed to answer those questions?"

Even before the infamous gun incident, Burress bickered with the Giants. He irritated the team by saying he would skip practices because he wasn't happy with his contract. Burress then battled more injuries during the season, but the Giants followed their Super Bowl year strong by starting 11–1.

Then two nights before a road game against the Redskins, Burress and linebacker Antonio Pierce went to a New York City nightclub, the Latin Quarter. Burress had an expired license to carry a concealed weapon in his home state of Florida, but he did not have a permit to carry a gun in New York. He also had a Glock tucked in the waistband of his pants.

Having grown up in a crime-filled neighborhood where he was used to armed drug dealers mixing with the rest of his neighbors, Burress was one of many NFL players who couldn't shake the instinct to protect themselves when they went out. He was also one of many who did not use their ample financial resources to hire a bodyguard, at least that night.

The gun fell and went off. Burress was shot in the thigh, and he and Pierce went to New York Presbyterian Hospital, starting a storm of controversy. Eventually Burress was sentenced to two years on a plea deal that led to a charge of attempted criminal possession of a weapon.

New York City Mayor Michael Bloomberg, a staunch gun control advocate, pressured prosecutors by publicly saying, "It would be an outrage if we don't prosecute to the fullest extent of the law."

The initial aftermath also caused the city to question the hospital for not reporting the incident as required by law and challenge the Giants for doing the same. The team later said it had immediately reported the incident to NFL security, and co-owner John Mara expressed resentment over the accusation.

Pierce, too, was investigated for allegedly taking possession of Burress' weapon, but he was cleared. So was a nightclub security guard who, it was later discovered, had taken the gun to the car Pierce used for the hospital trip. Prosecutors reportedly decided hospital personnel and the guard were guilty of a "screw-up rather than a cover-up."

Without their most talented receiver, the Giants still won the NFC East and the conference's top seed but dropped three of their final four games. The Eagles then shocked them with a 23–11 win in the first round of the playoffs to end their Super Bowl title defense.

"Obviously it's hard to replace [Burress]," general manager Jerry Reese said after the game. "The guy has a presence out there, and when you lose that, teams play you differently."

The Giants were initially open to a return for Burress, who wouldn't be sentenced until 2009. But even before his sentencing, the Giants, frustrated with Burress' lack of communication, released him.

The two-year sentence, deemed too harsh since Burress had only injured himself, drew sympathy from many of his teammates and fans. Others felt the importance of restricting guns was a valid enough concern to merit the punishment, even if Burress was used as an example.

"I'm truly remorseful for what I've done," Burress said after exiting the court room.

As shown in the *News*' photos and videos in September 2010, Burress looked thin and humbled—so far from the man who cocked his head and predicted the Giants would shock the NFL the week of Super Bowl XLII.

Burress hoped for another chance to play upon his release in 2011, whether it was with the Giants or another team.

"I feel like I let a lot of kids down," he told the *News*, vowing, "No one would be more dedicated than me" to win another title. "It's something I can't erase. All I can do is get back to the football field and play at a high level. That's the only way I can redeem myself, so to speak."

Of course, football doesn't provide redemption on its own, as Burress' quick trip from Super Bowl star to prisoner shows. But Burress has said he would like to speak out on gun control, and he appeared determined to move on from the biggest mistake of his life, which came nine months after his biggest catch.

84 "Better Not to Make the Playoffs at All"

The Giants knew they couldn't blame everything on Plaxico Burress. Even without him, they had earned the No. 1 seed in the NFC following the 2008 season. Without him, they had put themselves in a strong position to defend their Super Bowl title.

And without him, they had given it all away in a 23–11 first-round shocker to No. 6 seed Philadelphia that left them feeling as though they shouldn't have bothered accomplishing a darned thing.

"I think shock would be an understatement," center Shaun O'Hara told reporters after the game amid a nearly silent locker room. "When you look at the season we had, the number of games we won, the way we won them, I can't even fathom not continuing to play. To have it taken away now, it's the worst feeling ever. You almost wonder if it's better not to make the playoffs at all than to exit the way we did."

The Giants had outscored opponents 427–294 and started the year 11–1 before Burress' gun incident helped derail them and they lost three of four to finish the season.

But this one, in the playoffs, would be another stunning, bitter defeat to the Eagles, who seemed so set on delivering defeat to the Giants over the years. Twice in the season's final weeks, Philadelphia beat them at home, this time labeling the Giants as the first No. 1 seed to lose to a No. 6 since the playoffs expanded in 1990.

Giants coach Tom Coughlin put the loss on his shoulders, which is where some of the blame surely rested after some odd moves, including using veteran kicker John Carney instead of a

"76 Lambuth Special" 86ed Season

The last time the Giants tried to follow a Super Bowl run, their season also ended against Philadelphia. The Giants didn't have as strong a Super Bowl showing in 2000 as the 2007 team, getting routed by the Ravens. Nor did they have as impressive a team.

But the 2001 Giants (7–7) were still mathematically alive when they went to Philadelphia (9–5) in Week 15. The teams had exchanged big plays—and Michael Strahan closed in on the single-season sack record by getting 3½ all in the first half.

But the Giants trailed 24–21 at their own 20 with seven seconds left. They tried the "76 Lambuth Special"—a play named for the small Tennessee university that receiver Ron Dixon had attended. It called for quarterback Kerry Collins to throw a short pass to receiver Ike Hilliard. He would lateral to Dixon, who would cross behind him, sprinting for the opposite sideline.

But Hilliard had problems getting open, and running back Tiki Barber did not, so Collins dumped it to Barber, who flipped it to Dixon.

The Eagles zigged. Dixon zagged—all the way down the left sideline—almost. Six yards from an exhilarating win, Eagles safety Damon Moore knocked Dixon out of bounds. The game was over, taking the season with it.

"For what it meant and how we lost it," Giants GM Ernie Accorsi told reporters the next day, "it was heartbreaking."

now-healthy Lawrence Tynes, who had kicked the game-winning field goal in the previous year's NFC title game.

Although in fairness, the rest of the Giants' playoff stars from the past year weren't exactly effective. After asserting himself in postseason play during the Super Bowl run, Eli Manning went just 15-of-29 for 169 yards with two interceptions. Brandon Jacobs was more effective on the ground but inexplicably not used enough.

The Giants' defensive line, unlike the previous year, didn't pressure Eagles quarterback Donovan McNabb, failing to sack him once. It all added up to one of several frustrating first-round defeats in the Coughlin era.

"I'm in disbelief right now," tight end Kevin Boss said, speaking for the rest of his team as well as its fans. "I thought we were playing well enough to make another run."

85 The Rivals: Teams You Love to Hate

The Giants' biggest rival has sometimes depended on the season and the circumstances, from division opponents who have battled twice annually; to playoff foes like the San Francisco 49ers, who traded knockout blows during the 1980s; to their long-standing fellow franchises who share their grand tradition, such as the Bears and Packers.

The rivalry with the Washington Redskins may have peaked in the 1980s when both teams were competing for division titles and Super Bowl bids. The Dallas Cowboys may have sickened New Yorkers with their "America's Team" success in the 1970s when they stole band wagon-jumping fans from the struggling Giants—and received their comeuppance when the Giants beat them to return to the playoffs in 1981. The rivalry may have re-ignited when Michael Irvin taunted Lawrence Taylor and again when the Giants stunned Dallas and sent Tony Romo back to his actress girlfriend Jessica Simpson for the winter.

San Francisco might have served as the perfect 1980s foe, Bill Walsh's high-octane offense vs. Bill Parcells' power football, and Giants fans can marvel at their team's ability to punish Joe Montana.

But the team that has boiled Giants fans' blood the most and for the longest period of time is the one that's closest. You may stray and fall into other rivalries, Giants fans, but you will always return your venom to the Philadelphia Eagles. The heart wants what it wants—to dislike.

Why Eagles-Giants, which was ranked fourth on SI.com's list of all-time greatest NFL rivalries? It's simple. It fills the needs of any good rivalry.

Figures to dislike? Check. See former head coach/bounty hunter Buddy Ryan and hard-hitters Andre Waters, Brian Dawkins, and Chuck Bednarik.

Heart-breaking moments that stoke your aggravation? Here. See Bednarik's vicious (but clean) hit on Frank Gifford, Randall Cunningham's elusive moves, Herman Edwards' fortune in picking up Joe Pisarcik's Fumble, DeSean Jackson's punt return, and playoff losses in 2006 and 2008.

Triumphant moments to make sure it's not one-sided? Present. See the 56–0 rout in the teams' first game in 1933, a 62–10 thrashing in the 1970s, a playoff upset in 1981, and another playoff victory in 2000.

Here's a quick look at some highlights from rivalry moments not featured in other sections of the book.

Philadelphia

When: October 10, 1988

Where: Veterans Stadium, Philadelphia

The Final: 24–13, Eagles

The background: Of all the folks the Giants loved to hate, Eagles coach Buddy Ryan earned his place high atop the list. As bold as his son, Rex, would be with the Jets, the Giants also found Ryan to be dirty with his reputation of placing a bounty on players his defense could knock out.

The play: Eagles quarterback Randall Cunningham was as mobile as they come, but when Carl Banks appeared to knock him down—and Cunningham managed to put a hand on the ground, get up, and still fire a touchdown pass, it was a bit too much for the

Giants to take. It didn't help that Cunningham, who also punted, hit a 91-yard punt a few years later in another win. Talk about kicking a team while they're down.

When: November 20, 1988
Where: Giants Stadium
The Final: 24–17, Eagles
The play: Ryan's hated Eagles were back, but the Giants seemed okay when Lawrence Taylor blocked a 31-yard field goal attempt in overtime. Instead, the ball bounced to Philly lineman Clyde Simmons, who returned it 15 yards for a game-winning touchdown. The Giants lost to the Jets in the season's final game and missed the playoffs with a 10–6 record.

When: January 7, 2001
Where: Giants Stadium
The Final: 20–10, Giants
The play: Donovan McNabb and the Eagles looked to knock off Jim Fassel's Giants, but Ron Dixon's 97-yard opening kickoff for a touchdown quickly added to Philly's workload. The game is most remembered though for showcasing the athleticism of cornerback Jason Sehorn, who tipped a McNabb pass, fell to the ground, batted it straight up in the air, caught it and took off for a 32-yard touchdown to give the Giants a 17–0 lead. "After I saw it on the replay, I didn't know how I did it," Sehorn said after the game, grinning. "They can keep playing it as many times as they can. I'll watch it every time."

When: January 7, 2007
Where: Lincoln Financial Field, Philadelphia
The Final: 23–20, Eagles
The skinny: Tiki Barber saved Tom Coughlin's job by running for 234 yards and three touchdowns against Washington the previous

week, but the Giants would lose another heart-breaker to the Eagles in the playoffs. Plaxico Burress caught a touchdown pass from Eli Manning with 5:04 left to tie the game, but Eagles running back Brian Westbrook helped lead the Eagles into field-goal range for David Akers, who made this one from 38 yards out to end the game, the Giants' season, and the Giant careers of Barber and GM Ernie Accorsi.

When: September 30, 2007
Where: Giants Stadium
The Final: 16–3, Giants
The skinny: The Giants didn't just punish their rivals with an NFL-record 12 sacks and an eye-popping, team-record six by Osi Umenyiora. They set the stage for their vaunted pass rush to later lead the way in shocking the Patriots and the football world in Super Bowl XLII. Evening their record at 2–2 while pummeling Philadelphia—and fill-in left tackle Winston Justice, who was repeatedly beaten by Umenyiora—the Giants stunned themselves. "I'm going all the way back to Pop Warner, and I've never seen anything like that," linebacker Antonio Pierce said after the game. "Really, he dominated the game by himself." Well, he did have some help from Mathias Kiwanuka's three sacks, a pair by Justin Tuck and one from Michael Strahan.

Washington
When: December 3, 1939
Where: Polo Grounds
The Final: 9–7, Giants
The skinny: Controversy ruled when referee Bill Halloran deemed a last-second field-goal attempt by the Redskins no good to decide the Eastern Division title on the season's last day. The rivalry had already grown the past two seasons when the teams exchanged routs on the final day of the year to clinch division crowns. But

Redskins owner George Preston Marshall had brought thousands of Redskins fans as well as a 150-piece marching band with him in 1939. Redskins head coach Ray Flaherty, the former Giant whose number had been retired, was furious and fights broke out on the field with one Redskin swinging at the official. Like the kick, the attempt missed.

Dallas

When: November 2, 1986
Where: Giants Stadium
The Final: 17–14, Giants
The skinny: The Giants helped establish themselves as true contenders with the second victory in what would be a 12-game winning streak through their Super Bowl championship. After losing the opener in Dallas when Herschel Walker rushed past an out-of-shape Lawrence Taylor for the winning touchdown, the Giants faced fellow 6–2 Dallas knowing they needed a win to keep from getting buried in the division. Instead, thanks to the second straight 181-yard rushing game by Joe Morris and a vicious hit by Carl Banks that knocked out Cowboys quarterback Danny White, the Giants were on their way.

When: September 15, 2003
Where: Giants Stadium
The Final: 35–32, Cowboys
The skinny: It was sickening for Giants fans to watch Bill Parcells celebrate a mind-boggling win at the Meadowlands as a member of the hated Cowboys—especially since the Giants had come so close to humbling him. The Giants trailed 23–7 but rallied in the fourth quarter when Kerry Collins threw two touchdown passes and Matt Bryant hit a field goal for a 32–29 lead with just 11 seconds left. Amazingly, the Cowboys came back when Bryant's kickoff went out of bounds and Dallas connected on a 36-yard pass. That set

up a 52-yard field goal by Billy Cundiff—his sixth field goal of the game. His seventh in OT won it.

When: September 20, 2009
Where: Cowboys Stadium
The Final: 33–31, Giants
The skinny: The Giants delighted in spoiling the debut of Cowboys owner Jerry Jones' new $1.2 billion football palace. Lawrence Tynes kicked a game-winning 37-yard field goal, and Eli Manning threw for 330 yards and two touchdowns. But it's what Manning did after the game that caused the Cowboys to throw a fit. Manning signed the wall of the visiting locker room, along with the score and the phrase, "First win in new stadium." "We won't forget that," Cowboys linebacker Bradie James said. "It just makes for a more intense game." Manning said he was asked to sign the wall by a locker room attendant and didn't exactly seem ready to offer any apologies. "Yeah, I kind of heard a few things about it," Manning said. "I figure they'll eventually get over it."

86 Drive the Bus, Conduct the Train

Want to know what to do when you start to feel pressure? Well, you could follow former head coach Jim Fassel's lead and take charge with a bluster-filled speech. He knew his job was on the line, so Fassel decided to cross it that day in November 2000.

His Giants dropped back-to-back games, and the New York media and fans converged as the Giants fell to 7–4 and risked falling out of playoff contention. Fassel made a move that amused some and shocked others. He guaranteed his team would make the playoffs.

And while his rambling, mixed-metaphor speech wasn't exactly as smooth—or as bold—as the more famous New York football guarantee made by Joe Namath in 1969, it showed just who was ready to shoulder the load for the stumbling Giants. "I'm raising the stakes right now. If this is a poker game, I'm shoving my chips to the middle of the table," Fassel said at a press conference. "I'm raising the ante; anybody wants in can get in. Anybody wants out can get out. This team is going to the playoffs."

He spoke in a more even-keeled nature than most NFL coaches' famous rants but still earned a spot on ESPN's list as the sixth-greatest tirade ever. He went on to say he was driving the bus, conducting the train, and a few other images of bravado, none of which connected to the one that came before.

The New York media reacted cynically, thinking it was a contrived attempt by a desperate man who surely knew he would lose his job if his team missed the playoffs, regardless of his speech.

Back in Montana, Fassel's old junior college coach Hal Sherbeck who had taught him to "stick by your beliefs" cheered when he saw his former quarterback's speech. "Go get 'em!" Sherbeck screamed. "Let it all hang out!"

That's just what Fassel and the Giants did down the stretch, rolling into the playoffs as the No. 1 seed in the NFC with five straight wins to finish the season. A 20–10 win over Donovan McNabb's Eagles in the first round impressed some. A 41–0 thrashing of the Vikings—who had ended the 1997 Fassel team's season with a heartbreaking playoff defeat—clinched a trip to the Super Bowl.

The ride ended there when the Baltimore Ravens' ferocious defense led by Ray Lewis dominated in a 34–7 rout.

Fassel's time with the Giants ended with even less success. After earning Coach of the Year honors in his rookie season with a playoff appearance in 1997, and going on the Super Bowl run in 2000, his team had one of the franchise's worst playoff collapses in a 39–38 defeat to San Francisco in 2002. The Giants led 38–14 before falling. They followed up that season with a 4–12 season in 2003 and Fassel was let go.

But Fassel will always own a place in Big Blue lore for the speech and the surprise Super Bowl appearance in a year when he called his team full of cast-offs and redemption projects not "America's team" like the Cowboys but the "American dream."

87 Jeremy Shockey

He arrived with as much bombast as he had potential. Jeremy Shockey shook things up almost from Day 1. He had barely been a rookie when the Giants' talented tight end balked at a training camp hazing ritual in 2002, sparking a fight that left his head coach Jim Fassel slyly smiling at the fiery nature of his newest star.

When Shockey took a swing at linebacker Brandon Short—after the pair sniped over Short's order for the rookie to sing his alma mater's fight song at lunch—Fassel gleefully recognized a fact he took as a positive at the time.

"When the fight was going on, all I could think of was, 'My man is here!'" Fassel later told *New York* magazine. "'My man has arrived!'"

Time validated Fassel's instinct about his new tight end's signature moment. It did not necessarily prove the moment was worthy of celebration. Shockey had torn into the low-key Giants tradition like a modern but mythic figure, his golden locks evoking images of Thor and his mouth providing the hammer as much as his play.

Of course, the man-child was wickedly talented, a combination of size, speed, and strength even the Giants' best tight end, Mark

Bavaro, never possessed. That's what had inspired the Giants to break from their tradition and trade up a spot to pick him out of the University of Miami with the 14th overall pick in the draft. But what Shockey offered in raw gifts he often sacrificed in unnerving moments—in front of a digital recorder or on the field.

He was just giving the people what they came for, he figured. "People pay money to watch people get hurt," Shockey told *Sports Illustrated* before his second season. "They're looking to win, but you ask nine out of 10 people and they'll say, 'I'd rather see Jeremy Shockey run over somebody and break his arm or leg than see him catch a touchdown.' They pay all that hard money for their seats? I'm going to give them what they want."

By his second year, after he had burst on the scene with an All-Pro rookie season that featured 74 catches and two touchdowns, Shockey had already displayed the volatile side Bavaro always kept raging under the surface but never allowed to bubble over into anything but a battering ram of a block or broken tackle.

In the Giants' historic collapse in the 39–38 playoff loss to San Francisco after the 2002 season, Shockey scored a touchdown and skipped around the end zone on one play, dropped a pass there on another, and finished off the mixed bag of a day that typified his tenure by throwing a cup of ice water at some fans and making an obscene gesture at the 49ers—earning him $15,000 in fines.

Despite all that, Giants general manager Ernie Accorsi, while acknowledging Shockey did not fit with the more staid Giants tradition, recognized the vibrant style of play combined with untapped potential that had Giants fans racing off in record numbers to snap up No. 80 jerseys.

"I thought it was an extraordinary rookie season," Accorsi said after the year was over. "He gave us a vitality we lacked. Certain players make everyone else better just by walking on the field, and he's one of those players. I think the sky is the limit on him, and we've only seen a small part of that."

The most naturally gifted tight end the Giants had was just starting to raise a ruckus. In the ensuing years, he would spar with former Giants coach-turned-analyst-turned-coach-again Bill Parcells, responding to criticism by calling him a gay slur. He also created gossip page headlines by dating stars like Tara Reid.

He created havoc on the field as well, of course, often showing the talent that made fans rally around while others wanted to run away. He ran over opponents he thought disrespected him, once running right over Colts safety David Gibson. He had his infamous battles with Eagles hard-hitting safety Brian Dawkins, and those events added yet another layer to the teams' rivalry. But Shockey could also let opponents get in his head as passes bounced off his fingers.

Shockey could be as polarizing a figure as there was around the Giants, the younger generation of fans was eager to embrace a star more in their mold, the older generation was irritated by the departure from the team's relatively low-key performers.

The irony was that Shockey found his closest ally on the Giants in the form of owner Wellington Mara, the man known for setting the tone of class the organization had always strived to follow. When Mara was near his death in 2005, Shockey and running back Tiki Barber were the players he invited to his home.

"We had a connection," Shockey told the *New York Daily News* in 2010. "My grandfather and he were about the same age. We would always talk, chit-chat, little things."

Shockey felt such a connection that he later said when Mara and co-owner Robert Tisch died weeks apart, "a piece of me left, as well." The Giants at that point were under disciplinarian and old-school coach Tom Coughlin, who was more focused on having the tight end block than catch passes, and several personnel were different.

"It was just different," he said. "It was a rough couple of years."

Two years later, the Giants' greatest moment would be one of Shockey's worst. It would ultimately lead to a divorce. Shockey was

Jeremy Shockey stormed into the Giants' world full of talent and controversy. The tight end surprisingly bonded with conservative owner Wellington Mara, but his relationship with the team eventually soured and he was traded. (AP Photo/David Drapkin)

hurt during the 2007 season and relegated to the sidelines propped up on crutches. As the Giants heated up to make a playoff run down the stretch, some media members wondered whether the team fared better with the less talented rookie Kevin Boss at tight end. The theory went that for all of Shockey's talent, his dominating personality ruffled Coughlin's team-above-all theme and also stifled rising young quarterback Eli Manning's leadership.

When the team reached the Super Bowl without him, Shockey's frustration reached a fever pitch. He was irked by the fact he had to fly commercial—the team had offered him to join them from New Jersey but Shockey flew in from South Florida where he was rehabbing. He was irritated by the fact he was relegated to co-owner Steve Tisch's luxury box instead of being able to stay on the sideline where the Giants' policy banned injured players for fear they could get hurt trying to get out of the way of a play.

For all of Shockey's big plays, one of the lasting images of him as a Giant was sitting in that box with beers in front of him as Boss made a key catch that got the Giants back in the game and on the way to their stunning upset of the Patriots. Shockey, who did not join in the victory parade, finally erupted in a locker-room argument with GM Jerry Reese the next year, demanding a trade.

The Giants said they did not want to make a deal but finally realized it would be for the best. Shockey ended up in New Orleans reunited with former offensive coordinator Sean Payton, now the Saints' head coach. He would get to be part of a Super Bowl, this time an especially active part—he caught the touchdown pass that put New Orleans ahead for good in their 2010 victory over the Colts.

He had never fulfilled that sky-is-the-limit potential in New York, but he had moved on, as had the Giants, each of them winning a Super Bowl without the other.

88 What to Think About the Jets

The Giants and Jets have always had a relationship best described in the character-cutting Twitter world as "frenemies." The teams' fans don't hate each other as much as Yankees and Mets fans do. Neither are they overly fond of hearing each others' boasts.

The Giants fan's traditional role is to remind Jets fans their team hasn't won a Super Bowl since 1969. The Jets fan usually then offers a four-letter reply that is not J-E-T-S. Not that the Jets haven't inflicted some pain on the Giants over the years.

Here's a quick look at the intra-city rivalry:

1959—Giants cut receiver Don Maynard. New York Titans pick him up. He develops into a Hall of Famer.

1969—Fresh off their Super Bowl III win, the Jets and Giants play their first exhibition game at the Yale Bowl. The Giants, still not respectful of the AFL, are humbled 37–14. The Giants soon fire head coach Allie Sherman.

1981—Jets beat Green Bay on season's final day to clinch playoff spot for both New York teams. Giants coach Ray Perkins toasts the Jets. Jets quarterback Richard Todd roasts the Giants with a smile. "I think the Giants should really appreciate us," he said. "Well, they backed up into it. They didn't give us anything. We gave it to them."

1988—Jets receiver Al Toon catches a last-minute touchdown pass on the last game of the season, costing the Giants a potential playoff berth.

1998—Giants cornerback Jason Sehorn is knocked out for the 1998 season and his career is altered when he tears his ACL and

Sharing the Stadium

The Giants partnered with the Jets on their new stadium in 2010, but this time the Jets didn't have to share "Giants Stadium." Instead, they were in a 50–50 arrangement, and the clubs used temporary end-zone displays and wall coverings to allow each team to showcase their colors. In the gift shop, Jets merchandise can be seen lurking behind the Giants' stuff on Big Blue game days and vice versa.

Jets owner Woody Johnson immediately set out to prove the Jets were tired of being the Giants' little brother, issuing a barb-filled statement to NFL commissioner Roger Goodell when he awarded the Giants the stadium's first regular-season home game via coin flip. The coin flip flap was especially odd because Goodell initially shot down the Jets suggestion to hold one and later made the flip without a rep from either team present.

"An NFL coin toss has a few fundamental elements that are missing here, most notably the presence of the teams involved," Johnson said in a statement released by the Jets. "That's how it's always done in the League, whether it's determining the order of the draft or deciding who's going to kick off the game."

The Jets, who had played the final game at Giants Stadium—much to the Giants' chagrin—were given the first Monday night game, the day after the Giants opened with their win over the Panthers.

MCL in his knee returning a kickoff against the Jets in a preseason game.

1999—Bill Parcells is greeted with three touchdown passes from Kerry Collins to Amani Toomer in a 41–28 Giants win as Parcells returns to the Meadowlands as a Jet.

2003—Giants linebacker Brandon Short knocks Jets quarterback Chad Pennington out for six weeks in a preseason game.

89 Bob Sheppard: "Welcome to ..."???

His regal intonation was most predominantly recognized for greeting fans in the Bronx with a seemingly perfect voice for a stadium known as a baseball cathedral. "Good afternoon, ladies and gentleman," Bob Sheppard said countless times in a cadence which inspired just as many imitations, "Welcome to Yankee Stadium."

For 18 years, that salutation by the legendary public address announcer applied to Giants fans, as well, when the team called Yankee Stadium home. For 30 more years, Sheppard welcomed fans to Giants Stadium, where he maintained his role as the Giants' PA man from the building's inception in 1976 to his football retirement in 2006. Sheppard, who died in 2010, had a strong connection to the Giants even if he was more often associated with the Yankees.

"Bob Sheppard was the most distinguished and dignified voice in all of professional sports," Giants co-owner John Mara said upon Sheppard's passing. "We are very proud of the fact that he was the voice of the Giants for so many years. Bob was a true gentleman and the consummate professional. There will never be another one like him."

Granted, Sheppard even acknowledged he was not perfect. He occasionally flubbed a name or two. And on October 10, 1976, he provided a bit of trivia that goes down as part of old Giants Stadium lore.

After 51 years of playing in shared ballparks, the last 18 of which were at Yankee Stadium, the team relished the thought of finally having its own home. So you can imagine the double-takes that followed after they turned to the golden-voiced Sheppard to get their new Giants Stadium off to a proper start.

"Welcome," Sheppard greeted fans entering the Meadowlands, "to Yankee Stadium."

Despite the rare gaffe, Sheppard had plenty of better days to celebrate with the Giants. In the 1986 season, he announced the starting lineups for their NFC Championship Game prior to the win over Washington. He did the same for several other playoff wins and special moments.

Regardless of the site, Sheppard's bond with the Giants was considerable as evidenced by the response he once gave then-Yankees broadcaster and former player Phil Rizzuto. Known as the Yankees' No. 1 fan, Rizzuto asked Sheppard for his favorite Yankee Stadium moment.

"The day Pat Summerall kicked the field goal in the snow in 1958," Sheppard said, flooring Rizzuto.

Like Wellington Mara, Sheppard was known as a gentleman amid a rough business. But also like Mara, Sheppard's professionalism and passion didn't keep him from making a sharp point when needed. At Sheppard's eulogy, John Mara recalled a story about his father and Sheppard, who also had been a speech professor at St. John's University. Needing to make a speech, Mara asked Sheppard for advice.

"Remember Lou Gehrig's farewell address?" Sheppard said. "It was 90 seconds. Keep it brief."

90 The Return After the Attacks

The league wisely canceled games that first week, and the Giants helped push them to do so because they asked themselves a question answered by taking a look across the river into lower Manhattan.

What good can a game do when real life is so utterly heart-breaking and raw?

The nation had been attacked on September 11, 2001, and from their stadium 10 miles away, the Giants could see what too many New Yorkers, New Jersey residents, and people all over the country could—all those clouds of smoke billowing from the spot where terrorists flew a pair of jets into the Twin Towers, eventually causing them to fall and killed nearly 3,000 people.

Another plane flew into the Pentagon. Yet another, United Flight 93, took off from Newark Liberty International Airport only hours after the Giants arrived, following their season-opening loss in Denver. Flight 93 crashed in a Pennsylvania field, the passengers on board learning of the other hijacked planes and fighting their hijackers literally to their death to prevent even more tragedy. Their actions, along with those from all the cops, firefighters, and emergency personnel who went running toward the burning towers to the rescue workers who dug through debris at the site known as Ground Zero, offered yet another example of why the Giants' actions on the field, no matter how impressive, should never be labeled heroic.

"Pressure is going into a 110-story building when it's about to collapse on you," linebacker Michael Barrow said. "Pressure is having 2,000-degree temperatures coming down on you. This is a game."

The week after the attacks, Giants head coach Jim Fassel first went to visit the site and see what small role his team could play in the healing. The Giants later sent a group of players to visit with the rescue workers as they dug through the debris for the folks still considered missing. The Giants were humbled by the reaction.

"We're visiting construction workers, cops, firemen," defensive back Sam Garnes said. "You respect them so much and feel so bad for them, everything they've seen. You're surprised that they talk to you about football…. You realize that what you do really is important to some people."

The most painful, personal loss came for legendary Giants announcer and former cornerback, Dick Lynch. His son, Richard, was among the lost, forever breaking a piece of his father's heart. "We sat there waiting to hear from him," Lynch told the *New York Daily News* years later. "We're still waiting."

The Giants were to resume playing on September 23 at Kansas City, grateful the league canceled the previous week's games after some deliberation. Lynch showed up, too, calling the game though listeners heard the pain in the usually affable announcer's voice.

That surreal period of pain left sports in a subdued role, but the Giants took their responsibility to represent the city seriously. Two days earlier, they watched New Yorkers rejoice at Shea Stadium as baseball returned to New York with a kickline of firefighters and cops singing "New York, New York" with Liza Minnelli, and Mike Piazza hitting a home run to beat Atlanta and give Mets fans a moment to cheer.

The Giants wanted to provide one, as well.

"To have those guys hug you and break down on you and actually say, 'Guys we need you to play this Sunday. We need you to divert our attention from what is going on here in the city,'" receiver Joe Jurevicius said that week, his voice overcome with emotion. "If that doesn't motivate you, I don't know what will."

Chiefs fans unfurled banners that declared Kansas City loved New York. It was proclaimed "New York Day."

Fans held hands over the railing with players who donned the caps of New York City police, firefighters, and Port Authority workers. Together, they cried during the National Anthem. Together, they sang "God Bless America."

Then they played a football game, most of them on this day wanting nothing more than to honor and serve the people who left them in awe earlier in the week.

The Giants did just that, earning a 13–3 win.

"We could not let our fans down," Barrow said later. "If we're going to wear NY on our helmets, we have to be fighters like the firemen and police who are true heroes."

Ron Dayne scored the only touchdown; Jurevicius, who only wanted to "divert their attention" back home for a little bit, caught seven passes for 90 yards.

"We just wanted to make New York proud," Fassel said.

91 Visit the Pro Football Hall of Fame

Granted, it's a bit of a road trip if you're a New York/New Jersey-area Giants fan, but along with all the other history lessons you can learn in Canton, Ohio, there is plenty to see particularly about your favorite team. Start with the Maras, of course, as Tim and Wellington became the first father-son duo to be enshrined when Wellington was inducted in 1997—34 years after his father went in with the inaugural class.

The Hall contains not just the dusty black-and-white newsreel type of memories but also visions of the team's recent glory. At one time, an exhibit included the helmet David Tyree pinned the football against on what is now considered the greatest play in Super Bowl history. Along with Tyree's helmet was the one belonging to Eli Manning, who scrambled out of trouble in an eye-popping display before heaving the ball downfield to the leaping Tyree.

But there has been plenty to explore for serious history buffs, as well, including a melon-shaped ball, leather helmet, and Giants jersey from the 1920s. The latter looks more like a Montreal Canadiens hockey sweater than a traditional Giants jersey since it's red with blue across the middle.

Giants in the Hall

Name	Role	Year Enshrined	Years with Giants
Harry Carson	LB	2006	1976–88
Benny Friedman	QB	2005	1929–31
Lawrence Taylor	LB	1999	1981–93
Wellington Mara	Owner	1997	1937–2005
Arnold Weinmeister	DT	1984	1950–53
Sam Huff	LB	1982	1956–63
Red Badgro	End/DE	1981	1930–35
Tuffy Leemans	HB/FB	1978	1936–43
Frank Gifford	HB/FL/DB/WR	1977	1952–60, 62–64
Roosevelt Brown	T	1975	1953–65
Andy Robustelli	DE/GM	1971	1956–64
Y.A. Tittle	QB	1971	1961–64
Ken Strong	HB/FB/DB/K	1967	1933–35, 39, 44–47
Emlen Tunnell	DB	1967	1948–58
Steve Owen	T/Head coach	1966	1926–53
Tim Mara	Founder/Owner	1963*	1925–59
Mel Hein	C	1963*	1931–45
Cal Hubbard	T	1963*	1927–28, 36

Hall of Famers with Giants' Experience

Name	Role	Year Enshrined	Years with Giants
Tom Landry	DB/Def. coach	1990	1950–54/55–59
Larry Csonka	FB	1987	1976–78
Don Maynard	WR	1987	1958
Fran Tarkenton	QB	1986	1967–71
Ray Flaherty	TE/coach	1976	1928–29, 31–35
Vince Lombardi	Off. Coach	1971	1954–58
Hugh McElhenny	HB	1970	1963
Joe Guyon	HB	1966	1927
Arnie Herber	QB	1966	1944–45
Jim Thorpe	HB	1963*	1925
Wilbur (Pete) Henry	T	1963*	1927

*Inducted in Hall's inaugural year

Traveling down the timeline, fans could have also checked out the trophy the Giants earned for their 1934 Sneakers Game championship win over Chicago, Y.A. Tittle's cracked helmet after the infamous hit that nudged him down the road to retirement, and the helmet Michael Strahan wore when Brett Favre graciously handed him the single-season sack record.

There are plenty of plaques to read as the Giants boast 18 Hall of Famers who made the most of their notable accomplishments with the team and 11 more who had at least some role with the Giants at one point in their careers.

92 Pick a Back: Bradshaw or Jacobs

The Giants faced a difficult decision after the 2010 season when running back Ahmad Bradshaw's contract was up. Could they afford to keep both Bradshaw and Brandon Jacobs and maintain one of the game's best tandems?

For fans, the debate is not eased regardless of the Giants' decision. Together or apart, Jacobs and Bradshaw are destined to leave Giants fans going back and forth on the merits of each back.

Bradshaw, a compact, muscular back in the mold of Tiki Barber, has the most big-play ability—and the culpability of too often fumbling the ball as Barber often did early in his career. Jacobs, at 6'4" 256 pounds, is more of a grinder—but his occasional reluctance to bowl over someone on the field can be as maddening as his fits of temper off it.

Sure, in an ideal world the Giants could always watch the pair perform in perfect harmony as they first did in the coming-out party for each of them in the team's playoff-berth-clinching 38–21

Brandon Jacobs (pictured) teamed with Ahmad Bradshaw during the Giants' 2007 Super Bowl run, with Jacobs grinding out tough yards and Bradshaw breaking big runs. In between competing for playing time the last few years, the running backs became close friends. (AP Photo/Dick Druckman)

win over Buffalo in 2007. That's when Jacobs (in his first year of replacing the retired Barber) and Bradshaw (then a rookie who fully introduced himself in this game) ran all over the Bills and gave the Giants the best of their complementary worlds. Jacobs bulldozed the Bills for 143 yards. Bradshaw ripped off an 88-yard run during a 21-point fourth quarter that put Buffalo away.

The pair continued to flourish in the playoffs. Jacobs wore down defenses, picking up tough yards like the 1-yard touchdown to beat Dallas and the fourth-and-1 that kept the final Super Bowl drive against New England alive. Bradshaw churned those strong, fresh legs late and scampered around and over folks—that 52-yard touchdown burst against Green Bay still visible in Giants fans memories—even if it got called back on a penalty.

By 2010, Bradshaw earned the starting role to begin the season and gave it up again in late November after coughing up six fumbles and frustrating Coach Tom Coughlin. Granted, as Coughlin pointed out, the Giants had used more of a rotation with the reserve getting only a few less touches, not a permanent spot on the bench.

But in between losing and regaining his job, Jacobs snapped at the media and threw his helmet off the Giants' bench and into the stands in Indianapolis—he apologized for that immediately and said it was an accident. He denied reports he wanted a trade while saying in a statement, "The only demand I am making is of myself right now, to be the best player I can be." Jacobs did not seem as harmonious after the season when he snapped at photographers in the team's locker room as the players packed to go home. "You're all getting pictures of Brandon Jacobs leaving, wondering if he'll ever return," he said, storming off. "That'll be your caption tomorrow. [Bleep] you all."

The pair combined for 2,058 yards and 17 touchdowns (Bradshaw had 1,235 and eight; Jacobs had 823 and nine).

And for all the intrigue of competition, the pair remained close. You could see it in the way they would joke with each other in the locker room, playfully teasing each other, or how they celebrated together after touchdowns.

"He's become that big brother that I lost when [Ronell] died," Bradshaw told the *New York Post*, comparing Jacobs to the brother he lost when he was 10. "He looks out for me, gives me courage, and makes sure I'm doing the right thing.... I love the guy."

Said Jacobs, "On most teams, guys that go through the situation Ahmad and I just had, the friendship is going to break down. But that's not the case here...our friendship is going to outlast all of it."

93 Enjoy a Super Week in 2014

Before the Giants and Jets could unveil their new stadium at the Meadowlands, they provided a perk Wellington Mara could never have imagined as a boy and could only have dreamed of as a man. The Super Bowl would come to New York. Well, technically New Jersey of course, the long-adopted home of the Giants. But when the NFL announced that Super Bowl XLVIII in 2014 would be played at the Meadowlands, there was no mistaking the Big Apple's draw as well as the enthusiasm showed by New Jersey.

"I think this is a unique opportunity to play the biggest game in the world on the biggest stage in the world," Giants co-owner John Mara said after the announcement was made in Dallas on May 25, 2010. "We're very excited about it. It's going to be great for New York, great for New Jersey, and certainly great for the National Football League."

Mara and co-owner Steve Tisch swapped compliments with Jets owner Woody Johnson after earning the bid in May 2010 and beating out South Florida and Tampa.

The concept of breaking from the norm of a warm-weather climate for a one-time special occasion had been broached back in 2001, after the September 11 terrorist attacks. Many league owners considered the idea of rewarding the area for its sacrifice. The idea faded for a while as many were turned off by the idea of exposing the biggest game of the year to wintry weather in New York.

But Johnson especially pushed the idea when the Giants and Jets agreed on sharing the new stadium in 2005, and their efforts were rewarded by the NFL. While Johnson's immediate efforts surely played a huge part, the legacy of Wellington Mara, who had helped the league grow sometimes through personal sacrifice, also played a role.

While the idea of the country's biggest sporting spectacle taking place on its largest stage surely excited many Giants' fans, the reality of the modern sports world will leave many of them forced to temper their enthusiasm.

A miniscule amount of tickets will be available for Giants season-ticket holders. Suite holders will have access to 109 of the 219 club suites, according to ESPN.com. But for regular season-ticket holders, the NFL's usual allotment for the host city is 5 percent. They will bump that to 6.2 percent, but the Giants and Jets will split that, meaning just 3.1 percent of Giants' season-ticket holders will have access to tickets.

However, fans can expect to take part in plenty of Super Bowl events through the week, which usually involves everything from concerts to sessions with legendary players and football-related games for kids. And of course there's one more way the rare glimpse at a local Super Bowl could send the area into more of a buzz—and provide the opportunity for more tickets.

"We'll try to be in that Super Bowl together," Johnson said after the announcement before turning to a member of the Giants' front office. "Am I right?"

94 Visit the Legacy Club

It's a Willy Wonka Chocolate Factory for Giants fans, a cornucopia of collectibles that can leave fans star-struck as the memories of their youth come flooding back. For all the negatives of leaving Giants Stadium and the tradition that seemingly left with the exit, the Legacy Club at New Meadowlands Stadium is one of the team's attempts to cushion the blow.

Okay, so it won't exactly make up for the PSLs...but that's another story. What the Legacy Club—the Giants' mini-museum—will do is give fans something they had long sought.

"The history behind it—it's all over the place," 27-year-old Giants fan Fabricio Mantilla said. "Everywhere you go, there's something historic. Something that made the Giants what they are now. Everywhere you go, you say, 'This looks important'— and it is."

The room, with its soft blue and red lighting and interactive displays, has modern appeal while inviting visitors to look past the comforts of today and explore anything from leather helmets and tattered jerseys to Yankee Stadium bleacher benches all the way to items from the Giants' most recent Super Bowl.

The room is chock full of history, recognizable—such as Phil Simms' No. 11 jersey—or previously unseen up close, like Wellington Mara's desk or Michael Strahan's locker.

"I imagine him being there and getting ready for a game," Mantilla said of Strahan. "I felt like, 'Oh, man.' It was like he was just there."

Regardless of whether you want to relive a piece of Giants' history or learn more about it, this is a must-stop on game day.

95 Do Not, Uh, Pucker Up

The Giants had just beaten Washington to finish 10–6 in a 2010 season filled with wasted opportunities. Despite the win, the Giants were eliminated from playoff contention when eventual Super Bowl champion Green Bay beat Chicago on the season's final day.

"We did our part, okay?" Giants coach Tom Coughlin told his team in the locker room after the game. "We did our part, okay? That's all I can ask you to do. Hey, from the bottom of my heart and everybody's, we have a 10–6 season. A 10-win season in the NFL, okay? And they can kiss my a--, okay? They can line up and kiss my a--. It's not a easy thing to do."

It was the type of private moment between a coach and a team that often occurs when coaches too frequently believe they need to motivate their team with an us-against-the-world mentality. But the footage was shown on Showtime's *Inside the NFL*. And while Coughlin may not have seen it before it was shown, he's been around long enough to know when cameras are there. A Giants spokesman also approved the footage before it was released.

Giants icon Phil Simms, in his role as a television analyst, praised Coughlin, saying he "loved it."

"Let it out, tell everybody how you really feel," Simms said on the air. "And I think it's deserved. For all the people who just constantly said, 'Oh, Tom just can't relate to the players,' I don't see that when I watched that."

It reminds you that players and coaches often buy into that us-against-the-world mentality even at the expense of respecting the fans so determined to cheer for them.

Granted, Simms makes some solid points. If you watch the video instead of simply listening to the inflammatory words, you

To Boo or Not to Boo?

The Giants' sensitivity to criticism extended beyond their coach and into the locker room during their roller coaster 2010 season. Safety Antrel Rolle created a controversy earlier that year when he criticized fans for booing a subpar first half against Jacksonville.

He compounded the problem by comparing football players to soldiers.

"We risk ourselves out there on the field each and every day also," Rolle said. "When soldiers come home from Iraq, you don't boo them. I look at it the same way. I take my job seriously."

Granted, football is an extremely dangerous game that comes with its own risks that reach far beyond a player's career. But it is not war, regardless of how many bad analogies have equated it with that. Rolle later apologized at least and labeled the remarks "inappropriate."

As to whether fans should boo?

In New York, where ticket prices and PSLs are at an all-time high, parking is a challenge, and mass transit options can create long lines to and from games…well, let's just say fans should be reasonable about their expectations and not be abusive.

But a simple booing?

Just ask Rolle's teammate, Justin Tuck. "If I paid as much as they paid for tickets and you play like we did in the first half," Tuck said that week, "I would have booed, too."

can see Coughlin speaking less with anger and more with the protective fatherly nature many of his players have praised him for from his college coaching days to the present.

And given the shots he'd taken from an ex-player who doesn't quite agree (Tiki Barber), the ones he would later take from a current young player proficient in running off at his mouth (Antrel Rolle) as well as all the rumors about his job security, it's somewhat explainable.

In a season in which the Giants opened their brand new stadium and introduced costly Personal Seat Licenses during a rough economy—all but excising a decades-old waiting list for season tickets because folks couldn't afford them—the team had one of its worst collapses in team history. The Giants gave the fans one of the worst losses in franchise history, losing a late 21-point lead against Philadelphia to blow the NFC East in a 38–31 loss. They followed that with a 45–17 thrashing by Green Bay the next week when they could have clinched a playoff berth on their own.

Given all those factors, Coughlin actually was not hard enough on his team. The players did not fully do their part. So if he wants critics to pucker up, Coughlin's best bet is to go earn himself another Super Bowl ring.

That's something any Giants fan would gladly kiss.

96 Stop Wondering About Jimmy Hoffa

You can keep wondering of course since it was a macabre tradition and part of Giants Stadium lore for 20 years. But the answer is further than ever from getting definitively discovered by Giants fans who have heard the likely tall tale about mobster Jimmy Hoffa's remains dwelling far beneath the west end zone of the old stadium.

The rumors have been, well, buried.

When Giants Stadium was demolished as the team prepared to move into New Meadowlands Stadium in 2011, the spot Hoffa was rumored to be in was covered with concrete, according to Frank Amicizia, the vice president of the company that tore down the stadium.

"If he's down there, he's going to be down there deeper," Gramicizia told the Associated Press.

The FBI didn't find the initial story in 1989 credible and hadn't given it any more respect due to the growing rumors by 2010 when

Giants Stadium came down. So the bureau did not oversee the demolition. Not that the site was free of criminal intrigue. At least five other bodies were dug up during the project, the AP said. But Hoffa's wasn't one of them.

The story was as intriguing as it was morbid. A self-proclaimed hit man named Donald "Tony the Greek" Frankos had a solid (if not a bit confusing) mob-style name. But the FBI found his facts didn't add up when he told *Playboy* magazine Hoffa's body had been cut up and buried under Section 107 by the west end zone during construction of Giants Stadium in 1976. The tale grew anyway because no one knew where Hoffa ended up after disappearing in Michigan in 1975.

The Giants themselves got in on the act with punter Sean Landeta providing the best line at one point. "It gives a whole new meaning to kicking into the coffin corner," Landeta said.

97 Look for the Ring of Honor

In 2010, the team with one of the most storied histories in the NFL joined several of its fellow traditional powerhouses in setting up a tribute ring in its inaugural year at New Meadowlands Stadium.

Of course, given the digital age and the Giants need to share a stadium with the Jets, the ring was not designed in a traditional way. On Giants game days, Giants members of their Ring of Honor are shown, while it flips to a Jets ring on Jets game days.

Regardless of the modern arrangement, fans had clamored for the franchise to put some of its rich history on display for a long time, and their requests were finally answered when 30 Giants

Giants' 2010 Inaugural Ring of Honor

Offense:
QB Charlie Conerly
QB Phil Simms
QB Y.A. Tittle
RB Tiki Barber
RB/WR Frank Gifford
RB Tuffy Leemans
RB/QB/P/K/WR/DB Ken Strong
WR/RB/TE/CB Joe Morrison
WR Amani Toomer
T Al Blozis
T Rosey Brown
T Steve Owen
C Mel Hein
K Pete Gogolak

Defense:
DE Andy Robustelli
DE Michael Strahan

DE George Martin
LB Jessie Armstead
LB Sam Huff
LB Harry Carson
LB Lawrence Taylor
DB Dick Lynch
DB Emlen Tunnell

Executives/Coaches:
Owner Jack Mara
Owner Tim Mara
Owner Wellington Mara
Owner Bob Tisch
GM George Young
Coach Jim Lee Howell
Coach Steve Owen
Coach Bill Parcells

(22 players and eight non-playing personnel) were introduced on October 3, 2010.

Among the Giants whose contributions were honored in the initial ceremony were owner Wellington Mara, Lawrence Taylor, Frank Gifford, Y.A. Tittle, Phil Simms, and Bill Parcells. Michael Strahan, who was working as a broadcaster for FOX, was allowed by his supervisors to scoot out just in time to make the ceremony. His former teammate, Tiki Barber, arrived as well but was greeted with boos after adding to his list of criticisms of his former coach, Tom Coughlin.

The rest of the Ring of Honor class was appreciative of just how far they had come.

"We didn't have a Ring of Honor at the Polo Grounds, that's for sure," said Frank Gifford, who played there in the 1950s. "When we played at the Polo Grounds, we would outnumber the crowd. When you think about what this means, it's just a great honor for all of us."

98 Special Teamers to Know

Here's a look at some special teams players who stood out but were not mentioned prominently in other sections of the book.

It took Jeff Feagles 20 years and five teams to reach the Super Bowl, and when he finally did with the 2007 Giants, he set a Super Bowl record as the oldest player to appear nearly one month shy of his 42nd birthday.

"There are not too many firsts that I haven't done being around as long as I have," Feagles said. "It's like being a rookie all over. I'm happy for it. I'm as giddy as a rookie."

Of course, after all that time his record stood only three years when the Colts' Matt Stover took the title in 2010. Such is the underappreciated life of a punter, whose presence on the field isn't often applauded considering his team has just failed to move the ball.

Which is why the amount of respect Feagles earned in his 22-year career, including the last seven with the Giants, is all the more impressive. When Feagles announced his retirement in April 2010, Giants coach Tom Coughlin said the punter was, "in my opinion, one of the greatest Giants of all."

And that was well before rookie punter Matt Dodge showed just how valuable Feagles' ability to keep a ball from a dangerous

Punter Jeff Feagles was one of many Giants punters to stand out through the years. The 22-year veteran savored the challenge of kicking in the challenging winds at the Meadowlands. (AP Photo/ Photo File)

return man could have been in the 2010 season when Dodge kicked the ball straight to Eagles punt returner DeSean Jackson and Jackson beat the Giants with…okay, you don't need to hear that anymore. You've suffered enough.

Feagles retired at 44 having played in an NFL-record 352 consecutive games, not missing a single one in his career. He also owned three major NFL career punting records, totaling 71,211 yards on 1,713 punts and having 554 punts downed inside the 20-yard line.

More impressive was that ability to nail teams deep in their end with coffin-corner kicks that bounced out before reaching the end zone.

"I will forever in my mind have a vision of Jeff Feagles, who is an incredibly talented directional punter," Coughlin said after Feagles retired. "My vision is of Jeff lofting the ball down into the corner of the field inside the 5-yard line and [former Giants special-teamer] David Tyree catching the ball before it goes out of bounds and before it goes into the end zone."

Feagles thrived on the crazy, swirling gusts at the old Giants Stadium, saying he loved the challenge it presented to "defeat the wind." He also loved using his brain rather than just looking to amp up the power in his foot, tricking punt returners by sending the ball where they did not expect—and "helping" opposing punters by offering "guidance" before games.

"I used to tell them to look at the flags—that's the way the wind's blowing," Feagles said when he retired. "It's the complete opposite."

* * *

Dave Jennings is part of the fabric of the Giants, the long-time punter a New York institution from his time not only with Big Blue but with the crosstown Jets. Jennings is one of the Giants' all-time greatest punters, averaging 41.7 yards per punt in his 11 years with the Giants and leading the league in yards in 1979 and '80 along the way to two of his four Pro Bowls.

Unfortunately, Jennings is one of the many Giants who played in a predominantly losing era and left before the 1986 Super Bowl. His last season with the Giants was 1984, but he played his final three years with the Jets and spent his entire 14-year career in New York. Jennings became a long-time and well-respected broadcaster for the Jets and later had a short stint with the Giants.

In 2005, Jennings revealed that for the past 10 years, he's had Parkinson's Disease, the neurological disease that affects Muhammad Ali and actor Michael J. Fox. Jennings, who looked to spread awareness after going public, showed the type of straightforward approach in dealing with the disease that had endeared him to Giants fans over the years.

"Something has taken hold of me, and I'm going to beat it," he told the *New York Daily News*. "You don't die from Parkinson's, you die with it."

* * *

Dave Meggett was one of the most electrifying members of Bill Parcells' Giants, thrilling fans with his punt returns and his ability to burst out of the backfield to catch a pass on third down.

After running back Rodney Hampton was injured in the first round of the 1990 team's Super Bowl run, Meggett teamed with Ottis Anderson to give the Giants a change of pace in the NFC Championship Game and the Super Bowl.

But mostly Meggett's playing days are remembered for watching the 5'7" return man scoot through holes on the way to six punt returns for touchdowns and one kick return in his six years with the Giants—including one in each of his first three seasons and two in 1994.

A Bill Parcells favorite, Meggett eventually ended up playing for the coach in New England on its Super Bowl team and later with the Jets.

Meggett's post-football life took a dark turn. The former fan favorite is no longer as well-received after arrests for several sex-related crimes, the last of which prompted a sentence in 2010 of 30 years for criminal sexual conduct and burglary in South Carolina.

* * *

Don Chandler came perilously close to going down in Giants infamy when he nearly convinced roommate Sam Huff to quit their rookie season in 1956. Fortunately, Giants offensive coach Vince Lombardi tracked down the pair of players at the airport and pulled them back.

Huff became one of the NFL's greatest linebackers, and Chandler became a key contributor as a punter and later a kicker for the Giants' championship teams of the 1950s and '60s.

That rookie season featured the Giants first NFL championship in 18 years, and Chandler did his part to set up the team's talented defense by averaging 41.9 yards per punt.

Two years later, when the Giants returned to the NFL title game against Baltimore, Chandler led the league in punts and yardage, and he had the NFL's longest punt for 67 yards while averaging 44 yards a kick.

After kicker Pat Summerall retired, Chandler pulled double-duty, topping the league with 52 extra points on 56 tries in 1963.

99 Giant Origins

When the New York football franchise he purchased for $500 first took the practice field in 1925, owner Tim Mara wanted to offer a tribute to the imposing men before him and so he labeled them.... Well, no. That's not what happened. But don't blame me for trying to offer at least a little meaning to the nickname of one of New York City's most cherished franchises.

The actual story doesn't exactly allow you to nod in reverence to a hallowed tradition.

The Giants are called the Giants because they played in the Polo Grounds, which already hosted the—Giants. Basically, Mara searched his mind for a name that would establish his budding franchise as a force to be reckoned with in the city's sporting landscape, then he decided to just use the one the baseball team had.

The baseball team had been so dubbed as an ode to the city's towering skyscrapers, and Mara decided that was good enough for him and his new team. That's why you still sometimes hear old-time fans refer to the team as the New York Football Giants instead of simply the Giants. Before the baseball Giants left for San Francisco in 1958, the distinction was necessary to avoid confusion.

The Giants have also been called the 'Jints, G-Men, and Big Blue over the years.

At least the Giants were far from alone in their lack of creativity. As noted on the Pro Football Hall of Fame's website, in its early stages when baseball was king, the NFL had plenty of would-be "World Series" contenders with teams such as the New York Yankees, Brooklyn Dodgers, Cleveland Indians, Cincinnati Reds, and Detroit Tigers at one point or another.

Logos and Uniforms

The Giants have had 12 logos and 11 uniform/helmet combos. The club's colors have always included a combination of red and blue—except in 1934 when they were blue and silver. Letters on the Giants' helmet were first introduced in the 1960s with the lowercase "ny" similar to the one used today, with the "y" extending below the "n." In 1976, the Giants replaced a variation of the "ny" by spelling out their name and underlining it—GIANTS. A variation of that would last through the 1999 season, before the Giants switched back to the "ny" in 2000—just in time for their first Super Bowl appearance since 1990.

The team's logos have mostly been tied into the lettering of their helmets, although variations have included a picture of a quarterback with his arm cocked, towering over the stadium.

Looking for a little more meaning in a name? The Big Blue Wrecking Crew label was definitely earned in the 1980s with pounding defensive players like Lawrence Taylor, Harry Carson, Carl Banks, and George Martin leading the way to Big Blue's first Super Bowl title after the 1986 season.

100 Remember Donald Thum

Wellington Mara was getting besieged by increasingly angry fans in the 1970s, when many of his poor decisions helped the club sink into one losing season after another. But fan Donald Thum wrote to Mara not with outrage but advice. He studied draft books like fans might now analyze websites, endlessly looking for an edge that could help his favorite team.

In the midst of all that animosity for a struggling team, Mara and Thum formed a friendship that lasted until Mara's death in 2005.

"My father wrote to him over 30-some-odd years," Donald Jason Thum said. "He would go down to training camp with him, eat lunch with him. He was more of a personal friend. He used to go through the draft books with him. He would send letters on who he wanted for the draft and stuff. Wellington would listen to him quite a bit."

It is a tribute to both men that they were able to reach an ideal that sports fans usually can envision as children but roll their eyes at as adults. The owner of a team not only took the time to listen to a fan—who approached with an optimistic outlook on how things could be improved instead of an angry demand—but befriended him.

It is hard to imagine now when increased ticket prices, parking, and Personal Seat License fees tear through a fan's sense of loyalty. It was not that much easier to see then when the gap between an owner and a fan seemed just as wide to a pair of young eyes.

"What are you doing there?" Donald Jason Thum remembers asking his father as a boy.

"Oh, I'm just writing to the owner of the Giants," Thum responded. "Just letting them know what players to pick and all that."

"What?" the boy said, his eyes growing larger.

This is not what should be the norm, of course. Too many fans think they know better than the men and women paid to operate teams. They are entitled to opinions and the right to voice them, but they are not entitled to a response to every suggestion, which is why the relationship between Thum and Mara was special. A combination of Thum's insight and Mara's open-minded willingness to listen allowed them to build a relationship any fan would dream of—but Thum refused to take advantage of fully.

Cheer on Your Own

The Giants are one of the few remaining teams in the NFL who do not have cheerleaders, dancers, or any form of sideline presence trying to put a surge through the crowd. While certain members of the fan base might find the fact disappointing, it's true to the soft-spoken nature of the Mara family, especially the late NFL patriarch Wellington Mara.

Mara was known for observing much about his team but saying little. He was so enamored of the sport that he saw little reason for the type of extra entertainment prevalent now.

"We have always felt that the game should be the focus of the day of game presentation," a message on the Giants' website reads.

The Thums were always invited to Giants Stadium or down to the sidelines at training camp. The state trooper sometimes took Mara up on it, eating lunch with his friend or some players, but at other times he turned the invites down.

"My father wouldn't take advantage of it," Thum said. "If he wanted to get tickets, he could have gotten tickets any time."

Thum represented the fan base the way Mara represented the team. An NFL Films production on the pair's correspondence is on display in the team's Legacy Club.

When Mara grew more ill before his death in 2005, Thum knew. "My father could see that his penmanship was getting bad," Thum's son said. "He could see he wasn't feeling too well."

When Mara died, Thum sent a note to the owner's son, John. "You could never find a better man than him," Thum said of Mara at the time. "He was one of a kind."

Five years and a few months after Mara's death, Thum died in December 2010. The Mara family sent roses for the funeral. There would be a phone call and another offer for the family to visit during training camp.

And, of course, there would be a letter waiting in the mailbox. "They're up in heaven," John Mara wrote to Thum's wife, Loretta.

The son of the Giants' No. 1 fan knows what advice his father would offer to Giants fans looking for things they should know or do. "If you're a Giants fan, always stay a Giants fan," he said his father would tell them. "Always be faithful to your team. Don't be a fair-weather fan."

It can be harder now. While the Giants treated Thum so well, it is not as easy for the countless fans that loyally remained season-ticket-holders for decades only to lose their seats because of the cost of Personal Seat Licenses. Their anger is understandable, their frustration during a dark economy justified. Over time, you can see fans continuing to turn as cold and detached to their teams as the teams are to them, making it completely about winning and demanding and less about simply rooting or hoping.

There is the increasing de-humanization of it all, straying so far from when the players and fans mingled at Toots Shor's in the city. Now a fan's loyalty can feel like a sign of weakness, a way for a pro sports team to attack with more exploitation of that passion.

For fans who feel as betrayed as Thum's family feels rewarded for his faith, it is more complex than simply remaining a fan.

But Thum's son can still remember his eyes growing wide when his father and the Giants owner cut through some of the cynicism by seeing a pair of humans instead of a customer and a business owner. It's a nice ideal, even if it's hard to imagine—even if it sometimes feels there's no way to connect through the big business world of pro sports anymore.

Donald Jason Thum will keep trying, if only because, in a different time, his father did. Because he saw it work.

"I'm actually going to start writing John Mara myself and keep up the tradition," he said. "I'm going to write to him and keep up the writing and the penpal-ship myself; follow in my father's footsteps."

Sources

Books

Barber, Tiki, with Gil Reavill. Tiki: My Life in the Game and Beyond, Gallery, 2007.

Bavaro, Mark. Rough & Tumble: A Novel, St. Martin's Press, 2008.

Baker, Jim and Bernard Corbett. The Most Memorable Games in Giants History: The Oral History of a Legendary Team, Bloomsbury USA, 2010.

Bendetson, William and Leonard Marshall. When the Cheering Stops: Bill Parcells, the 1990 New York Giants and the Price of Greatness, Triumph Books, 2010.

Burress, Plaxico, with Jason Cole. Giant: The Road to the Super Bowl, It Books, 2008.

Callahan, Tom. The GM: A Football Life, a Final Season, and a Last Laugh, Broadway, 2008.

Cavanaugh, Jack. Giants Among Men: How Robustelli, Huff, Gifford, and the Giants Made New York a Football Town and Changed the NFL, Random House, 2008.

Conerly, Perian. Backseat Quarterback, University Press of Mississippi, 2003.

Davis, Jeff. Papa Bear: The Life and Legacy of George Halas, McGraw-Hill, 2006.

Devito, Carlo. Wellington: The Maras, the Giants and the City of New York, Triumph Books, 2006.

Freedman, Lew. New York Giants: The Complete Illustrated History, MVP Books, 2009.

Gifford, Frank, with Peter Richmond. The Glory Game: How the 1958 NFL Championship Changed Football Forever, Harper, 2008.

Gordon, Robert. The 1960 Philadelphia Eagles, Sports Publishing, 2001.

Gottehrer, Barry. The Giants of New York: The History of Professional Football's Most Fabulous Dynasty, G.P. Putnam's Sons, 1963.

Greenberg, Murray. Passing Game: Benny Friedman and the Transformation of Football, Public Affairs, 2008.

Gutman, Bill. Parcells: A Biography, Carroll & Graf, 2000.

Klein, Dave. The Game of Their Lives, Random House, 1976.

Maxymuk, John, with Tiki Barber. Game Changers: The Greatest Plays in New York Giants History, Triumph Books, 2010.

Maxymuk, John. The 50 Greatest Plays in New York Giants Footall History, Triumph Books, 2008.

Miller, Stuart. The 100 Greatest Days in New York Sports, Houghton Mifflin Harcourt, 2006.

Pervin, Lawrence. Football's New York Giants: A History, McFarland, 2009

Richman, Michael. The Redskins Encyclopedia, Temple University Press, 2007.

Schwartz, Paul. Tales From the New York Giants Sideline, Sports Publishing, 2007.

Summerall, Pat with Michael Levin. Giants: What I Learned About Life from Vince Lombardi and Tom Landry, Wiley, 2010.

Taylor Lawrence, with Steve Serby. LT: Over the Edge: Tackling Quarterbacks, Drugs and a World Beyond Football, Harper Collins, 2003.

Vacchiano, Ralph. Eli Manning: The Making of a Quarterback, Skyhorse Publishing, 2008.

Whittingham, Richard. Illustrated History of the New York Giants, Triumph Books, 2005; What a Game They Played: An Inside Look at the Golden Era of Pro Football, Harper & Row, 1984.

Zipay, Steve. Then Bavaro Said to Simms ...: The Best New York Giants Stories Ever Told, Triumph Books, 2009.

DVDs

America's Game: 1986 New York Giants, Warner Home Video, 2007.

America's Game: 1990 New York Giants, Warner Home Video, 2007.

New York Giants: Road to Super Bowl XLII, Warner Home Video, 2008.

The New York Giants: The Complete History, Warner Home Video, 2004.

Newspapers

Los Angeles Times
New York Daily News
New York Post
The New York Times

Newsday
The Record
Newark Star-Ledger
USA Today

Magazines
ESPN
New York
Sports Illustrated

Team Publication
Giants Media Guide

Websites
AOL Fanhouse (www.fanhouse.com)
ESPN (www.espn.com)
Forbes.com (www.forbes.com)
New York Giants (www.giants.com)
NFL (www.nfl.com)
Pro Football Hall of Fame (www.profootballhof.com)
Pro-football reference.com (www.pro-footballreference.com)
www.jt-sw.com

Wire Service
Associated Press